Managing Distribution
and Change

Managing Distribution and Change

The Total Distribution Concept

Alan West

JOHN WILEY & SONS

Chichester · New York · Brisbane · Toronto · Singapore

Copyright © 1989 by John Wiley & Sons Ltd.
Baffins Lane, Chichester
West Sussex PO19 1UD, England

Other Wiley Editorial Offices

John Wiley & Sons, Inc., 605 Third Avenue,
New York, NY 10158-0012, USA

Jacaranda Wiley Ltd, G.P.O. Box 859, Brisbane,
Queensland 4001, Australia

John Wiley & Sons (Canada) Ltd, 22 Worcester Road,
Rexdale, Ontario M9W 1L1, Canada

John Wiley & Sons (SEA) Pte Ltd, 37 Jalan Pemimpin   05-04,
Block B, Union Industrial Building, Singapore 2057

Library of Congress Cataloging-in-Publication Data:

West, Alan
    Managing distribution and change: the total distribution concept
/   Alan West.
       p.   cm.
    Includes bibliographical references.
    ISBN 0 471 92259 5—ISBN 0 471 92260 9 (pbk.)
       1. Physical distribution of goods—Management.   2. Marketing
    channels—Management.   I. Title.
    HF5415.7.W47   1989   89-38741
    658.7'88—dc20   CIP

British Library Cataloguing in Publication Data:

West, Alan
    Managing distribution and change
    1. Goods. Physical distribution. Management
    I. Title
    658.7'88

    ISBN 0 471 92259 5

Typeset by Thomson Press (I) Limited, New Delhi
Printed in Great Britain by Courier International Ltd, Tiptree, Essex

Dedicated to Bea

Contents

Introduction—The Importance of Distribution

In 1992, customs barriers between EEC member countries will be eliminated and restrictions imposed by differing technical standards will be progressively removed. A year later, the rail link between England and France will become operational according to the EuroTunnel group—with the characteristic enthusiasm of most construction companies. Link these two events and it seems likely that Europe will experience another revolution in distribution as fundamental as the one that occurred in retailing when radical alterations in distribution channels compelled consumer goods manufacturers to reappraise many of their policies. Already, these imminent developments are fuelling change. Swiss manufacturers Suchard and Nestle made competing offers for the Rowntree Mackintosh group which controlled about 23 per cent of the UK confectionery market during 1988. BSN, the French food group, bought the HP sauce group from Hanson Trust in 1988 to gain a distribution network in the UK.

When EEC tariff barriers disappear, the advantage of operating within the Community will be greatly enhanced and companies with manufacturing and distribution facilities outside will be at a considerable disadvantage. This explains much of the enthusiasm of Suchard for the acquisition of Rowntree and the BSN purchase of HP. When Chunnel becomes a reality, it may be more realistic for large companies with continent wide markets to locate assembly plants and warehouses on mainland Europe in northern France, closer to the 'golden triangle' of the EEC—northern Germany, Benelux, and the Netherlands rather than in the south east of the UK. In the UK the events have only been noted, and discussion of their true ramifications has hardly begun, largely because of the poor understanding of the demands of continent wide markets, which are intimately connected with distribution issues.

Poor understanding of distribution is due in part to the failure to appreciate its relevance to a company's strategic planning. Odd though it may seem distribution is similar to marketing in this respect. Of marketing, I have written elsewhere that it should be viewed as an activity integral to the successful firm and that marketing managers should understand its strategic implications (see A. West, *Understanding Marketing*, Harper & Row, 1987). Yet if one takes the four 'P's of the marketing mix—Product, Price, Promotion, Place—it is the high profile issues—Product and

Promotion—that are the focus of marketing activity. In studying distribution as the fourth 'P' of the marketing mix it has seemed to me that it is regarded as having to do with lorries and warehouses rather than providing a long-term framework enabling a company to establish and maintain its market presence. Concentration on the humdrum, day to day aspects of distribution is not going to capture the imaginations of ambitious young managers needed to cope with the Europe of the future!

More appealing and more incisive is Peter Drucker's view. With justification, he has described distribution as one of the 'final frontiers' of management because it affects all aspects of the firm's long- and short-term activity and internal organization. His vision of the future of management sees fewer, more highly skilled, and less departmentalized individuals organizing and directing the high technology firms in the industrialized world. Distribution as a multidisciplinary skill will be an increasingly important component of the work of these skilled individuals. Reduction in labour forces and management will become the reality for the manufacturing sector in the 1990s and into the 21st century as capital investment in production plant reduces the numbers employed and makes greater demands on their understanding. For example, Uncle Ben's rice, part of the Mars corporation, supplies its entire US market and some export requirements from a Mississippi base with a capital intensive manufacturing plant employing 120 people and a management/employee ratio of about 1:5.

INFLUENCES ON DISTRIBUTION POLICIES

When one examines the influences on company policies it becomes quite clear that distribution does indeed involve more than lorries and warehouses, influencing and being influenced by a whole range of external and internal factors.

The market environment. Any company will have to decide how the structure of the market affects the distribution methods and techniques employed. How urbanized is the population, where are the main centres of population, how efficient are road and rail networks, are there alternatives? The relative importance of these issues about the market environment differs between the long-established company and one that is just entering the market. Nevertheless both will be equally concerned to monitor change over time.

Strategy. Planning is the key element in continuing company success as it involves the long-term relationships between the firm and its markets and its competitors. Distribution affects its approach to the market—the nature of distribution intermediaries; and the type of product it can offer. The likely impact on distribution channels of events like the abolition of tariff barriers within the EEC is one factor in this context.

Tactics. A more responsive distribution policy may enable the firm to react quickly to short-term changes in the market. A mass manufacturer of convenience foods may gain a tactical advantage over competitors by being willing to meet retailers' demands for increasing deliveries.

Profitability and cash flow. The cost of using intermediaries versus selling direct, the amount of investment to be made in such areas as stocks and transport systems, the

Table 1.1 Key distribution criteria

Factor	Distribution issue
Strategic issues	Service levels
	Customer contact methods—channel decisions
	Control over distribution
Product issues	Product requirements
Logistics	Production points
	Storage methods and location
	Transport
Support requirements	Inventory levels
	Communication and order processing
Management	Numbers
	Organization
	Skills
	Reporting systems

types of customers or intermediaries, all influence the supplier's profit margins on its goods or services and the rate of return (cash flow).

Organization and location of production and storage. Distribution policies affect the firm's organization and location. Dell Computers, the personal computer company, grew rapidly because it concentrated on selling equipment direct via mail order. This approach to the market needed a high level of service, spare parts and expertise at head office to deal with any customer problems. This contrasts with many other companies that sell via distributors, which rely on the distributors to provide the necessary service back-up.

Product qualities and packaging. The demands of the distribution system have implications for product packaging and manufacturing. Major grocery and clothing chains in the UK increasingly want suppliers to provide product ready for the sales floor. Suppliers must pack product specially for these customers.

This brief summary emphasizes the initial point—that there is more to distribution strategy than lorries and warehouses. It has instead a wide impact on a range of business operations (Table 1.1).

THE TOTAL DISTRIBUTION CONCEPT

Accepting a broader approach to distribution makes untenable traditional treatment of the topic: the 'Physical Distribution' and the 'Logistics' concepts. A look at standard definitions is enlightening in explaining the genesis of the lorries and warehouses view of distribution.

'Physical distribution involves the planning and controlling of the physical movement of goods from manufacturer to end user.'

'Logistics involves the planning and control of the interaction of materials management and the distribution of the finished product.'

The total distribution concept (TDC) is of greater value in a rapidly changing business environment. It involves all elements of the distribution system from the moment of manufacture to the final receipt by the customer. To supply customers efficiently and competitively with products or services, companies must define customer service requirements and the best methods of meeting them; they must decide how goods can be best transported to the customers or intermediaries; the stock levels and the packaging of the product necessary for the transport system chosen; and where these stocks should be produced and stored.

Together, order administration/information support, distribution channels, physical distribution decisions, warehouse location and production siting make up the total distribution concept. TDC is complex, involving a whole series of interlocking factors, each requiring careful consideration before a company can be sure that cost effective integration has been achieved. Its complexity ensures that optimizing a company distribution system will be both difficult and demanding as each component will be affected by company sales, investment and customer expectation. A whole series of trade-offs exists within individual components of the system and across the entire range of distribution activity as well. Only by understanding these interactions is it possible to develop an effective distribution policy.

Knowledge of the interrelationships of TDC is therefore essential to efficient management and this book is an overview of the concept. It examines the components of total distribution and analyses the strategic implications of action in particular areas giving special attention to the trade-offs that exist. For example, greater investment in stock inevitably increases cost but this will be balanced by a higher proportion of completed orders and a reduction in the incidence of orders lost through lack of stock. Total distribution, operating as it does at the interface of production organization, production scheduling, marketing, sales and finance, can be used to integrate tasks usually regarded as almost totally separate functions within the same firm.

Cost effective integration of distribution within the company can only be measured against some form of quantifiable standard—normally implicit in its objectives or goals which generally contain levels of market share, volume sales and expected level of profitability. The role of distribution is important in the organization's strategic options; changes in the structure of distribution will normally have major benefits in improving market share, profitability, or on many occasions, both. DuPont, the major American chemical manufacturer, reported improvements of over $300 million in profitability due to changes in its distribution system.

CASE STUDY MATERIAL

The impact of the total distribution concept is that it affects the company at all levels and cannot be isolated from broader company objectives, the effects of competition and other environmental constraints.

Specific companies will, however, encounter particular distribution problems relating to the market in which they operate or the implementation policies that they are trying to pursue. The case studies included in this volume are designed to improve the awareness of the way in which these problems can be systematically approached and handled *within* the confines of the overall company position. The main problems within cases relate to the general topics discussed in the preceding chapter, but no company faces single and clearly defined barriers. As a result the cases will require a range of issues to be analysed, with specific concentration on key areas.

Secondly, the cases are designed to show how important distribution decisions will be for the company's finances, demanding quantitative rather than qualitative assessment. The purpose of providing large quantities of data is to encourage the development of a more rigorous analytic approach than that often seen with cases— data evaluation is critically important in the distribution area no less than other areas of company activities.

Each case will require different treatment, and as cases tend to be used in varying ways, it would be too constrictive to suggest a common format. However a structured approach includes the following.

—The analysis of the problem, including the competitive environment, the strengths and weaknesses of the company, and the company goals both in the short- and long-term.

—What distribution management issues are most important in the case, such as distribution channels, sales organization, physical distribution, warehouse location, order processing, and inventory control.

—How they should best be organized to meet the objectives of the company.

—What financial implications such a reorganization would have for the organization.

DISTRIBUTION AND THE ROLE OF THE COMPUTER

As the contribution of information technology to the control of distribution has become increasingly important no book on the subject can ignore the range of software available to help resolve specific problems.

Though the range of available software is considerable a representative sample of programs is included at the end of each chapter to demonstrate the potential computer applications that are available in the late 1980s.

Chapter 2

The Scope of Distribution

The introduction briefly summarized the influences on distribution policy, outlining the scope of the factors that must be taken into account. This chapter expands certain of these initial ideas to stress the contribution that distribution can make to long- and short-term decision making. We shall concentrate on the distribution environment, the contribution of distribution to strategic development, the link between company tactics and distribution, and consider some of the cost factors.

THE CHANGING DISTRIBUTION ENVIRONMENT

All companies exist in an era of accelerating change, but because of the large number of interacting factors within the total distribution arena it can be said that distribution is more influenced by environmental change than many other areas of company policy. The pressures exerted by change on company distribution policy vary with the company but all companies will share the common effects of broader environmental conditions. In their distribution policy all companies will have to cope with new technology, the rising costs of personnel, economic volatility, higher bills for vehicle repair and maintenance. However, changes in the population age structure and in social trends will have a greater relevance to companies operating in the consumer sectors. Let us take a look at the likely effect of changes in key areas such as these on distribution policy.

New technology

New technology, astonishing because it is continually being refined and applied in different situations, is having a dramatic impact on distribution. Simply by *improving knowledge*—of sales, volumes, production lead times, current inventories and the like—manufacturers can reduce stockholding at plants, control inventories at suppliers, and change order processing procedure. They can more effectively define warehouse location, vehicle routing and loading. But the process does not simply end here. The alterations accompanying company application of new technology to distribution systems allow fundamental reallocation of company resources favouring improvements in profit. For example, new till systems allowed British Home Stores to reduce stockholdings in each individual store and to convert over 300 000 square feet of existing storage space to selling space during 1984/85. This was part of planned improvement in profitability.

The impact of new technology in the changing distribution environment has had other knock-on effects. There have been alterations between companies as well as within them. Thus buying organizations' use of microprocessor systems poses new problems for the supplying company. Bar code systems in supermarkets and the slowly growing technique of just-in-time stock provision in manufacturing industry make old systems of stock provision and maintenance less and less acceptable. Manufacturers using just-in-time manufacturing systems (which involves the arrival of raw materials and components at the exact moment they are required by the production process rather than being held in reserve within the warehouse) are inevitably more demanding on their suppliers, requiring a far greater accuracy in the timing of delivery and quantity delivered.

Viewdata (Prestel or cable television system) is another facet of new technology with the potential to change the way companies reach their end market in the 1990s because it offers direct access to end users or consumers. Research in the mid-1980s by the retailer W.H. Smith, which has interests in cable television, indicated that a cost effective distribution system could be achieved providing there were sufficient numbers of households in an area connected to the cable network.

Industrial concentration

In all major Western economies, industrial concentration or the ownership by fewer and fewer companies of larger and larger market shares proceeds apace. This has two important effects on suppliers. First, their profit margins will be put increasingly under pressure as large groups buying in large quantities will want large discounts. Less obvious, however, is that to continue to service these large scale buyers, suppliers will have to meet increasingly stringent and demanding distribution criteria. Let us look at exactly what has happened in the grocery sector.

The continuing expansion of market share by the major multiple retailers through-out Western Europe has radically altered the way consumer goods suppliers are approaching the market; since 1950 the grocery multiples have expanded their market share from below 20 per cent to over 60 per cent; Tesco and Sainsbury alone control over 50 per cent of grocery sales in the London area. These groups demand, and often get, major concessions on delivery volumes and destinations because of their dominant positions in the market. For the fast moving consumer goods manufacturer the market reality is that they are achieving a greater and greater volume of sales through a smaller number of accounts. This change influences the way suppliers organize and service their markets, with distribution becoming an increasingly key issue in effective market management.

Cost and complexity of stock holding

With steadily increasing sophistication in many product fields, the cost of holding stocks or inventory has increased in real terms. Furthermore, greater specialization and segmentation of demand has broadened product ranges. For example, coffee producers in the 1960s could blithely concentrate on powdered instant coffee. By the 1980s, they would have had to consider granulated instant, decaffeinated instant, ground filter coffee, ground percolator coffee and several variants of blend. When one links increasing product complexity and industrial concentration the result is that buyers expect a wider range of products in smaller quantities within the delivery cycle. This can put severe strains on any distribution policy. One industrial valve manufacturer reported that the cost of maintaining stock at the levels held in the 1960s had increased by over 40 per cent in real terms by the mid-1980s due to the growing sophistication of the product.

Speed of market change

The huge growth in competitive, international markets has played a key role in shaping the total distribution environment. Thus the pace of product replacement has steadily increased. For example, Hewlett Packard, the computer manufacturer, now obtains over 60 per cent of its earnings from products that were introduced in the previous two years. Indeed when one compares the markets of Europe, Japan and the US, it is possible to judge the competitiveness of the environment by the speed of product change and innovation. This measure makes the Japanese market by far the most competitive. Companies in high technology and/or consumer fashion have to respond more rapidly to changes in market trends and control their levels of inventory and product range accordingly. The growth of the citizen band (CB) radio market in the UK was followed by an equally rapid collapse. Some of the smaller companies went out of business by being unable to control their stocks effectively; Amstrad in contrast forecast the rapid rate of market decline and managed the problems in the market more efficiently.

Increasing costs of personnel

Labour costs rose steadily in real terms throughout the 1970s and 1980s. This could only be offset by higher efficiency and capital investment and in fact significantly improved UK output per head in the manufacturing sector where productivity per employee rose by 56 per cent between 1979 and 1985. Distribution remains very labour intensive for many firms and changes in distribution policy and organization often have a significant impact on staffing levels. Indeed much of the rationale behind the mid-1980s reorganization of ICI's bulk chemicals subsidiaries was the savings potential of reducing the large workforce employed in the distribution of the company's products. Over a thousand redundancies made a major contribution to improving group profitability in a very competitive industrial sector.

Rising fuel and vehicle repair costs

Fuel costs have continued to rise in real terms since the early 1970s. Repair costs have grown astronomically: average repair costs rose by 800 per cent between 1960 and 1985 (less in real terms). An amusing example of the effects of such trends has been the increasing use of real horsepower by UK local authorities for refuse collection and park maintenance. Young's Brewery, one of the more successful real ale brewers based in South London, are convinced that delivery within the local area by horse and dray is far more cost effective than using traditional motorized transport! The cost of fuel is causing companies to attempt to distribute and store in large quantities, even though this may conflict with such legislative trends as restrictions on the size of lorries on roads; and changing market demand—customers wanting delivery of smaller quantities of a broader range of products.

The optimal relationship between load size and market constraints requires constant monitoring because it changes from year to year. In many industries the inter-relationship between vehicle servicing and replacement costs similarly varies by year. Because old vehicles are fuel inefficient, this also affects the need for fuel economy if fuel costs make up a major proportion of distribution expenditure. To illustrate: the re-equipping of the world's airline fleets with fuel efficient aircraft became essential when the 1973 Middle East conflict resulted in rapidly rising aviation fuel costs.

Standardization

Once, transport and distribution systems were extremely inflexible. Road freight could not be transferred to the rail network, for example. A whole series of modifications which began with palletization make them increasingly compatible. This trend towards multi-modal transport systems, based largely around the concept of containerization, is again influencing the distribution environment. Many manufacturers had to invest heavily throughout the 1970s to improve warehouse design so that the growing amount of container traffic could be handled effectively.

Legislation

Changing attitudes towards the environment and working practices affect the distribution environment in various ways—from restricting the length of the working day for delivery drivers to limitations on load size and content for the different distribution systems. Legislation will, in addition, often influence how products are distributed in particular markets. As well as the regulations on delivery drivers' working day, maximum loads of lorries are set by individual EEC member countries; before its abolition the Greater London Council attempted to establish a precedent banning heavy lorries from the London area during the night. Drugs, explosives, and alcoholic drink are all subject to some degree of licensing controlling their sale in the UK. Benylin Expectorant was, for example, only available on prescription until 1986 and so it could be sold only in registered pharmacies.

Economic volatility

Changing exchange rates and rapid fluctuations in the cost of borrowing have been established features of the 1970s and 1980s. Partly by affecting the level of company working capital, they contribute to pressures on the distribution system by demanding much closer scrutiny of stock levels and other cash absorbent elements of the distribution system. Oil companies had to reappraise their distribution policies because of oil price volatility accompanied by fluctuations in supply and demand. Traditionally, oil companies were vertically integrated: they controlled the extraction facilities, the tankers or pipelines, the refineries and the final outlets to the consumer. Recent trends have been for the oil companies to disinvest from upstream activities (extraction and transport from the production point) and concentrate on downstream ventures, where they can more effectively control the effects of economic volatility than in the extraction sector.

Changes in infrastructure

A modern infrastructure is crucial to economic success. Western governments have modernized and developed road, rail, water, air networks to suit modern economic environments and obviously there have been ramifications for the users of transport infrastructures. The backbone of Victorian industry, the railways, had replaced the canals of another era only to be superseded in turn by the road network. In 1962 most of mainland Britain's towns were served by railway network, and only limited mileage of the dual carriageway motorway network (some of the M4 and M1) had been completed. By the mid-1980s certain stretches of the three lane M25 orbital network around London were already operating over planned capacity two months after opening, and manufacturers and retailers were applying feverishly to develop sites around the periphery which, if approved, would substantially alter the distribution environment of the entire south east of England.

Crystal ball gazers of the 21st century have made a series of predictions concerning the impact of the Channel Tunnel on distribution systems: that this will not drastically change the pattern of distribution methods. The past history of infrastructure alterations and change in methods suggests that any such forecast needs to be treated with substantial caution. The forecasters can, however, proceed with the sure knowledge that they will have retired by the time the system is in operation.

Government policy can also indirectly affect the distribution environment. The de-nationalization of Japanese railways is already altering the way that Japanese industry uses the railway network. French railways carry a higher percentage of national freight than British Rail since government encouragement of a freight role for the nationally owned railway has been more limited than in France. The prosperity of certain areas can obviously be directly affected by government decisions—the current chosen route of the new Paris to the Channel coast rail route will bypass the town of Amiens, and this has led to considerable local protest in an attempt to reinstate the original route.

Demographic trends

Rapid movements of population will affect distribution and so will changes in population age structure. New Mexico is a striking example. Population shifts in some of the southern states of the US have resulted in a five fold increase in its population over the last 25 years. The rising proportion of the elderly in the American population—there will be 13 million Americans over 85 by 1990—has been partially responsible for greater interest in the potential of mail order in the consumer sector.

Social trends

How consumers spend their leisure time is significantly more important to major retail groups in deciding where outlets should be located. Their decisions in turn affect the distribution policy of both retail suppliers and retail multiples themselves. Retailing commentators have identified a 'third wave' of retailing in the Western world with 'leisure' shopping in out-of-town centres becoming a major part of the affluent consumers' week. This perception of leisure shopping has created huge demand among retailers for out-of-town retail parks in the UK, an evolution of the highly successful retail mall concept of the US.

DISTRIBUTION AND COMPANY STRATEGY

Various studies have shown that the most successful firms are those that plan most effectively. Their decisions about company direction are taken logically through systematic steps designed to ensure that they understand the market more effectively than competitors. The point is that the planning process enables them to achieve a better understanding of how alterations in the market environment are likely to affect them, their competitors and their customers. Understanding how these changes affect company distribution policy is crucial because distribution will influence the ability of the firm to improve its competitiveness. In turn it will be influenced by the market and product policies that are, or can be, followed.

Competitive advantage in distribution

One option available to the firm wanting to improve its competitiveness is to alter its distribution policy. Other strategies involve changes in product and promotion policy. If the firm decides to change its distribution policy, various alternatives are available.

Service improvement

Service levels can be reappraised so as to improve the back-up offered to customers. This can be achieved in a number of ways. By improving stock control, both sales and customer satisfaction rise and ensure that the customer receives a more complete order than might be the case with the competition. By reducing end users' inventories

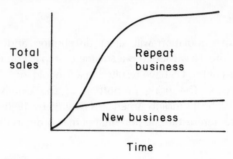

Figure 2.1   Repeat business versus new business

through speedier and more frequent delivery the company can improve its competitive performance. Improving the reliability of the delivery system can help meet the timing requirements of buyers. By maintaining stocks and delivery systems in distant areas of the market the company can supply distant customers more effectively than competitors. Probably more important is the contribution of the distribution system to keeping the customer, once a relationship has been established. Surveys indicate that the cost of developing a new customer can be up to seven times that of maintaining the relationship with an existing one. As the company grows in size it will need an increasing amount of repeat business (Figure 2.1), underlining the importance of keeping customers by providing a continuing high service level. Indeed in mature markets where demand levels are not growing rapidly, changes in distribution will be one of the few methods available to the company wanting to gain an innovative edge.

Higher service levels often allow the firm to charge a premium price either for the original product or for the products supplied via the distribution system. ACS, Automatic Catering Supplies, became one of the largest catering supply firms in the UK by offering a rapid door-to-door delivery service, initially unmatched by its competitors. Caterpillar, the leading American manufacturer of earth moving machinery, promises to supply spare parts worldwide within 24 hours for any equipment in the range. This service partly explains how the company maintains a substantial price premium over broadly similar competitive products.

Obviously, there are costs involved in better service levels. Companies like ACS must invest more heavily in the distribution network than the industry traditionally requires. Thus delivery on a daily basis might mean an investment in vehicles and drivers 40 per cent higher than a system operating a twice-weekly service. Improved service level provision is also an important marketing mix decision involving much more than a higher level of investment. Such a change will often reduce the level of goods out-of-stock to the end user and will enable the supplier firm to achieve a higher level of in-market sale. It will also allow a far higher level of market coverage and the consumer is almost certain to find the company's product in any outlet.

Emphasizing universal, or nearly universal, availability will be more important when the product is primarily an impulse buy item or one with a very short purchase cycle,

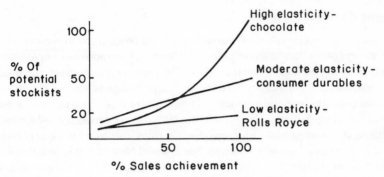

Figure 2.2 The higher the distribution elasticity the greater the requirement to ensure the widest distribution

where a high distribution elasticity exists. (Distribution elasticity refers to the relationship between product availability and sales.) In the case of chocolate bar manufacturers—a product sector with a high level of 'impulse' purchasing—and cigarette companies—a product sector with a very short purchase cycle—distribution levels of 98 per cent of available outlets are essential to maintain a high level of sales. Here the distribution elasticity is fairly steep. In contrast, manufacturers of premium hand tools find that a limited number of stockists out of the potential total will achieve a high level of sales. Here, the distribution elasticity is less severe (Figure 2.2.).

There will always, however, be a pay-off between the level of service that the company offers, and the demands upon the system, and it will become progressively more expensive for a manufacturer to service smaller and smaller customers. Most companies find 80 per cent of their business is generally achieved through 20 per cent of customers, a fact that is true of all sectors, and is often referred to as Pareto's law. Nineteen thousand grocery retail outlets (or 16 per cent of the total UK grocery outlets) account for 67 per cent of total grocery turnover. The implications are that reaching smaller businesses will be disproportionately and progressively costly. There is therefore a point at which the costs of distribution cross the profit objective line. This will vary according to the distribution cost and the nature of the strategic objectives.

Cost reduction to gain competitive advantage

Companies frequently ignore the contribution that distribution policy can make in gaining competitive advantage via reductions in overall cost levels. Often they prefer to concentrate on advertising and packaging, areas relatively insignificant when viewed in relation to their overall contribution to the cost of the firm's goods or services. Cost reductions achieved through changes in the distribution system are especially relevant to companies supplying low value added and high bulk goods (see below).

Changing distribution methods

A company can successfully generate demand for its products by experimenting with different ways of reaching the consumer or customer. Amstrad, for example, achieved its success in the business computer market by exploiting high street audio outlets rather than the traditional dealer network. In its struggle against Coca-Cola, Pepsi built up market share through the expanding vending machine sector, a part of the market that had been largely ignored by its rival. The 1986 merger between a fashion retailer, Next plc, and a leading mail order operator, Grattans, followed by the acquisition in 1987 of a chain of tobacconists, Finlays, has enabled Next to test a new distribution approach to mail order. It is using Finlays as a collection point for clients instead of delivering goods while clients are absent from home.

Product policy

Distribution policy must take account of the needs of the company's products and its particular approach to the market. Each developmental path followed by the company will in turn have implications for its distribution policy. A number of the various product policy strategies have implications for distribution.

Rapid change in the market place involves the introduction of new products and the withdrawal of obsolescent ones. A policy of product abandonment affects the distribution system because stock levels must be carefully controlled throughout the network to ensure a minimum of customer complaint and market disruption. The toy industry is bedevilled by the problems of product abandonment and how to handle the sale of unpopular lines. The collapse of the Airfix group in the late 1970s was partly caused by inability to handle product abandonment effectively. The group maintained stock levels of £20 million, mostly of slow or unsaleable lines against sales of around £40 million.

A company may be pursuing a market penetration policy to increase current product consumption amongst current customers. The distribution implication is the need to maintain higher stocks within the network. This could result in the need to use some form of distribution intermediary to provide additional stock storage facilities, and/or achieve a wider level of distribution coverage. The development of the successful magazine *Smash Hits*, for UK teenage pop enthusiasts, hinged upon the acquisition of more and more sophisticated production and despatch facilities to achieve a circulation level estimated at 500000 in the mid-1980s.

In a market development strategy, the company develops new markets for current products. This requires new distribution initiatives and a significant increase in the investment requirement of the distribution network. The renewed success of the Jaguar motor car company in the US in the 1980s is partly due to its policy of expanding and training a larger dealer network in the large American conurbations. Though the initial new business development will depend largely on promotional and sales efforts, the company will be unable to hold on to the newly established customers unless it has planned and provided for their continuing support via the distribution system. In the Jaguar example, therefore, the new dealer network in the US was supported by an improved speed of product flow from the UK manufacturing base to the market, a greatly improved spare part inventory in the market, and via training and motivation of the intermediaries, a much enhanced ability to service the customer.

A product development strategy involving the introduction of new products to the current customer group may also involve the firm in developing new distribution methods, especially if the new products have different handling characteristics from the old. Thus a company such as Twydale Turkeys, moving away from producing frozen turkeys to concentrate on fresh further processed items, must either maintain a fleet of delivery vehicles to distribute small quantities of the fresh product direct to each store or find customers among large retailers like Tesco able to guarantee an unbroken chilled delivery system from central warehouse to chilled cabinet in-store. This is because the perishability of the product means that the manufacturer to consumer storage period is five days at most, in contrast to deep frozen products with a shelf life of months.

The sale of entirely new products to new market sectors—a diversification strategy—can often involve completely restructuring a company's approach to the market. Lamentable product diversification failures in new market sectors by companies eminently successful in others can be attributed to inability to understand the complexities inherent in the development of an entirely new distribution approach. Management in these companies were used to operating successfully in a different market sector and attuned to the dynamics of a different distribution environment. The perfume and cosmetics industry has been a graveyard for many highly successful consumer companies unable to manage effectively the problems raised by diversification into the perfume market. Neither British American Tobacco with Yardley, nor Unilever with Atkinsons, could effectively handle diversifications into this consumer market sector.

PRODUCT REQUIREMENTS

The physical properties of products will be a major influence on a company's distribution structure. We have discussed the link between product development policy and distribution method in the case of Twydale where perishability of product required a new form of storage. But other product properties like the type of packaging chosen for soft drinks can affect the distribution points chosen. PET bottled drinks are appropriate where the distribution path between manufacturer and consumer is short because the barrier properties of the plastic are such that the product has a fairly limited shelf life. This type of packaging is therefore inappropriate for distribution channels where the product will not rapidly reach the final consumer.

If a product is fragile, this will obviously influence the packaging chosen. It will also affect the type of transport used, materials handling, storage, and distribution channels. Any packaging chosen will have to consider these factors. As major grocery multiples became increasingly important milk outlets, milk packers were induced to introduce cartons rather than glass bottles. There were breakage problems at checkout points but cartons also offered retailers improved shelf stacking characteristics.

Other physical characteristics such as weight, size and shape and chemical composition also need consideration. Bleach, for example, can break down in high ambient temperatures releasing the constituent chlorine under pressure, and in certain circumstances blowing open the bottle. Manufacturers shipping product to such areas needed to either redesign the cap to vent the gas and prevent its build up or ship in cool stowage areas. Safety and security will affect the distribution process as well. High value, low weight products such as diamonds or precious metals will require special emphasis on the security aspects of transport. Dangerous or hazardous products require additional protection. After long argument, British Nuclear Fuels arranged for a 300 ton locomotive to drive into a nuclear storage bin to demonstrate the ability of the design to withstand the impact of a collision.

TACTICS AND DISTRIBUTION

There are a number of short-term, or tactical, advantages associated with an effective distribution policy which can make a company more competitive than others in the market place. They may be necessary because of fluctuation in demand, competitive activity, or changing product demand.

Fluctuations in demand

When unforeseen fluctuations in demand occur, an efficient distribution system can be a great asset. To illustrate the point, firms supplying airports have to be able to cope with major changes in demand for certain materials. An airline strike might quintuple demand for catering products. Extreme weather conditions will affect other types of product requirement—toilet use increases in extreme temperatures.

Competitive activity

Responding quickly to competitive moves is of key importance in some market sectors. The ability to do this effectively can reduce the impact of the competition's promotions or new products or product tests. A common competitive response to many test markets is for a company to increase the stock levels of its existing product (often called 'stock pressure') at the wholesalers or intermediaries so that demand for the competition's new product is more limited than it might otherwise have been. This leads to poor results of the competitor's test market or promotional activity.

Changing product demands

As products age, the demands of the distribution system will change. The product life cycle (PLC) theory—essentially that products undergo a period of growth, maturity

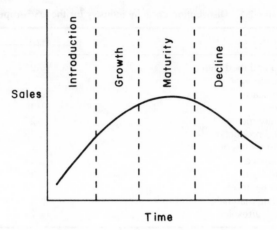

Figure 2.3 The product life cycle theory

and decline (see Figure 2.3)—suggests that firms should tactically change the distribution objectives at various stages in the cycle. When the product is first introduced, a company will want the widest possible distribution to gain product trial. As the product establishes itself during the growth stage, it would aim to maintain the distribution achieved to attain the maximum level of repeat purchase. During the maturity stage of the PLC, when the product is firmly established, the firm's objective is to maximize profitable distribution to achieve a positive cash flow for the product in its most profitable period. Once the product begins to decline in the market, selective distribution can reduce stocks and market commitment maximizing revenues. Although the PLC concept has been heavily criticized for its inability to predict change it remains useful as a method of defining how the firm should be evaluating the product's likely distribution requirements. Once a product is established, more and more intermediaries may be needed to stock it to ensure that the service offered to end users cannot be bettered by competitors. As sales volume drops, selective distribution via those intermediaries or outlets that provide the most profitable sales will be more important as a distribution criterion.

DISTRIBUTION AND COST

Company strategy, market position, market sector and product demands all influence the eventual cost of distribution and its contribution to the final cost of the product. For those producing light high value items, distribution costs will constitute only a small component of the final cost; for others it will, however, be substantial. The link between the variable and fixed costs of distribution is an important one. Normally it is only in the area of production that managers link the two. Because distribution is such a major cost centre in a large range of businesses (see below) an understanding of the

Table 2.1   Distribution costs by industry for the US/Europe

Industry—US	Per Cent
Food and food factors	27
Machinery	9
Chemicals	22
Paper	16
Primary metal	25
Wood products	16
Industry—Europe	
Aerospace	13
Agriculture	13
Beverage/food	31
Building materials	25
Clothing/textiles	23

Source: Adapted from US Department of Trade 1985, AT Kearney, 1988.

interrelationship between fixed and variable distribution costs is one key to improving company efficiency.

Variable costs

In most cases variable distribution costs constitute a far more significant proportion of the final selling price than might be expected given the lack of management interest in the subject. Variable distribution costs are the direct costs relating to each product unit from the point of manufacture to the end consumer. An American survey in the 1980s showed that the costs related to distribution made up a significant percentage of the final product price in many industries, with an average for all the industries studied of 19 per cent (Table 2.1). An earlier UK survey revealed that distribution costs made up 16 per cent of the final manufacturers' selling price in the same range of industries, and Japanese surveys show an average of 14 per cent. The difference reflects the smaller geographical area of the UK. Transport costs within the EEC, because of the delays at

Table 2.2   Main variable cost components in distribution
for the US (per cent)

Factor	Manufacturer's cost
Administration	2.4
Transport	6.7
Warehousing	3.8
Costs of stock (inventory)	3.7
Order processing	1.2
Cost of incoming materials	1.7

borders, was estimated by the Commission to make up a higher component of cost—20.5 per cent being the average for all industries—than in the US. As stated earlier, distribution costs as a percentage of final selling price are always greatest in low added value, high mass items, and least in high value, low mass production.

Rapid reductions in variable costs can be achieved by reviewing the major cost components that are involved in total distribution. The easiest way to do this lies in re-appraising the largest cost components. Within a typical industry with distribution contributing 19 per cent of the manufacturers' costs the US Department of Trade calculated the main cost components (Table 2.2). Of these, transport tends to be the highest, followed by stockholding and warehousing.

Fixed costs and the link with variable cost

Table 2.2 reflects the often high variable cost of distribution. The fixed costs, or investments that the company makes in its own internal infrastructure, are also important. They range from the smallest investment in storage areas to large-scale expenditure on vehicles, pipelines, warehouses, and order processing systems. There are various issues connected with determining fixed investment levels. Thus the volume of product transferred is a crucial one. The greater the volume being moved the more logical it is to increase fixed investment in an attempt to reduce the variable costs of shipment for each unit. This becomes possible because the greater investment in fixed costs can increase efficiency in such areas as labour, storage, fuel. The pipeline systems used by oil companies illustrate the logic of high volume movements paying the company to reduce the variable cost of transport. When one considers the alternatives to transporting liquids in this way, either by truck or rail, the additional unit cost of transport becomes clear. Increasing fixed investment to reduce variable costs applies not just to transporting the product (physical distribution) but to all other areas of distribution activity as well. Automation in warehousing, for example, is most effective as a method of reducing variable costs where high volumes are shifted and stored. This introduces one of the central features of distribution planning, that because of its complexity there are a large number of *trade-offs* that exist both within particular components of the distribution system, but also between them. The trade-off which we have just mentioned—investment in warehouse automation reducing labour and storage costs—is just one example of the many that exist. Later chapters will explore more of the trade-off issues in particular elements of the distribution system.

Fixed distribution investment costs also involves consideration of destination and/or product. Higher levels of fixed cost investment are more logical when there are low numbers of destinations/products involved in the distribution process. It will be less suitable where the product range and destinations are rapidly changing. British Coal supplies the majority of the CEGB's coal powered power stations by rail; the product itself and the permanent nature of its destination makes this a particularly appropriate method of moving product even though it involves a substantial investment in fixed distribution facilities. Consider an analogy in the public transport sector—electric trams versus diesel buses. An overhead cable network requires a considerable outlay for a system inflexible in terms of routes compared with independent diesel buses. However, the electric tram network is much cheaper to run and can handle much higher passenger numbers, permitting far greater control over the system. The old tram network in the centre of Hong Kong coped with a substantial increase in use as population rose from 1.2 million to the current 5.4 million. Only recently have the authorities had to invest in an underground—another fixed or inflexible link.

Investment in a distribution infrastructure, whether in plant—warehousing, vehicles—or people—distribution companies—will raise the company's fixed costs levels, that is those it has to pay on a continuing basis. Although fixed cost investment raises the point at which the revenue line crosses the fixed and variable cost line (the break even point), the variable cost of selling each individual unit will be reduced so that at higher volumes the unit cost will be lower, thus improving profitability. The logic underlying the purchase by manufacturing companies of their overseas distribution companies is based on this theory that by increasing their fixed cost investments they will achieve a reduction of variable cost as they broaden their product range. Both Guinness and International Distillers and Vintners have followed such a policy in the US. While they have increased their investment in fixed assets (warehousing, stocks, order processing systems) by this policy, they have increased the range of products moving through the distribution system. The greater volumes being handled lead to overall reduced costs and no longer having to provide the distributor's profit margin!

It is important to realize that the unit costs of distribution (cost per unit moving through the distribution system) do not necessarily change in a clean linear fashion: two units do not cost double one unit to distribute. This is a result of increasing fixed investments at various volume levels, and the effect of economies of scale. Thus there will often be substantial increases in cost operating in a step like fashion when certain volumes are exceeded (Figure 2.4). This type of non-linear cost behaviour underlines the need to understand accurately the interaction of all the components involved in the total distribution concept and how a distribution strategy should be evolved (see Chapter 15).

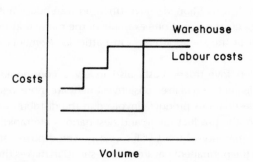

Figure 2.4   Increases in distribution costs with volume

DISTRIBUTION AS AN INVESTMENT ISSUE

Whether raised investment and higher levels of cost benefit a firm will, in the main, be influenced by the market environment pressures and the degree of risk measured against current or future market potential. Earlier discussion of the factors affecting distribution policy in a changing environment suggests that it is long-term objectives that must be considered when decisions are taken. Distribution is an investment issue. There are pay-offs between the level of investment and the improved control that the organization obtains; between the speed of return on that investment and the level of risk associated with it; and between the relationship between fixed costs, variable costs and the level of volume sales. Investment in the distribution process can be clearly associated with increased *control* of the market. One can define three broad company approaches to the market according to the level of distribution investment made.

In the first case, that of *low or nil investment*, different manufacturers offer end users or intermediaries large numbers of competing, and unknown, items in a product category. Intermediaries handle most of the physical distribution and the supplier cannot therefore control the destination of product or the types of products used. As there is no specific demand for any particular manufacturer's product the end users can freely substitute the supplier's goods with another's without fear of losing sales. Their ability to do this reduces the prices that the supplier can achieve and minimizes their independence from the end user. The industrial fasteners market (nuts, bolts, rivets) is an example of limited investment by manufacturers in controlling the distribution channels with over 300 companies in the market. The vast majority use wholesalers as intermediaries to handle physical distribution to end users.

A second approach to distribution involves *increasing levels of investment* where consumer or end user demand starts to be generated. Retailers or end users need to stock the product to achieve sales and the supplier is able to increase distribution without making major concessions on price. The supplier starts to service major clients direct—ensuring product range stocking, and is able to minimize competitive product availability. Supplier independence therefore increases. The computer software industry has demonstrated the importance of investment in the distribution process with companies such as Ashton Tate (Framework, D Base II and Javelin) concentrating on the development of dealer networks to expand sales.

The third approach is *heavy investment*. Manufacturers ensure that the product is carried by a substantial number of end users or intermediaries. Successful suppliers can achieve major economies of scale. For major suppliers, the percentage of sales revenue spent on investment in the distribution channel decreases in line with their considerably expanded distribution. Competition steadily intensifies between a few suppliers who effectively control prices. The suppliers now have substantial control over the end user or intermediaries unless similar concentration is taking place at the end of the distribution chain with end users becoming larger, fewer and more powerful too. Changes in newspaper distribution methods, begun by News International in 1987, illustrate the leverage that heavy investment in the market can achieve.

Historically, most newspapers were distributed via two national distribution networks, W.H. Smith and John Menzies. Both had considerable power over the levels of market coverage and speed of delivery. With its position as a major newspaper supplier— *News of the World, Times, Today, Sunday Times,* and the *Sun*—News International could renegotiate distribution arrangements to reduce cost and improve effectiveness of coverage. Smaller newspapers like the *Independent* and *Guardian* have found it far more difficult to achieve similar improvements in cost and performance. The car market shows continuing major manufacturer investment in establishing and maintaining a closely linked dealer network. This gives substantial leverage in determining the types of products sold and the price level charged and is crucial to maintaining market share.

Risk and distribution

The risk issues associated with distribution investment are very similar to those involved in other aspects of company investment plans. The greater the uncertainty of future events the greater the level of risk. It is inevitable that risk will be higher in many overseas markets and this will affect the distribution policy options that the company considers when it expands overseas (see Chapter 5).

CASE: ICI

Background

Imperial Chemical Industries, or ICI, is a leading international chemical company. It operates in over 150 countries, and in world terms is the fourth largest chemical manufacturer, after the German companies Bayer, Hoechst and BASF (see Table 2.3). Originally the company was formed from a combination of UK chemical companies and continues to maintain its head office within the UK and manufacturing facilities for all its range of products, even though it has become in definition a transnational corporation with less than 50 per cent of its assets in any one country.

By 1987, turnover had reached £11 123 million ($19 300) and was split geographically between the UK, providing 25 per cent of total turnover, Continental Europe 25

Table 2.3   Sales in $ billion 1986

BASF	25.64
Bayer	23.66
Hoechst	23.55
ICI	20.99
DuPont	17.60

Source: From company accounts.

Table 2.4   ICI 1983/7 (all figures approximate £ million)

	1987	1986	1985	1984	1983
Total sales	11000	10000	10750	9800	9400
Physical distribution costs	790	730	730	690	700
Per cent	7.2	7.3	7.2	7.0	7.4
Stocks	1800	1730	1750	1740	1500
Stock turn (sales/stock)	6.1	5.8	6.1	5.6	6.3
Individual divisions (sales):					
Pharmaceuticals	1100	1000	950	800	600
Paints	1300	800	750	600	600
Other effect products (dyes)	2000	1800	1700	1300	1100
General chemicals	1800	1700	1700	1600	1500
Plastics/petrochemicals	2600	2800	3600	3800	3000
Fibres	700	700	700	600	600
Agrochemicals	850	750	750	650	500
Fertilizers	800	900	1100	1100	800

Source: Adapted from annual reports.

per cent, the Americas 27 per cent, Australasia, Japan and the Far East 17 per cent, others (including India) 6 per cent.

In common with the other major chemical companies ICI originally concentrated on the manufacture and distribution of basic industrial feedstocks, products such as caustic soda and potash, and fertilizers for the agricultural community. ICI also became one of the major manufacturers of artificial fibres and basic plastics for this rapidly growing sector after the Second World War. All these products were relatively low in value and high in weight, which meant that the company had to pay substantial attention to the way in which it distributed and held stock. Since 1955 the company had progressively moved away from a concentration on such bulk products into speciality areas of chemical production. By 1987, a large contribution to turnover was made by speciality products (see Table 2.4), though distribution costs and the value of stocks held continue to be a major factor in the way in which the group plans its worldwide operations.

Much of the way in which ICI organizes its worldwide business can be explained by the specific distribution requirements of the individual business areas. In the high added value divisions such as pharmaceuticals and speciality chemicals the costs of distribution remain low in relation to the value of the product, and it is only where there are specific product demands in the market that the company has established production units (Table 2.5).

Where the company has large markets for bulk products, such as the agrochemicals and fertilizer divisions, it has to establish local manufacture operations to offset the high cost of inter-market transportation and storage. This is also true of markets where the customer base is extremely large as is the case in the paint division, where the long-

Table 2.5 Main centres of production for ICI by product type

	UK	Europe	Japan	America	Australia	Other Pacific
Pharmaceuticals	*		*	*		
Paints	*	*	*	*	*	*
Dyes	*	*		*		
Polyurethanes	*	*		*	*	*
Speciality chemicals	*			*		
Advanced materials	*	*	*	*		
Films	*	*		*		
General chemicals	*	*		*	*	
Petrochemicals	*	*			*	
Fibres	*	*		*		
Explosives	*				*	
Agrochemicals	*	*		*	*	*
Fertilizers	*			*	*	*

Source: Adapted from annual reports.

term stated strategy is to build the Dulux brand into a true world consumer product, similar to Coca-Cola or Lux toilet soap. In contrast, many of the industrial products are sold to specific end users, such as the manufacturers of blue jeans that use ICI dyes.

Not only does distribution play a crucial part in the long-term strategy of the group, it is also extremely important in the short-term as a major component of cost. Physical distribution costs make up over 7 per cent of the cost of sales, and are regarded as so important that they are identified as a separate element in the annual accounts.

The company also holds high levels of stocks in the majority of its operations, a much higher level than in many other manufacturing or service sectors. Control over these stocks will make a major impact on the overall profitability of the group; for example, reducing the stocks by 20 per cent would mean a reduction in finance cost of around £40 million (at 12 per cent interest) and this would feed through directly to profitability. Reducing its physical distribution costs by a similar percentage would mean an additional improvement of £160 million in profitability. Put in context, such changes in policy would mean that the trading profit of £1297 million in the financial year 1986/87 could be improved by 15 per cent.

Such figures underline the considerable financial impact that distribution and stock holding have for a company like ICI, and how important it is that the needs for particular stock holding, manufacturing and physical distribution policies are continually reappraised in relation to changing strategic directions.

DISTRIBUTION ASSIGNMENTS

1 Using company balance sheets, explore the contribution that decisions concerning distribution have made to the progress of a major company in any particular manufacturing sector over the last ten years.

2 A manufacturer of highly priced industrial valves has asked you to produce a report on the main problems that might be encountered in their expansion plans for the rest of Europe, from their current base in the Netherlands.

3 What major changes do you think that the completion of the Channel Tunnel will cause in the distribution environment in the EEC and the UK in particular?

4 British Aerospace, a manufacturer of aeroplanes and defence equipment, are in the process of taking over the Rover group, a manufacturer of mass market cars. What are the distribution implications for British Aerospace for this particular development?

5 A small company in the agricultural chemicals business is expanding outside the current customer base. What are the distribution implications of this change likely to be?

Distribution Channel Design—Some Broad Issues

Earlier discussion suggests that the total distribution concept firstly requires an understanding of a company's products, markets and the service needs of customers; and secondly an integration of stocks, delivery systems and order administration with these realities. The main objective is to serve its markets and customers more efficiently than the competition.

A first step is the definition of who is, in fact, the customer. This might appear straightforward—one might say that the customer for a tin of baked beans is a mass market consumer. However, reality for the manufacturer is that the customer is the retailer putting the product on the shelf. Here the manufacturer does not have direct contact with the end consumer, but uses an intermediary, the retailer. The baked bean manufacturer's distribution planning will therefore proceed with this in mind. This separation of the concept of the customer and the consumer is an important difference between basic marketing concepts and the reality of distribution. The marketing department will concentrate on the *segment* of the market which the company can best serve. In this case, it is the buyer of the can of baked beans who is the consumer. The distribution system will concentrate on the best *customer(s)* to service this segment of consumers. As we have said, it is the retailer who is the customer.

Finding an efficient method of reaching the final consumer and deciding whether or not it should be through intermediaries is vital initially. It involves choosing the most appropriate *distribution channel*. A distribution channel can be defined as the way in which goods move from the supplier to end user. They can be direct, where the supplier has immediate contact with the end user or consumer; or indirect, where there are intermediaries between the supplier and end user or consumer (Figure 3.1). Through the process known as distribution channel design, the firm selects a distribution system most appropriate to those realities mentioned at the beginning. It should be remembered that there are not just the intermediary stockists to be considered in developing a distribution channel—there is also the management of physical distribution intermediaries if they are involved in the transport of goods from manufacturing point to end user. Physical distribution intermediaries can be involved

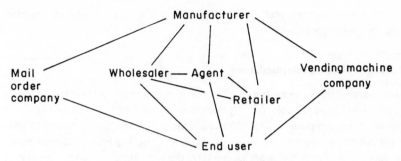

Figure 3.1   Distribution channels

in any of the transfers between manufacturer and end user. Whether it is direct—from manufacturer straight to end user; or primary—from manufacturer to an intermediate warehouse; or secondary—from intermediate warehouse to the end user. The issues involved in the choice of physical distribution channels will be discussed in Chapter 12, as part of the management of the movement of product from manufacturer to channel member.

Each channel, whether direct or indirect, will involve the physical movement of the product from the manufacturer to its final destination (end user or consumer) and a number of additional movements as well. Information flow is important: manufacturers will supply information about product availability and in return channel members will supply information about the product's performance in the market. Payment flows relate to intermediaries/end user purchase of the goods and the transaction results in an ownership movement from the manufacturer to the component of the distribution channel; investment flows involve continuing manufacturer investment.

Investment is a central problem for distribution channel design: cost versus benefit. In other words, what level of investment and consequent raised fixed cost will provide what level of control and improvement in profitability. The correct design will aim at a balance cost and benefit. To maximize benefit, the correct distribution channel must be compatible with the firm's objectives in respect of market share, profitability, growth and new product development. The implications of using a direct or indirect distribution channel have to be carefully evaluated. Thus use of some form of indirect channel will affect such areas as stock-holding, pricing, control over the market. The chosen distribution channel will also need to be continually monitored and reviewed as market factors change.

INDIRECT DISTRIBUTION

The company opting for a system of indirect distribution must consider various issues. Whatever the channel design selected there are bound to be problems as well as opportunities and, in common with other areas of the company's distribution system, the planner must achieve a balance between the advantages of one approach and its inherent disadvantages and decide upon a policy appropriate in meeting the company's strategic objectives.

Advantages of using intermediaries

In summarizing the varied services supplied by an intermediary one has to remember that not all will be applicable to every company, nor will the importance of each be the same for every company. Intermediaries will generally help the company to widen its market coverage: in some instances they can increase the local customer base via a sales force whose overheads are covered by the wide product range handled. A firm can also obtain assistance in developing its approach to the market, getting local sales promotion and advertising, product testing and development through intermediaries. In export markets particularly, they can adapt product in such a way that it becomes acceptable to the local market—often termed 'breaking bulk'. They can in addition provide a local level of buffer stock which copes with fluctuations both in supply to the market and within the market. Use of intermediaries also offers a certain adminis-trative simplicity by reducing the paperwork involving the supplier—one customer instead of dozens. Such simplicity extends to other areas: providing credit to the end user and reducing the credit risk to the supplier by dealing with all the individual accounts and perhaps improving the supplier's cash flow. A further financial advantage for the export supplier is reduced distribution costs through shipping in bulk. Intermediaries will also take the responsibility for setting local prices and discounts if the market is distant from the supplier's manufacturing point or if it faces specific local pricing problems.

Disadvantages of using intermediaries

Intermediaries are usually companies in their own right. Like their suppliers, they too are operating to make profits. Since an intermediary has its own profitability criteria, it may choose to price product at uncompetitive levels, either reducing potential market share or encouraging parallel trading, which is the interference of other intermediaries within the market sector due to variations in pricing policy (Figure 3.2). Similarly, when a company uses intermediaries, pricing structures will be more complex as they will have to allow for both direct and indirect purchase. Pricing structures will also have to be adjusted to include a profit margin for the intermediary and this may well reduce the supplier's profitability, although it is an essential part of maintaining and motivating intermediaries as key components in the supplier's distribution process.

Intermediaries tend to handle a wide range of products which may be comple-mentary or direct competitors to those of a particular supplier. Conflict is inherent in this situation although it may not be immediately apparent. The intermediary, acting in good faith, begins by handling products that do not overlap. But change occurs in the market over time and, over a ten year period, product range A of manufacturer A becomes identical to product range B supplied by manufacturer B. Competitors

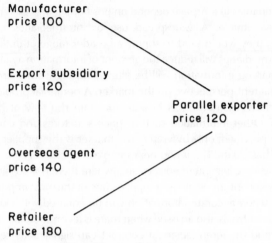

Figure 3.2 Parallel trading

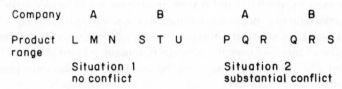

Figure 3.3 Conflict between product ranges

encroaching on each other's sector of the market fail to perceive this and accordingly adjust their distribution intermediaries (Figure 3.3). Where this is happening, the intermediary may respond by concentrating on the most immediately profitable products giving little attention to developing new products.

A further complication arising where intermediaries handle extensive product ranges is conflict between their own promotional plans and those of their suppliers. An intermediary may decide to concentrate on ice cream in the summer rather than soft drinks, for example. The soft drinks supplier will have to take this into account in the timing of a promotional campaign. The use of intermediaries also influences the supplier's promotional expenditure patterns. Part of its promotional budget must be allocated to persuading intermediaries to stock or maintain product—the so-called 'push' promotional techniques used to ensure a product's presence in the distribution channel; rather than promotional material aimed purely at the end user— the 'pull' promotional techniques to persuade the end user to take stock out from the distribution channel or direct from the supplier.

For the manufacturer relying on very accurate market segmentation problems may also arise from the frequently broader approach of intermediaries. For instance, perfume companies like Arpege depend on positioning in premium outlets as part of their exclusive image. A widespread use of intermediaries might weaken this exclusivity as they would tend to supply a broader range of outlet type.

Using intermediaries will reduce the amount of information available to the supplier about the market: information will be filtered through other firms which have an essentially different perspective on the market. A perennial problem in the management of overseas distributors is how to maintain the flow of monthly stock and sales reports. Other information such as price structures and competitive pricing is rarely if ever provided; only by visiting the market is the supplier company likely to receive such basic data. This is another example of the loss of *control* that the supplier experiences when using intermediaries and, where there is a considerable geographic distance between intermediary and supplier, one of the most important—living as we do at a time when accurate information can be equated with power.

Decreased control is also an issue when there is a contractual relationship between the supplier and the intermediary: a contract can significantly reduce the flexibility that the supplier company will have in the market place as replacing one intermediary with another or some form of direct delivery may take over a year. These are some of the considerations which resulted in Seagrams, the owners of Sandeman port, taking the policy decision to concentrate distribution of major brands in the French market via an owned sales subsidiary instead of using intermediaries in the distribution process. The changeover from the previous distributor entailed the loss of product distribution and sales which could only be recouped by substantial promotional investment.

DIRECT VERSUS INDIRECT DISTRIBUTION—REACHING A DECISION

Whether or not a company should use intermediaries in the distribution system is therefore a complex decision. It involves both benefits and risks which vary from product sector to sector and market to market. However, there are various product and service related criteria that can be used as general indicators of whether direct or indirect distribution will be *more appropriate*. This will always have to be modified in the light of the firm's strategic requirements (Table 3.1).

The underlying logic of the Table 3.1 grid is that wide distribution in terms of numbers and locations is costly and may best be served by using some form of intermediary. If the product is complex, with a significant service element and installation requirements it is unlikely that an indirect distribution channel will be able to supply essential expertise. Furthermore, if there is a significant requirement for sales information and substantial negotiation in price the process cannot be effectively left to an intermediary. A similar approach separates the channel environment into three subsets, long, medium and short distribution channels (or red, orange, and yellow) in the fashion shown in Table 3.2. But these rule of thumb or 'heuristic' approaches to defining distribution paths must be analysed in conjunction with the firm's strategy. Thus there may, for example, be a competitive requirement to provide a high level of

Table 3.1 Direct versus indirect distribution—some decision making criteria

Factor	High	Low
Geographical concentration	Direct	Indirect
Number of buyers	Indirect	Direct
Complexity of product	Direct	Indirect
Unit price	Direct	Indirect
Standardization	Indirect	Direct
Servicing requirements	Direct	Indirect
Price negotiation	Direct	Indirect
Sales information	Direct	Indirect
Frequency of purchase	Indirect	Direct
Perishability	Direct	Indirect

Table 3.2 Long, medium and short distribution channels

Factor	Long	Medium	Short
Replacement rate	High	Medium	Low
Gross margin	Low	Medium	High
Degree of necessary adaptation	Low	Medium	High
Speed of consumption	Rapid	Medium	Low

direct delivery when the logic of our discussion would indicate that an indirect channel was a far more satisfactory arrangement.

TYPES OF INTERMEDIARIES

The company's market and product sector are the main considerations determining the relative importance of intermediaries. When tackling a new market or developing a channel for a new range of products, the distribution planner has to identify the presence or absence of the main alternative intermediary types. These include wholesalers, retailers, mail order firms, agents and distributors, franchisees, licensing, industrial co-operation agreements and management contracts. The main characteristics of each will be summarized in the remainder of this section with the aim of emphasizing the complexity and variety inherent in each. Wholesalers like retailers, for example, range from those handling a wide product range in a particular sector to those with a much more specialized range requiring a higher level of technical expertise.

Wholesalers handle goods supplied either directly from a variety of manufacturers or from other intermediaries. They act as a stock holder or distributor for the final end user. They are independent of both the manufacturer and the end user and achieve their profit from the difference between the price at which they buy product and the price at which they sell. Typical companies include cash and carry wholesalers that service the retail trade and do not deliver; delivered wholesalers which provide credit and deliver to their client base; and specialist wholesalers providing specific product ranges. The exporter must also consider the variations between countries. Japan is an example of a market where three layers of wholesalers exist, each providing a steadily wider market coverage. Countries with large geographical areas such as the US also have an important wholesale sector. Wholesalers will vary as to the type of product ranges stocked, and the degree of market coverage; national wholesaler chains are increasingly common throughout Western Europe and North America.

Retailers are intermediaries selling direct to the consumer and are normally independent of the manufacturer. They vary considerably in size and specialization. In many markets there are clear-cut divisions between the various types of retailers. Thus national multiple chains maintain a large number of outlets, being established in the majority of regions in the market. In contrast, regional multiple chains will own a number of outlets in a single region of the market. There are independent general stores with a small number of branches and a broad product range; and independent specialist stores with a small number of branches and a limited product range. A supplier may, however, be more interested in the voluntary chains consisting of small independent stores which band together under a common operating umbrella. Finally there are independent stores operating single outlets.

In certain sections of the consumer market, mail order operators are very important intermediaries. For example, overall mail order accounts for around 6 per cent of total spending by consumers on clothing in the UK. It has been suggested that the role of mail order may become more important as the Western industrialized economies become more diverse. In certain specialized sectors vending machines may provide an important distribution method. In Japan, much of the growth of pot noodles was achieved through vending machines as meals vending is far more widespread in that market than Western Europe or the US. Vending machines also continue to provide an important distribution channel for cigarette manufacturers in pubs and clubs even though in the major towns the advent of the convenience or late opening store has reduced their importance elsewhere.

Agents have a contractual relationship with one or more manufacturers to distribute particular products in a geographical area. The level of support that they provide may vary from the commission agent—which does not carry stock and merely passes orders from end users to the manufacturer; through stocking agents— that carry spare parts or the entire range; to full service agents or dealers fully equipped to deal with all service problems.

With the expansion in the service sector of modern industrial economies, franchising has become an extremely important method of achieving rapid expansion. Franchised intermediaries are independently owned companies which enter into a close contractual relationship with the manufacturer to distribute a specific product or service within a clearly defined geographical area. Franchising, though not new in concept, is one of the most rapidly growing sectors of the UK economy; an estimated one in three people employed in retailing will work for a franchise by 1992, as is already

Table 3.3   Important franchised outlets in the UK

Name	Type of operation	No. of outlets
Service Master	Carpet cleaning	195
Prontaprint	Printer	284
Kentucky Fried Chicken	Fast food outlet	225
Wimpy	Fast food outlet	350
Benetton	Retail clothing	260
Body Shop	Retail cosmetics	90
Apollo Window Blinds	Kitchen fitting	110

Source: Franchise Directory, Franchise Development Association UK, 1986.

the case in the US. Many other areas of the economy will also be involved but retailing is likely to remain the most important sector in this area (Table 3.3). The growth of franchising has significantly blurred the interrelationship between the supplier and the outlet in many companies. Some continue to follow the policy of owning all the retail outlets for which they manufacture—an example would be the Tandy Corporation in computers or Laura Ashley in clothes. Such organizational structures are known as corporate vertical marketing systems or CVMS. Others operate a mixture of company owned stores and franchise outlets. From the supplier's perspective the degree of control that they are able to exert through franchise agreements may in reality mean that the franchise system operates entirely under very clear guidelines on product, price and presentation. The decision whether to franchise or not then merges into investment requirements and the degree of risk involved in the rapid expansion of franchised outlets. Body Shop, one of the most successful franchised operations in the UK, chose that route because of the lack of available funds—establishing franchises for them was the only possible expansion method, whereas Laura Ashley, with a better cash flow, have been willing to expand more slowly with directly owned outlets, thereby accepting a higher level of return over a longer time period.

Licence agreements, industrial co-operation agreements, and management contracts are common methods of achieving distribution in overseas markets and are discussed in detail in Chapter 5. Here we shall simply summarize their main characteristics.

Licensing is a distribution method whereby the manufacturer or supplier licenses the use of its technology or brand name in return for a royalty on sales. Coca-Cola is the classic successful example of licensing. It operates a worldwide network of licencees bottling the Coca-Cola range and buying the concentrate from the parent company in the US; and in the 1980s successfully expanded the use of the Coca-Cola brand name into a wide range of clothing and other products such as umbrellas.

Through an industrial co-operation agreement, two companies may contract to swap material or finished goods and sell them in their respective markets. Industrial co-operation agreements can also include the creation of some form of joint venture which is often regarded as a separate type of distribution channel.

A management contract is a distribution channel whereby the supplier takes management responsibility for the particular operation. There are many sectors of industry where the use of management contracts has grown; international hotels, work camps, and farming projects being examples.

DISTRIBUTION CHANNEL ANALYSIS AND DISTRIBUTION PLANNING

Distribution channel analysis is often called *dissection* implying that the distribution channel can be cut open and laid bare in a clinical fashion. Readers should be aware that channel evaluation is more of an art than a science, relying on the subjective assessment of all the contributions that a particular channel can make to achieving the company's distribution objectives. Any analysis must acknowledge that each channel in each market will have its own characteristics and that these change over time. We have already examined the various types of intermediaries. Here we make the point that the characteristics of each channel in each market will need evaluation to avoid basing distribution action on the perilous assumption that what works in one market will work in another. For example, voluntary groups such as Spar and VG have had a far more important role in the distribution network in the Federal Republic of Germany than they have had in the UK, where the co-operative movement was always stronger. Some key distribution planning issues are outlined in this section.

Market coverage

The desired level of market *coverage* is an important aspect of distribution channel analysis. For each market two measurements of coverage of the total available customer base exist. *Numerical distribution* measures the percentage of total outlets supplied. *Weighted distribution* measures the distribution related to the importance of the outlet. For example, a distribution channel might provide 60 per cent numerical distribution but only 30 per cent weighted. This would mean that the channel concentrated on small outlets and missed out on accounts that provided the bulk of the turnover in that market sector.

Product distribution factors

The chosen distribution channel affects the *completeness of product range* that will be carried. In each channel there are wide variations in the ability to provide and maintain an entire product range. For companies supplying technical or complex products a full range of accessories may be an important service issue when selecting a distribution channel. A complaint about high street electrical stores selling computers is their unwillingness to stock large quantities of essential back-up product such as disks, printer ribbons and other peripherals.

There is therefore an issue of the degree of *expertise* and back-up that the distribution channel can bring to the sale of the product. Thus the amount of product knowledge and experience between each channel varies considerably—a vital issue for those making channel decisions for selling complex or premium products, especially where any type of post sale warranty or service agreement is necessary for the effective marketing of the product. Part of the success of the Our Price record chain rests on the employment of young record enthusiasts who could knowledgeably sell products to the target market of 14–25 year olds. Expertise in the distribution channel is also important if product properties require delicate handling, or special equipment because of size or weight.

Stock holding and service to the end user

Earlier discussion mentioned the variations in *levels of stock holding* offered by different intermediaries. This is another issue that must be examined in the context of distribution channel selection and planning. A range of stock holding capacity is apparent: from the agent that will not carry stock as part of the agreement with the manufacturer, to large wholesalers that specialize in maintaining significant volumes of stock against possible fluctuations in demand.

A related issue is the *speed* with which a distribution channel can service the final customer: important for perishable goods and spare part provision for technical equipment. Brake Brothers, the delivered wholesaler, grew rapidly because of rising demand for rapid delivery of frozen food products. The frozen food market had expanded but many outlets were unable to stock substantial quantities of frozen food.

Conflict and distribution channel leaders

There is conflict in each distribution system between companies fighting to achieve maximum profitability in the market; wholesalers against wholesalers (an example of horizontal channel conflict); suppliers against end users (vertical channel conflict); and wholesalers against retailers (inter-channel conflict). Manufacturer, intermediary and end user all have a number of differing objectives the resolution of which will be determined by the amount of power each can exert (Table 3.4). For the distribution planner there are various points to consider.

In all likelihood, there will be a *channel leader* in each channel exerting a major influence and often acting as an incubus of conflict. The channel leader, usually the

Table 3.4 Varying objectives within the distribution channel

Manufacturer	Intermediary	End user
Market share	Margin	Choice
Widest market penetration	Exclusivity	Convenience
Cash flow	Credit	Value for money
Widest product range	Stock turn	Availability
End user promotion	Trade promotion	Discount

company with the largest market share, is occasionally the company that is most innovative. It will tend to determine the price levels operating in the market with the competing companies reflecting the price levels of the market leader in their pricing policy. For example, the Belgian retail group Colruyt, with about 9 per cent of the total grocery market, uses a group of market researchers to continually monitor prices in the two larger retail groups, Delhaize and GB, with 12 and 22 per cent respectively. Colruyt then sets local store prices in relation to the prices charged at these stores.

The channel leader can play an important role in expediting the diffusion of new products or concepts. It will furthermore influence the conduct of negotiations and the level of promotion that is demanded by the entire sector. The concentration of UK wholesale activity among a smaller number of companies has substantially increased the promotional demands within this channel of distribution. Particularly active in this respect have been Linfood and Nurdin and Peacock. The speed of own or private label development is normally heavily influenced by the stance that the channel leader takes. Channel leaders in Spain such as Cortes Ingles have been slow to develop own labels and a result own labels are under-represented in Spain compared with the rest of the EEC.

Vertical conflict has been a noticeable feature of increased retailer power in the consumer sector. Less noticeable, though just as relevant, is the concentration of industrial activity in many sectors. Retail (and end user) purchasing power has affected the ability of the manufacturer to distribute products in a number of ways. So although there is a trend towards a greater market segmentation, store buyers are tending to reduce the range of products stocked within each segment. Because of their great size, retailers and major end users are increasingly acting as manufacturers in their own rights.

An additional feature of vertical conflict is that, for the supplier, new products face a steadily shorter proving period. Whereas retailers found it acceptable to allow a new product between six and eight months to become established in the 1970s, this proving time for many retailers is now down to three. Indeed, Marks and Spencer, the largest retailing group in the UK, requires any new product to achieve a substantial turnover in the first week of introduction. Similar concentration on exploiting only successful products and those lines that provide a rapid return has been part of the revitalization of the J.C. Penney retail chain in the US. This example illustrates the emphasis now given in retailers' strategies to turnover per square foot. For other end users the emphasis is on reliability and other profitability criteria.

When linked with end user purchasing power, these developments influence the supplier's pricing strategy and may have the effect of lowering the profitability within the distribution channel for the supplier. Higher levels of service demand also complicate the supplier profitability issue as end users adopt further cost-cutting strategies like delivery at higher frequency, buffer stocks being held by manufacturer rather than end user, provision of specially marked packs for the retailer or end user.

Horizontal conflict is increasingly a feature of many market sectors in the developed world due to the growing market share of major intermediaries. Thus in the Belgian market, where 70 per cent of grocery sales is in the hands of four chains, there is intense conflict in the market to improve market share. The four demand steadily increased promotional expenditure to increase and maintain their customer base; they wish access to the supply of exclusive product (partially served by the expansion of own label products). Furthermore, there is a search for greater control over suppliers through the purchase of competitive supplier companies; and pursuance of a policy of continual expansion of market share by the purchase of minor competitors which further increases these retailers' purchasing power.

Inter-type conflict is less apparent in most market sectors but becomes more relevant as the groups in each of the major channels reach the limits of growth and seek opportunities for expansion by entering new market sectors. Makro, the Dutch based chain for example, operates in many of its European markets as a wholesaler/retailer. Although it is officially classified as a wholesaler, getting a Makro card allowing access to the store is fairly simple for consumers having some contact with clubs, associations, or interest groups. Such wide ownership of cards means that many of them use Makro as a retail outlet.

Rigidity in the distribution channel

The channel servicing a particular market sector may become static over time; this may be caused by any one of several factors and has important implications for any new supplier or intermediary trying to enter the market. Distribution channel rigidity occurs in a number of ways.

Where a distribution channel demands *high levels of fixed costs* the likelihood of other companies being able to enter the market is reduced, fixing the distribution system. The international air courier business is one area requiring high investment in local offices, and transport systems. Companies such as Federal Express from the US and DHL from Hong Kong have these networks established. For new market entrants the investment required would be considerable.

Where *high levels of current expenditure* are needed to maintain distribution there will also be barriers to new entrants. The popular music record industry seems to be one where new companies can rapidly become established, with over 3000 independent labels in existence in the mid-1980s. Production costs are low and margins high so fragmentation appears inevitable. However, in 1972 six companies held 60 per cent of the market. In 1983, even after eleven years of rapidly changing fashion in music, seven companies (the same six plus one newcomer Virgin Records) held 66 per cent of the market. Distribution remains the key to market domination. Newly successful groups are often signed by the small independent labels for their first disc, but it is the major record producers who offer guaranteed promotion on the radio—70 per cent of purchase decisions are made following radio 'plugs'; and have the widest distribution throughout the trade. Almost inevitably the successful group moves from the independent to the major label, reinforcing market strength of these companies. Virgin Records joined the major companies by concentrating on building up its own retail outlets to provide instant distribution for its artists. Virgin could now hold on to successful groups.

Legislation can have the effect of creating channel rigidity. UK drug wholesalers cannot buy standard branded drugs from other EEC countries where prices are often lower. There is a government licensing requirement that all drugs must be obtained from suppliers licensed by the Department of Health and Social Security. The effect of this legislation prevents new intermediaries entering the market without DHSS approval.

Contractual control enables suppliers to maintain distribution channels by contractual undertakings. Thus managers of 'tied' public houses were required until a court ruling in the 1980s to purchase all their catering requirements from a single source. By providing frozen food cabinets on loan to retail outlets, frozen food manufacturers like Walls and Lyons Maid ensured that competitive products were not stocked. Contractual control therefore often has major implications for development in new markets. The takeover by the Elders IXL group of the Courage chain was bedevilled by the fact that a rival group, Grand Metropolitan, had contractual rights to the production of the Fosters brand through the Watneys chain.

Market conservatism can cause inflexibility in the distribution channel where specific historic or cultural influences are resilient to change. Cars are, for example, mainly sold door to door in Japan, and attempts to set up dealer networks along the lines of Western Europe have been successful only at the upper end of the product range. Asda, the supermarket group, attempted to alter car retailing systems in the UK by selling them through selected grocery outlets. The experiment failed partly as a result of consumer perceptions about the wisdom of buying cars with groceries.

Demand for product *exclusivity* in a distribution channel can create resistance within the channel to new products and concepts available outside it. Distribution channels differ in the extent of their interest in product exclusivity. In general the smaller and more specialized the distribution channel the greater the need for exclusivity, as it is this which allows specialized groups to charge the premium prices necessary for the normally higher overhead levels than the volume, mass market channel members. Breuval, the Distillers distributor in Belgium, partly resolved the problem caused by supermarket groups selling its leading brands at prices below those offered to the specialist wine merchants, by splitting its product range into two: one stocked by the supermarkets, the other by the specialists.

The Breuval example also suggests that *pricing demands* can also become a factor in channel rigidity. Large channels, particularly one with a dominant channel leader, will have considerable price leverage over the supplier. Small channels with a fairly homogeneous membership will have lower levels of price demand.

Durability, image and channel change

A minor consideration in channel design is whether the channel has long-term future in the market: its durability in effect. Specialized mail order and retail outlets have a particularly high failure rate, and companies using these channels must take such considerations into account in their distribution policy.

End user perceptions about available distribution channels differ considerably and this has an important influence on their efficiency and impact on product positioning. Inappropriate channels can cause considerable damage to the image and product positioning of particular brands. This is of especial concern for companies trying to dispose of end of lines or remaindered stock, which if sold at a discount into an open market will often appear in inappropriate outlets, thus damaging the overall perception of the supplier.

Long-term study of distribution within a particular market sector shows that the dominant companies within that sector will alter over time. The classic example of such a change is retailing in the US, dominated in turn by mail order, department stores, variety stores, town centre supermarkets, hypermarkets, and finally discount stores. Two broad theories have been proposed to explain this change. The wheel of retailing concept is a five stage theory reminiscent of the product life cycle theory mentioned in a previous chapter. The first stage involves the introduction of the innovative concept operating on high profit margins with low overheads. In the second stage there is rapid growth of the successful formula followed by a plateau as growth slows as market share increases, in the third stage, when promotional and other overheads increase. During the fourth stage the business ceases to be innovative, and becomes more interested in maintaining market share and profitability. Finally, an innovative competitor appears in the market.

The second explanation of change in the retailing market is the specialist–generalist–specialist theory. This takes the view that firms succeed because they initially specialize in narrow market segments, then they branch out into other market areas becoming what might be termed 'a Jack of all trades but master of none', and are in turn replaced by another specialist firm that is more accurately meeting the market needs.

Though these theories relate primarily to the retail sector they are relevant to explain the likely changes that take place throughout the distribution channels available to a company.

CASE: GASCOFIX

Introduction

Gascofix was founded in 1984 by an industrial chemist Gurindar Shah, aged 52, who had developed the concept after several years of trial and error while working part time at a technical college in East London.

The product that was finally perfected was a new form of sealant for motor vehicle gaskets. Gaskets are seals between the engine block and the cylinder head to prevent the leakage of gases and water. They are made of a variety of materials—often asbestos with a thin steel or copper covering. The gasket has to be fixed to the block with some form of adhesive, and this adhesive has to face severe conditions of heat, (ranging from $-20°C$ to $+250°C$) pressure and corrosion which will often be sustained over a long period of time. The larger or more powerful the engine, the greater the forces on the sealant.

The new adhesive had two particular advantages over the competition: by using certain industrial waste as raw material in the production process it was substantially cheaper to manufacture and had greater resistance to both heat and pressure. Because of the basic nature of the product, the company could not take out a patent on the new adhesive, but Gurindar Shah was of the opinion that the research that had been put into finding the exact production process and combination of raw materials would require a substantial research programme and the product could probably not be copied within eighteen months.

The production process

Gascofix could be simply produced from dry raw materials in 50 kg (for practical purposes 50 kg contained 50 000 ml of product) quantities in single air-tight reaction vessels electrically heated and magnetically stirred over a five hour period. The product could then be extruded via a simple filling machine into a range of containers ranging from 50 ml to 250 ml, or supplied in the reaction vessels themselves for local filling. Contact with air hardened the product which would then set rigid in two hours.

A 50 kg container of the finished product cost around £100 including labour; the cost of tube containers ranged from 2p for a 50 ml tube to 5p for a 250 ml unit. Gurindar Shah had facilities with the local branch of Remploy to fix these tubes on to instruction cards at 5p per unit. When established in a small warehouse in East London, the company had the ability to produce 100 kg per day, all of which could be successfully passed through the filling machine and fixed on to backing plates via Remploy.

Gurindar Shah was able initially to handle the entire production process on his own but would be able to employ his two sons and other family should the production need to be increased.

Because of the nature of the production process overheads were very low (Table 3.5).

Gurindar Shah had no specific experience of running his own company as he had been involved in research for most of his working life. He had been developing this

Table 3.5   Gascofix overheads

Rent	£2000
Rates	£750
Power	£500
Telephone	£300
Miscellaneous	£1000

Table 3.6 Gascofix—income and expenditure

	1	2	3	4	5	6
Sales	450	650	1300	2200	2600	2800
Revenue	—	—	300	700	1200	1500
Materials	90	150	260	440	520	560
Rent and rates	1375	—	—	—	—	—
Wages	500	500	500	500	500	500
Other	150	150	150	150	150	150
Interest and repayment	100	100	100	100	100	100
Equipment	1500	—	—	—	—	—
Cash flow	(3715)	(900)	(710)	(490)	(70)	190
Cumulative	—	(4615)	(5325)	(5815)	(5885)	(5695)

process over a number of years and he had to turn to the local authority for finance as he had no security to borrow money from the bank. The local authority had provided him with £7500 start up finance, repayable over 5 years.

Company progress

Tables 3.6 and 3.7 supply details of the company's progress.

The market

The market for a gasket sealant was a potentially large one, as the product could be used by both the manufacturer of the original engines and by engine reconditioners and repairers. The main sectors within the UK are identified in Table 3.8.

A rough guide suggested that DIY repairs would use around 50 ml on each occasion whereas other users would use in the region of 150 ml.

The market was obviously also one that was potentially worldwide including the EEC, the US, Japan and many other countries with well developed road transport systems and fairly substantial vehicle repair sectors. Since the armed forces through-

Table 3.7 Gascofix—six months balance sheet (unaudited)

Sales	£10 000
Materials	£2 000
Overheads	£2 200
Wages	£3 000
Selling expenses	£1 200
Interest	£500
Loan repayment	£500
Profit (loss)	£600

Table 3.8   Gascofix—main sectors of the UK market

Sector	Numbers of vehicles per year
OEM (cars)	1 913 000
OEM (goods/transport)	116 000
OEM (others)	55 000
Reconditioners	500 000 (est.)
Repairs (professional)	300 000 (est.)
Repairs (DIY)	350 000 (est.)

NB OEM figures include imported and exported units.
Source: Trade estimates.

out the world required high specifications in their engine design and maintenance as a result of the greater demands for performance and reliability, this sector also provided favourable market opportunities.

Each of these sectors was serviced in different ways.

1. *The Office Equipment Manufacturer (OEM) sector* bought direct, a small number of large volume manufacturers such as Ford, GM, making up the bulk of the production of both cars and goods vehicles. These companies varied considerably as to the degree to which they were vertically integrated (producing components in-house), but were all currently in the process of attempting to reduce the number of component suppliers with whom they dealt. Because of the large volumes produced, OEM companies bought in bulk and demanded high quality specifications. It often took suppliers two or three years to be accepted as a potential source of components. The price at which these companies bought was uncertain but was thought to be around £10 per kilo. They also demanded highly favourable credit terms of around 100 days.

2. *The overseas military market* was handled by a number of international agents that co-ordinated the purchase of materials for the armed services throughout the world. The going price for this market was considerably higher than that for the OEM manufacturers; the product would tend to be available in small quantities with appropriate language instruction.

3. *The reconditioning market* consisted of a large number of medium sized companies that had regional bases servicing the surrounding market. It was estimated that there were around 150 such firms in the UK each handling between 200 and 1500 engine repairs a year. They bought gasket sealant in fairly large quantities direct from the manufacturers, and were paying around £2.30 for a 250 ml tube. They were fairly erratic payers and average credit periods were of the region of 90 days.

4. *The DIY repair market* was serviced via retail and wholesale outlets. It was estimated that there were around 3000 outlets that specialized in this market sector; the largest, Halfords, owned by the Ward White group, had around 21 per cent market share. The rest of the market was characterized by independent retailers which either bought direct from individual firms, one of the five major distributors in the motor accessories

market or via the growing number of specialized wholesalers. The price charged the consumer was the highest, with competitive 50 ml tubes priced at £2.40 retail. This included a 35 per cent gross margin for the retailer and a 15–18 per cent wholesale margin. Credit terms varied according to the type of outlet, with 60 to 100 days being common. There was also a fairly high level of bad debts.

There were a number of independent sales agents that serviced the motor accessories market, making an income from a 15 per cent gross commission on the sales achieved, the supplier company taking all the credit risk involved for the particular account.

5. *The professional repair sector* was partly carried out in the 5000 garages that provided a full service facility, and also via mechanics who serviced cars at home for individuals. Approximately 9 per cent of all repairs were carried out by a mechanic working on the car at the home of the owner. The buying pattern of this group varied considerably.

(a) Dealers were required to buy product direct from the manufacturers and only manufacturer approved material could be used for repairs. This made up around 60 per cent of this sector.

(b) Independent garages bought either direct or via the wholesale sector. There was no reliable information as to what percentage bought in which fashion.

(c) Individual mechanics would on the whole buy direct from the retailer.

The competition

There were a variety of companies that produced gasket sealant, and a number that produced gasket replacement products that could be used for small gasket areas, but not in the case of the cylinder head. The market leader was Hermetite, a product produced by one of the major multinational chemical combines which was estimated to have around 37 per cent market share. There were two other major forces in the market and then a number of concerns that supplied specific customers with product to their specification (the suppliers to the OEM sector, for example).

Because the production process used by companies currently in the market was broadly similar, pricing was fairly inflexible. Though there was no information as to the profitability of the competitive products it was considered in the trade that 40–50 per cent gross contribution on a typical retail product would not be unusual.

The exhibition

In early 1985, Gurindar Shah had around 30 reconditioner clients to whom he was selling direct at around £2.15 for a 250 ml tube though terms varied between each customer. He was also selling a small quantity of product through local retailers and via an advertisement in *Exchange and Mart*. As these selling activities were now taking up a considerable amount of time he decided to invest in attending one of the main motoring manufacturing exhibitions, the Motor Accessories Fair. After this event and once potential customers had evaluated his product he received the following offers.

Motor Spares Ltd, one of the leading distributors in the country covering 1900 outlets with a sales force of 15, offered to distribute the product under their own label and pay a royalty of 15 per cent. They estimated that they would be able to achieve a 20 per cent market share in the DIY and reconditioner market within 18 months. To achieve this they demanded exclusivity over a three year period both in the UK and overseas where they had some, though limited, interests.

Mazel Tov, one of the leading international suppliers to the world arms market offered to buy the product in bulk at £4 a kilo for international distribution. They would initially want to take around 30 tons per year, but were not prepared to enter into a definite contractual relationship stating that Gurinder Shah would not be able to pursue independent action overseas.

Halfords offered to distribute the product via their outlets as an own brand provided they had exclusivity within the UK market. They would buy product in 50 ml tubes for £1.25.

A number of independent sales agents also approached the stand offering to represent the company in various areas throughout the UK: D. Evans Associates, based in Dartford, Kent, covered the south east counties of England and claimed to sell to 400 accounts in Kent, Sussex and Surrey; Arlex Ltd, based in Bracknell, called on around 600 accounts in Berkshire, Surrey, Hampshire; James Motor Factors, based in Uxbridge, claimed to call on 800 accounts in the London area.

All these companies would be prepared to operate as wholesalers selling at an agreed wholesale price which they thought should be between £1.30 and £1.45 for a 50 ml tube on which they would get 15 per cent gross commission.

Kasgai Ltd, the major supplier to the Japanese motor trade, had also approached the stand with the proposal that they would pay a $2\frac{1}{2}$ per cent commission on sales of the product in the Japanese market which was worth around eight times that of the UK market, and of which Kasgai had 60 per cent. The proposed agreement would last initially for two years, with an additional two years option available. It would require Gurindar Shah to reveal his production formula.

DISTRIBUTION ASSIGNMENTS

1   Evaluate the type of intermediaries that would be required for the manufacturer of: (a) frozen food and ice cream, (b) hand held power tools, (c) picture frames.

2   A company operating in the fast moving consumer goods environment is considering moving from wholesale to retail distribution. What are the implications of such a decision on the type of distribution system that will need to be employed?

3   Your company, currently operating as a specialist caterer, is considering acquiring a manufacturer of vending products. What implications would this have for the distribution channels that the company would choose?

4 Compare the distribution of various types of watch in retailers within a large town. Why have particular suppliers of watches chosen these retailers as their distribution channel? Do you think that some of the distribution channels have been inappropriate?

5 ` Collect details of all the franchised operations in your immediate area and identify what you regard as the reasons for the success of particular franchise operations. What other types of local service would be ideally franchised?

_Chapter   4__

Distribution Channel Design—Output Criteria

Designing, managing, and changing a distribution channel is an evolutionary process involving various steps.

—Deciding on the most suitable distribution channel in general.
—Choosing the specific channel members.
—Establishing close or broad agreements with the channel members.
—Motivating the chosen channel members.
—Evaluating channel member performance.
—Redefining distribution channels and channel members.

For the supplier there are distinct advantages in adopting a systematic approach to distribution channel design. It makes possible effective setting and co-ordination of company distribution objectives as part of its overall strategy (discussed in greater detail in Chapter 15). The tasks being implemented in each part of the distribution channel will be specified ensuring that these too are consistent with overall distribution and company strategy. In addition, a systematic approach will define the investment criteria for evaluating each channel. Finally, accurate definition of distribution channels and their specific functions will reduce conflict potential in the distribution channel and ensure that the distribution process works as smoothly and effectively as possible.

BROAD OUTPUT CRITERIA FOR THE DISTRIBUTION CHANNEL

The characteristics of the distribution channels available at home and overseas determine what they can or cannot achieve; and the level of investment and management time they will require. The output criteria—that is, what the channel can achieve—are an important aspect of distribution channel design because they allow the company to decide on the channel most appropriate to its product and market strategy. The importance to the company of the various output criteria and their ramifications must therefore be carefully and systematically evaluated. In the following discussion of various output criteria it becomes plain that it is essential for a company to be clear about what its distribution goals are.

Volumes, stock holding, market entry

In examining output criteria, most companies will be concerned to select a channel that is appropriate to their volume requirements. The type of channel determines the volume it can handle and this has implications for production management and the provision of working capital to fund any potential increased level of activity. Thus for a small company the mass market may be an inappropriate channel decision because it will be unable to fund the required stock levels, warehouse and systems requirements.

This illustration also indicates that a company must evaluate the channel's stock holding requirements. Different channels make different stock holding demands on the supplier. Wholesalers, for example, carry large levels of buffer stock, whereas many of the multiple chains expect suppliers to maintain high levels of stock.

But in any case, the channel may operate in such a way that it is difficult for newcomers to enter. In order to sell to large and dominant members of a particular distribution channel the supplier will often have to meet rigid quality control and stock maintenance requirements. This ultimately means that these channel leaders will only deal with well established companies that provide a high degree of support. The lesson is that it can often take a newcomer longer to become established in one channel than another.

Products

Discussion in an earlier chapter drew attention to the need to harmonize the requirements of company products with the distribution channel. Many of the issues raised then remain relevant in the context of output criteria—where, for example, a company producing highly sensitive and expensive technical equipment must opt for a channel with technical expertise to provide service back-up.

We also considered the issue of distribution channel and the image of a product in the market, that is, its product positioning. The company producing premium quality product will be looking for a distribution channel consistent with its product positioning strategy. If, for example, Gucci handbags were sold through multiple retailers, they would rapidly lose the scarcity value which, in addition to quality and price, determine the premium position that they hold in the market.

Different distribution channels also alter the product range mix. Mail order outlets, for example, will buy only one item of a possibly extensive range of sizes and varieties; small grocers will tend to buy products in smaller sizes than the large supermarkets. Industrial wholesalers will require product in a certain size or configuration different from that supplied to the franchisees.

Some suppliers, especially those with export markets, may be more concerned about their ability to control the final destination of a product. In other words, they want to be confident that the distribution channel selected will indeed be serving the market it says it is and that products supplied for one market will not end up in another where the company may be pursuing different product and pricing strategies. Suppliers using wholesalers also often find that they lack control over the type of final end user and where the product will be stocked.

The level of competitive exposure might be a cause for concern for the company examining output criteria. Certain channels will be far more liable to expose the company's product range to competitive action. Mass market exposure will be particularly relevant in this respect; entering the core markets for major competitors may produce a violent response whereas other more specialized channels will generate less conflict.

Cash flow and diverse costs

Obviously, every supplier is concerned about how quickly it is paid for its goods or services and there are variations from channel to channel. In theory, payment is more rapid the smaller the end user; for whereas large intermediaries are often allowed payment terms in excess of 70 days, smaller accounts will often be on limited credit. However, this advantage is offset by the often higher cost of collecting revenue from smaller accounts.

Certain channels are more expensive to administer. In general administration costs rise with the number of accounts involved, but there may be certain channels that cause particular debt collection problems that are higher than might be expected from the total number of accounts that are involved; the office equipment and construction sectors are particular examples of this.

Higher selling costs may be a problem with a particular channel. When, for example, a company establishes and maintains a distribution channel consisting of a large number of small independent outlets, the costs will generally be higher than selling to national multiple chains. The relationship between the sales force and the distribution system is further discussed in Chapter 14. There are also costs associated with the level and type of promotional investment demanded by a particular distribution channel. The acceptance of point of sale material, for example, will be limited in the multiple retailer but possible in the independent specialist.

Pricing and revenue

Any evaluation of output criteria for distribution channels must take account of profitability. There are considerable variations between channels in the level of pressure they can exert on the supplier's pricing policies. So the channels used will affect the eventual revenue of the supplier company. Suppliers obviously will not obtain the final end user price when intermediaries are involved in the distribution process and the more intermediaries the larger, in general, the differential. For example, Table 4.1 shows the relative price levels obtained by the manufacturer from different channels.

Table 4.1 Relative price levels obtained by
supplier from different channels

Specialist retailer	112
Multiple retailer	100
Independent retailer	105
Wholesaler (primary)	90
Wholesaler (secondary)	95

A manufacturer supplying the specialist retailer via a primary wholesaler would make a much lower profit than the manufacturer supplying the specialist trade direct, though obviously the selling costs will be lower in the first case than in the second. The pricing demands of the chosen distribution channel will therefore have a considerable influence on the net revenue that the supplier company will obtain for its goods and services. Some surveys show that for many manufacturers the supply of stock to the more powerful components of the larger distribution channel may not in fact be more profitable than supplying the smaller channels; volume in other words will often not be compatible with profitability. This is partly caused by the reduced price levels obtainable from dominant members of large distribution channels and partly by the increased promotional and management demands.

Flexibility, seasonality

When evaluating alternative distribution channels, a company might want to retain the maximum freedom of manoeuvre in the future. In the context of output criteria there are two issues of concern. In an earlier chapter we mentioned that certain channels are far more flexible than others and will adjust more readily to a proposed change in distribution arrangements. Where there are contractual obligations distribution channels respond more slowly at great cost to the suppliers; where arrangements are looser, as with wholesalers, flexibility will be greater. It is also perhaps relevant in a discussion of flexibility to consider the issue of the permanence or resilience of channels—some will be far less likely to survive over a period than others.

The second issue of flexibility relates to exclusivity. Certain distribution channels are far more demanding in the degree of exclusivity they require. Suppliers have to consider carefully the likely exclusivity requirements before becoming committed to particular distribution channel arrangements.

On the issues of seasonality of demand it is the case that certain distribution channels can either accentuate or decrease an underlying market seasonality. The use of mail order as a channel will often concentrate the purchase of particular line into a narrow time band after the despatch of the catalogue.

SPECIFIC OUTPUT CRITERIA

We began by stressing the advantages of a systematic approach to distribution channel design and drawing attention to its role in setting and co-ordinating

Table 4.2   Weighting output criteria by channel

Factor	Weighting (on 1 to 10)	Channel 1	Channel 2	Channel 3
		Per cent probability of achieving objectives		
Volume				
Product positioning				
Product range				
Physical requirements				
Stock holding				
Control				
Competitive exposure				
Cash flow				
Selling costs				
Debt collection				
Pricing				
Ease of change				
Exclusivity				
Promotional investment				
Seasonality				
Barriers to entry				
Permanence				
Final positions				

distribution objectives that are consistent with overall company strategy. The eventual choice of one or more distribution channels will flow from careful analysis of the general output criteria which help the company to clarify its distribution objectives—partly by ensuring that it considers some of the ramifications of the channel under consideration. One of the advantages of using a broad approach to output criteria consistent with the total distribution concept is that it allows the channel designer to systematically align distribution objectives with company strategy. It highlights those market factors that are particularly important to the firm and those that are less relevant at a particular time. It then becomes possible to evaluate the impact of the distribution channel on company strategy through some form of checklist and weighting system that compares one distribution system with another. As each channel will offer advantages not available in others the final decision will always require the weighing of benefits against disadvantages (Table 4.2). The weighting and evaluation system outlined in Table 4.2 enables the distribution planner to identify those channels most appropriate for the particular objectives of the company.

MULTI-CHANNEL PLANNING

For many firms a multi-channel approach will be essential to attaining their goals as no single channel will suffice. In a multi-channel system, each will yield differing volumes

Table 4.3   Establishing the revenue pattern for individual distribution channels

Revenue analysis	Channel 1	Channel 2	Channel 3
Market share			
Volume			
Price			
Revenue			
Selling costs			
Promotional costs			
Net contribution			

and revenue and must be analysed individually for the final total company distribution plan. The advantages of the multi-channel policy are that the company will be able to reach more segments of the market, essential for a mass market manufacturer like Kelloggs or Heinz. Secondly, the manufacturer may be able to improve profitability by splitting the product range between channels—making available one part of the product range to one channel and not to the other, thereby reducing price competition. An example of such an approach is that of the Distillers company in Belgium supplying specialist liquor stockists with premium products while limiting the highly competitive multiple grocers to standard products.

Implementing such a mixed strategy does, however, often imply higher promotional costs and it will be necessary at this stage to identify the likely investment requirements for all types of promotional expenditure, including selling costs (Table 4.3). Though required level of investment in such areas is generally considered to be outside the scope of the distribution plan, this calculation is essential because promotional and selling investment in a particular channel may be so high that it effectively disqualifies its use. This is because promotional expenditure in certain channels may demand a major commitment over a long period of time. If the company is unwilling to provide this investment, promotional requirements will act as a major barrier to the use of the channel. Similarly developing a sales force, especially a specialist one, will require long-term planning. Here are some illustrations of company distribution channels to clarify the point. Mars, manufacturers of Pedigree Petfood and Mars confectionery, spent £46 million on advertising in 1987 (£23 million on petfood and £21 million on confectionery), and have continually been one of the highest spenders on media advertising since the company started operations in the UK during the 1930s. A competitor thinking about entering the mass market distribution channel in which Mars operates would need to consider a similar level of expenditure. Continental Canners, the manufacturers of Tex dogfood and the fourth largest petfood producers in Europe, announced their intention in 1988 to expand distribution of both dogfood and catfood, accepting the necessity to spend heavily and continuously on advertising to become established. Thompson Bull, the French computer company (which merged with Honeywell, the American computer company, to form a new organization Honeywell Bull), has been successful against large American companies in the European market because of the investment that it continued to make in training and developing a highly sophisticated sales force. Companies endeavouring to compete in this sector of the market would have to equal such long-term commitment.

We will return to the issue of channel planning in greater detail in later chapters when the other service issues have been discussed—stock levels, warehousing, physical distribution and order processing costs, which will all be influenced by the choice of distribution channel, but it is essential at this stage to realize that the selected channel also affects many other areas of company activity.

SPECIFIC CHANNEL MEMBERS

Assume that a distribution channel designer has narrowed the range of alternatives, having examined the broad output criteria for channel selection and carried out some form of weighting exercise. A method for identifying specific channel members must now be found. Different market sectors pose a range of difficulty in defining the specific channel members. In some such as mass goods consumer retailing the choice is self evident and present in any high street. For other companies operating in more specialized sectors the choice is less obvious and the channel members more difficult to find. Though the supplier will have chosen a particular distribution channel because it has the most appropriate general characteristics, specific channel members will have individual strengths and weaknesses. Output criteria that will help the channel designer to evaluate these become essential.

Of these a number are relevant to every company. Thus everyone considering using a specific channel member will want to know the exact nature of the market coverage provided in terms of the percentage of the market that the channel member services. Equally relevant is the exact geographical area covered by a particular distribution channel member. There are also various output criteria for evaluating the level of service that a supplier might obtain through a particular channel: how frequently are end users contacted, for example. How professional a service does a particular channel member provide in such areas as display, sales and service?

Further questions highlight other areas of concern. What level of stock holding and/or service commitment does the channel member provide? Are the complementary or competitive lines held by the channel member acceptable to the supplier? What degree of conflict exists between the particular channel member and others within the same distribution channel? How the distribution channel member has developed in the recent past will be an important issue in determining its acceptability as an intermediary. For example, should the channel member be marketing orientated, or only interested in sales volume achievement? Thus a key selection factor among French and German firms looking for overseas distribution is whether or not the potential distributor has a marketing orientation. UK firms overseas do not tend to use this as a criterion.

Finding potential distribution channel members

Evaluating a potential, specific distribution channel inevitably involves an information search. There are sources of information about potential channel members at home and overseas. We have said that it will not be difficult for companies operating in mass consumer products to identify potential channel members for all they have to do is walk down the nearest shopping street. For companies operating in specialist sectors of the market, finding intermediaries may be far less straightforward. Various sources can be used to identify channel members.

Most developed markets have well established, fully indexed, and fairly comprehensive trade directories which will provide the most effective initial method of finding appropriate channel members for specialized products or services. In addition, many companies operating in broadly similar areas maintain lists of stockists or local service agents, which can often serve as a useful means of identifying potential channel members for companies providing broadly complementary products or services. Many potential channel members in specialized sectors of the market are often obtained via personal contact with some member of the organization. The collection of market information to aid in the development of channels and the choice of channel members is an important part of the management task (see Chapter 14).

Banks can assist in certain market sectors at home and overseas; and national and overseas trade associations may provide lists of potential agents/distributors or publish magazines which provide a means of advertising in the local market for representation. Chambers of Commerce vary in importance from industry to industry and market to market. The British Chamber of Commerce in Mexico, for example, provides a detailed back-up service for firms interested in developing overseas. The London Chamber of Commerce supplies details of potential agents to subscribing members. Local Chambers of Commerce may also allow firms interested in export to meet firms currently established in overseas markets which can provide introductions to possible overseas agents and distributors. The International Union of Commercial Agents and Brokers maintain lists of agents/distributors in overseas markets which are available for purchase.

Should all these avenues fail, the firm can consider the use of advertisement either in a trade journal, or by exhibiting at an appropriate exhibition.

Evaluating potential distribution channel members

In our discussion of specific output criteria we have mentioned many of the issues which will interest the supplier searching for a potential channel member. A useful evaluation method is a selection profile, similar to one that might be used for the recruitment of personnel, defining what is *essential* in a channel member and what is not essential, but *desirable*. Such a selection profile for a supplier of top of the range personal computers is given in Table 4.4.

The amount of research that the supplier company carries out on the status of the

Table 4.4   Channel member selection profile

Factor	Essential	Desirable
Market coverage	50 mile radius	—
Customer type	Offices	Education
		Factories
Expertise	Systems design	Installation expertise
	Servicing	Software advice
Speed of response	Working day	3 hours
Stock holding	Spare parts	All systems
	Main range	
Financial standing	Strong	
Management	Computer experts	Sales expertise
Competitive lines	No product A	No product C
Complementary lines		Printers

potential channel member depends on the degree of risk involved in the appointment. Where a long-term contractual relationship between the two is proposed, it would obviously be sensible for the supplier to carry out detailed checks on credit worthiness and selling policy, in all cases. Where the image of the product and company relies on the expertise of the channel member this will pose a risk which will need to be considered—much of the success of the McDonalds franchising operation has been in the care taken in appointing franchisees as one unsatisfactory restaurant may damage the reputation of the entire chain.

Where the supplier company is actively searching out intermediaries—in contrast to McDonalds where it is the franchisee that approaches the company—it will have to be prepared to invest time and money in the preparation of material to promote its brands. This is especially relevant where there is a shortage of intermediaries (most industrial manufacturers will always comment on how few effective technical agents there are, both at home and abroad) where the supplier is competing with others for a scarce resource. In other instances, where the channel is large, the preparation of detailed investment plans for the product and its support will be, as mentioned, an essential prerequisite of operating in such markets.

Channel agreements

We have seen how the broader parameters of the total distribution concept can be realistically applied to distribution channel design. We have shown how through the use of various output criteria it is possible to bring system, order and method to the complicated tasks of first identifying appropriate channels for a company's products and then finding specific channel members to handle them. The output criteria are important in helping the designer to be realistic about whether the company's requirements of a channel are compatible with what the channel can in fact achieve. The process of selecting, appointing and then evaluating specific channel members is one which must therefore be managed with care, especially if the decision involved has long-term implications, such as the appointment of agents or distributors in overseas markets, the appointment of franchisees or licencees or the choice of partner in an industrial co-operation agreement. The agreement mentioned in Chapter 5 between Xerox and the Rank Organisation is a case in point: the wide scope of the agreement is considered to be greatly in favour of Rank and against the best interests of Xerox.

Types of channel agreements

The type of channel chosen is fundamental to the type of agreement adopted by the supplier and the channel member. As mentioned previously, the more important the channel by market share, the greater the channel member's power, and the greater the need to define accurately the relationships between supplier and channel member. Take, for example, the supplier of components to the chemical industry in Germany, compared with one operating in Italy. In Germany, the market is dominated by three major multinationals Hoechst, Bayer and BASF, the world's three largest producers of chemical products. Sales of components and raw materials to these companies would comprise well over half the market in such products. In contrast Italy has a highly segmented chemical industry with, apart from companies such as Montedison, a large number of manufacturers. Supplier policies in Germany would be dominated by the Big Three's requirements and it would have to work in close agreement with them to survive in the market. In contrast, the lesser power of the smaller Italian chemical producers reduces the need for close relationships.

Options open to the supplier range from loose unstructured or verbal agreements to contractual relationships with the distribution channel. Their exact nature affects the level of supplier investment in a particular channel and is important in determining the more general role of motivating and controlling the distribution network as we shall see in later discussion. Within the broad span of agreements, the two most important specific types of agreement are *trade marketing agreements* (often called vertical marketing agreements); and agency and distributor agreements.

Trade marketing agreements

In trade marketing agreements the distribution channel member is offered certain benefits in return for specific sales targets, in an attempt to reduce the level of conflict (see Chapter 3) that exists in the distribution channel. The type of benefit offered can vary enormously from product sector to sector but the main alternatives are given in Table 4.5. For these concessions the channel member will commit itself to maintaining certain volumes, prices and shelf space, and agree the type of promotional policy that should be followed (Table 4.6). In the UK, Lever Brothers, the detergent arm of the multinational Unilever, have a series of agreements with major retailers. They lay down expected levels of sales volumes, discount levels across the product assortment sold

Table 4.5   Major components of trade marketing agreements

Price factors	Promotion factors	Exclusivity
Trade discounts	Advertising allowances	Territorial protection
Quantity discounts	Premarked goods	
Seasonal discounts	Promotional material	
Free goods	Display investment	
Credit	Training	
Size of delivery	Sales planning	
Mixed stock order	Demonstrator provision	

Table 4.6   Contents of a trade marketing agreement

Sales issues	Stock issues	Promotional decisions
Volume	Stock turn rate	Space allocation
Price	Minimum stock levels	Promotional material
Discounts		Media schedule
Sales training		Store location decision
Sales visits		

by the outlet, together with agreed levels of promotional support and discounts for special promotional activity throughout the year.

Trade marketing agreements become increasingly important as the number of buyers in industrial and retail sectors contracts and the larger companies seek longer-term agreements. Their main feature is the reduction of potential profit for the supplier in return for guaranteed sales volume and pricing levels. The trade marketing agreement will, however, provide a much more structured relationship than that existing in the free market. The main differences between the two are summarized in Table 4.7. Trade marketing agreements involve a degree of compromise by the parties

Table 4.7   Comparison of the main factors operating in markets either controlled by trade marketing agreements or as free market forces

Factor	Free market	Trade marketing agreement
Level of negotiation	Individual deal	Annual plan
End user goals	Sales increase	Total profit
	Profit margin	
Supplier's goals	Volume	Long-term market share
	High margins	Long-term profitability
Conflict within channels	Often high	Low and controlled
Conflict between channels	Often high	Low and controlled

Table 4.8 Pay-offs within a trade marketing agreement

Party	Promotion	Price	Sales
Supplier	Media schedule Points of sale Special packs	Range discounts Guaranteed price	Delivery points Minimum delivery size Delivery frequency

Channel
  member
	Timing of
	  store promotion
		Minimum price	Volume

involved but the balance of compromise depends on the power or influence of the supplier in relation to the distribution channel member. The main typical areas of compromise are highlighted in Table 4.8. From the perspective of distribution planning, trade marketing agreements offer an ideal method of reducing costs, providing that distribution problems are taken into account at the time of discussion. The opportunity to increase the percentage of direct delivery, from factory to customer, and the ability to reduce the overall stock holding requirement in the warehouse due to lower fluctuations in the demand pattern (see Chapters 9 and 10) will allow substantial savings to be made in many areas of the distribution system.

Trade marketing agreements are subject to local laws concerning fair competition. These lay down clear limits to how far such agreements can go with respect to price, product availability and promotional support. With the growth in the power of large multinationals and the concentration of retailing strength in a small number of hands, they are becoming a more contentious issue as the smaller operators perceive that they are being excluded from special deals that are only available to the larger companies. This has in certain circumstances led to legal action, and is likely to become a major issue of contention as Europe moves towards a common tariff policy in 1992.

Agency or distributor agreements

An agency or distributor agreement is a commercial contract involving a long-term binding agreement between supplier and local representative. Since contract law differs from country to country there can be no hard and fast approach to the drawing up of agency documents in overseas markets. However, as a general rule the more specific the document, whether it relates to overseas markets or those at home, the better for both parties as this limits the scope for misinterpretation. Because of the large potential areas for confusion even for agents or distributors in the home market, an agency or distributor agreement has to be clear on such key issues as those in Table 4.9.

Table 4.9   Main components of an agency or distribution agreement

(a) *Parties.* Identification of contracting companies.
(b) *Territory.* The territory on which the agreement is based.
(c) *Exclusivity.*
    (i) How the principal and agent handle orders placed direct with the supplier—there may be some established customers that the supplier wishes to continue to service directly.
    (ii) How the principal and agent handle orders for the territory arising outside the market— orders from an international head office requiring delivery in the local market.
(d) *Competitive lines.* The rights of the agent to handle competing lines and what constitutes a competitive line.
(e) *Products.* The exact products covered by the agreement. It is in the interests of the supplier to state clearly that new products and new activities are not covered by some blanket agreement.
(f) *Duties of the distributor.* In particular:
    (i) servicing and guarantee arrangements,
    (ii) the provision of sales information,
    (iii) whether the distributor provides part of the promotional budget and if so how it is calculated,
    (iv) what clearance procedure the local distributor must follow for local publicity material,
    (v) what stock holding the distributor needs to maintain,
    (vi) the degree of freedom in setting price levels in the market and if there are stipulations on the maximum level of gross margin that the distributor can add to the product,
    (vii) the degree of freedom in disposing of stock at below list price—obsolescent stocks, for example.
(g) *Duties of the principal.*
    (i) Supply of replacement product for faults in previous shipments.
    (ii) Provision of spare packaging material and labels to deal with goods damaged in transit.
    (iii) Translation costs of brochure material.
    (iv) Speed of dealing with orders.
    (v) The amount of notice that needs to be given for price rises.
(h) *Duration.* The length of time that the arrangement will remain in being in the first instance and then the length of time the contract will be renewed on an ongoing basis provided that both companies are in agreement.
(i) *Commission.* Where commission is payable:
    (i) when it is payable, quarterly, half yearly;
    (ii) the rate of payment payable on different categories of goods and the basis on which it is payable;
    (iii) the rate of payment on orders received from organizations that cancel orders or become bankrupt.
(j) *Termination/problems with the agreement.* This will need to include:
    (i) amount of notice that either side will need to give for termination of the contract;
    (ii) the rights of either party to dispose of remaining stock,
    (iii) effects of change of ownership of the agreement either on the supplier or on the distributor,
    (iv) what body should be involved in arbitration should the agreement break down.
    (v) The laws under which the agreement is administered. This has important implications. Contracts within countries operating a system of common law can limit actions and liability to issues stated within the contract. In other countries operating a civilian system (such as France) there will be overriding statutory provisions outside what is specified in the contract.

Source: West, *Marketing Overseas*, Pitman, 1987.

Motivating channel members

It is important to understand that an agreement between a supplier and a specific member of a distribution channel marks the beginning of a relationship that will be mutually beneficial if it operates successfully. Once an agreement is reached, a successful, profitable working relationship becomes the objective for the distribution channel designer—channel members must be encouraged or motivated and their performance continually monitored. The more distant the channel member from the supplier, as when markets are overseas, the more difficult the problem: distance creates its own isolation which, unless a supplier is very careful, can lead the distributor to conclude that the supplier is not particularly interested in its activities. The predicament of the overseas channel member can be taken as an extreme example of the need for motivation but it highlights the fact that motivation is a form of support and if a supplier fails to give such support, such attitudes will appear in channels in home markets as well. Should this occur, the channel may well cease to be of use in helping the supplier to achieve some of its broader distribution goals.

This can be seen from analysis of the benefits to the supplier of properly motivated channel members. The channel will operate more effectively in a number of ways: better sales; more effective service to the customer; greater receptivity to new product development; improved information flow since the channel will be more willing to provide market information about competitive products, pricing and the like. Of greatest long-term importance perhaps is the fact that the well motivated channel member is unlikely to consider competitive products, and will therefore act as a substantial barrier to entry to other companies trying to enter a particular market sector.

Issues in the motivational mix

A supplier may well be operating in different market sectors having different goals for each. As a result each distribution channel member will need different types of support and may well respond differently to particular types of support. The manufacturer will have to develop a *motivational mix* for each channel member which will vary according to the importance of the channel and the size of the channel member. The relationship between the supplier and the channel member(s) is of crucial importance and many of the issues mentioned in the remainder of this section are also fundamental to the trade marketing agreements we discussed earlier. In general the supplier's motivational mix will concentrate on certain key areas for maintaining a good working partnership with all channel members.

Improved information flow from the channel to the supplier is one advantage of channel motivation. A supplier can assist greatly if it maintains an efficient information flow to its channels. It is practically impossible to motivate people who are not well informed about matters involving them. The continuing provision of information concerning pricing, changes in specification and packaging will affect the performance of the product in overseas markets. Many firms are notorious for the very limited information that they give to intermediaries who are then demotivated and perform less well.

Not only do many firms provide very limited information, but they are then often unwilling to compromise over the promotional material that is supplied. Many intermediaries have active promotional programmes in their local markets which may not exactly fit the supplier's promotional preconceptions. Compromise and the willingness to provide material suitably modified will engender a measure of goodwill towards the supplier.

In addition to information back-up, adequate technical support is essential even where a problem appears simple and straightforward. For example, a British firm exporting worldwide found that sales in minor markets like the Middle East doubled after a simple information system was introduced to ensure that agents were kept informed of product availability and pricing. Where technical products are involved the amount of training that the supplier provides will have an important bearing in motivating channels and maintaining their interest and support for the supplier's products.

A supplier must also ensure that its trade policies are clear cut and consistent. Confusion and reduced performance are likely when channel members perceive that competitive channel members or members of other channels are receiving support or other benefits which are at variance with their total sales achievement. Clear trade policies on pricing and discounts will be particularly important if the company has adopted a multi-channel strategy.

Market visits are essential for a number of reasons. They increase the knowledge of the market, particularly the problems that the distributor or agent is facing. They also allow the supplier to influence and train the sales force in particular product areas. Finally they are important to convince major customers of the supplier's commitment to the market, often a crucial factor in sales development.

There are instances where competitions between channel members are useful, but more normally competitions within the sales force or awards to channel member employees can be very effective in improving the relationship between supplier and intermediary. For example, Asbach, the German brandy firm, gives an award to individuals who have worked for an overseas distributor for more than ten years, which is presented at a dinner attended by an Asbach director.

The development of joint plans for the market by supplier and distributor ensures a common commitment to a genuine partnership between supplier and channel member. This is of course central to trade marketing agreements (see above). Ensuring that the packaging in which the goods are supplied meets the demand of the channel can be important in maintaining effective motivation. Case sizes and identification methods will, for example, affect the acceptability of consumer products in large outlets throughout Western Europe and will, if unsuitable, involve the intermediary in extra work and reduce the effectiveness of the product range.

Table 4.10   Performance criteria for channel members

Sales performance measures
Sales achieved versus budget
Market coverage achieved versus planned levels
Inventory levels against planned stock holding levels
Selling skills and expertise against planned levels

Current channel member/supplier interaction
Attitudes and co-operation of the channel member over the past planning period
Competitive lines; changes in stocking procedure

Future channel performance
Growth prospects

Monitoring channel members

Throughout this book we speak of distribution in a broader environment; of distribution objectives within the context of broader company strategy. When, as part of a planning process, a company sets goals over a period of time it will also establish procedures for monitoring progress or lack of it. Distribution should be no exception and management must measure performance of the current channels against company objectives and decide upon the necessary response to either success or failure—whether to change channel members, the entire channel or to alter the motivational mix. For example, disappointing sales in the Spanish market led a British toy company to approach the major department store Corte Ingles. By changing the motivational mix of the previous channel the company substantially improved total sales in the Spanish market.

To make such decisions a supplier needs procedures to identify success or failure. Criteria for judging performance will vary from company to company making it impossible to supply a common framework. However, some of the evaluation criteria common to most are outlined in the Table 4.10.

CHANGING DISTRIBUTION CHANNELS

Most firms will have faced the dilemma of whether or not to replace a distribution channel member for failing to meet its expectations. Changing channels often demands major structural reorganization and must be carefully evaluated and planned. The company considering changing distribution channels has to resolve a number of problems.

The costs of terminating an existing agreement will include both the compensation that may be payable to the current channel member(s) and the interval between leaving one channel and starting distribution via another. European legislation can lead to distributors or other intermediaries being able to claim substantial compensation for the loss of distribution rights, thereby causing further delay in litigation. Whether the proposed change in distribution is not a potential case of 'frying pan to fire'—replacing a current problem with a long-term one—also deserves careful thought. Thus, substantially increased investment in the current channel may be a more cost effective solution in the longer term than termination and re-establishment of another channel.

A proposed change in channels might in addition reduce control over the market. For example, a British company changed from using wholesalers to a direct distribution system to major outlets. As a result, demand fluctuations increased as major outlets bought the major proportion of their stock on promotion, and the by-product was that gross margins fell. The overall result was an increase in sales volume, but a decline in net profit. Furthermore, in a situation where competitive pressures are strong the effect of the changeover to new distribution channels may be to allow competitor companies to become established in core markets.

Where large companies are involved in major changes in the market which lead to redundancy, or where overseas companies change local distribution channels, there will often be substantial resistance within the local community. This can create long-term problems.

CASE: DOORLARM

Introduction

At the end of 1985 Doorlarm Ltd had been established for 16 months, manufacturing and selling two entirely new products to the home security market. Through the efforts and skills of the three founder directors a great deal was achieved in a short time, but within eight months of the launch Polycell had introduced similar products, seriously threatening the new company's position. The fragmented nature of the market, however, meant that the company had a fair chance of success with a good product but limited distribution prevented it becoming a highly successful one.

The directors were aware of this weakness and had recruited John Hughes, an ex-area manager of a car accessories company, as marketing director. Hughes was given a free hand as the founder directors felt they did not possess the necessary skills or experience to compete with Polycell.

Hughes was asked to study all the documentation provided and produce a new marketing plan with a justification as to why his new approach would be more successful than the company's current one. The other directors were particularly concerned about investment levels required to pursue any new objective and sources of funding.

Hughes was asked to give particular attention to:
—distribution policy,
—promotional policy including all aspects of sales force expansion.

The problems were acute as the company had grown rapidly. From its initial base in a small unit on an industrial estate in North Tyneside, Doorlarm Ltd had had to move within six months into a larger 2000 square feet unit. Full time production staff had increased from two to eight at the time of writing. One salesman, a personal friend of the directors, was based in Newcastle where he lived.

The directors had initially taken on positions as managing director, production director and sales director. All three had agreed, however, that the sales function was not as strong as it needed to be and Brown, the sales director, agreed to take on the new role of financial director to allow the position of marketing director to be filled by Hughes. They had differing views as to the potential direction of the company. The managing director, James Goodley, wanted to minimize overheads to ensure that investment levels could be maintained in new product development, which he saw as essential to the company's continuing success.

Products

Doorlarm Ltd produces two products, both easy-to-fit, external door alarms. They are battery operated, emitting a loud 105 decibels when an external door is opened.

Doorlarm 1 (size 4″ × 1″ × 1″) is an easy to operate alarm using a simple on/off switch (m.r.p. £9.99).

Doorlarm 2 (size 5″ × 2½″ × 1½″) has an additional exit and entry delay alarm feature for operator use, and is operated by means of a key (m.r.p. £12.99).

Both products are made of attractive, heavy-duty white plastic and do not require wiring of any sort.

The end users of the products are male householders in the B/C/C1/D socio-economic groups, and with a DIY orientation.

A third product, Doorlarm 3, is just about to be introduced. It is of a similar size to the Doorlarm 2 model but instead of a key control, a code operated on/off facility is used. The alarm has eight push buttons enabling a personal four digit code, from a selection of 1680 different combinations, to be chosen. It has an additional feature of emitting a visitor entry bleep which would be suitable for shop or waiting room use (m.r.p. £16.99).

The home security market

The market had grown significantly over the past five years thanks both to the increase in the number of households and the steady year on year growth of reported crime, especially in the area of household break-ins which have escalated (Table 4.11).

The involvement of the insurance companies and the growing popularity of household watch schemes contributed to the increasing willingness of the house-holder to invest in household security. Since the early 1980s, some of the larger insurance companies were introducing schemes to reduce premiums in return for the installation of 'approved' home security devices.

Table 4.11   Trends in the security market

	1976	1977	1978	1979	1980	1981	1982
Households (million)	18	19	19	20	21	22	23
'Serious crime'							
percentage growth	17	5	6	7	11	13	11
Market size (£ million)	55	60	65	72	85	87	89
Locks/latches (%)	90	89	83	76	70	68	66
Alarm systems (%)	10	11	17	24	30	32	34

Market shares and other companies operating in the market

There are three broad sectors identifiable in the market, each with distinct product attributes, namely locks and latches, alarm systems and DIY installations. The market overall is very segmented with over 200 companies having some form of national presence; in addition there are numerous locally based operations.

Locks and latches

The market splits into two sectors: cylinder locks, which are more DIY oriented, and mortice locks. Ultra sophisticated, electronic lock systems had only started to appear in some prestige developments such as hotels and were unlikely to pose any substantial threat for the rest of the decade. The market was dominated by a few large companies with large sales forces and wide distribution (Table 4.12).

Alarm systems

Chubb and Automated Security Holdings (Modern Alarms) are believed to be the market leaders with around 15 per cent of the market each, followed by Securicor with 11 per cent and then AFA Minerva with around 7 per cent.

A high level of customer service is required to operate successfully and many companies like Doulton Glass and Dolphin Showers entered and left the market as the going was tough. The insistence of insurance companies that clients install alarm

Table 4.12   Major suppliers of locks and latches

	Mortice % value	Cylinder % volume
Union	60	25
Yale	10	55
Legge	10	10
Others	20	10

systems during the 1970s and 1980s had meant that this sector of the market had grown considerably; whether growth would continue was of major concern to the large companies.

DIY alarm systems

There are no market share figures for this sector. Companies in this sector supply mainly kit-type systems at around £140. In recent years companies like Hoover, Philips, Pifco and more recently Polycell have entered this market, bringing with them their consumer oriented marketing expertise.

Doorlarm Ltd is thought to hold an 8 per cent share of this sector in value terms. At present (besides Polycell), only a few small companies offer a product of a similar nature and their individual shares of the market are smaller than Doorlarm's. With the decreasing cost of electronic systems it is likely that the market will become more competitive over the next few years as the major companies, facing a downturn in office and shop installations, turn their attentions to the home market to maintain growth. This increased competition will inevitably affect pricing and profit margins. Such had been the experience in the institutional market where gross profit margins fell from 65 to 30 per cent over three years.

The lock and latches and alarm systems sectors show only moderate growth. It is the DIY alarm sector that is the potential growth area with current relatively low sales.

The growth rate in the security industry market is naturally influenced by the rate of burglaries per year and the gradual, if reluctant, consumer acceptance of the need for home security. The number of reported burglaries has steadily increased over the last decade. The most recent figures show a 27 per cent increase between 1981 and 1982.

By 1985 Polycell was the largest competitor to Doorlarm Ltd having introduced comparable products within eight months of the Doorlarm launch. The products are heavily branded and merchandised, fitting neatly into an existing range of security products such as Polycell window locks.

The presence of Polycell in this sector was not unexpected but the major obstacle presented is the company's well established distribution network, enabling the competing products to gain shelf-space alongside other items in the Polycell range within a very short time. Polycell have obtained distribution through large DIY stores where it is usual to find an eight foot rack displaying the extensive range of the company's home security products.

In addition to Polycell there are a few small companies that supply generally low quality door alarms. These are, on the whole, badly designed and poorly packaged and do not pose a threat to Doorlarm Ltd.

Production facilities

Output is steady. Roughly 3600 units of Doorlarm 1 and 5400 units of Doorlarm 2 are produced per month. The maximum production capacity of the factory with the

Table 4.13   Doorlarm Ltd shareholding

Managing Director	30%
Production Director	27%
Financial Director	27%
Marketing Director	16%

present workforce is roughly 11 000 units a month. This workforce can be increased to a total of ten before factory floor space available becomes a restricting factor. If the workforce were raised to ten, the maximum production capacity would be roughly 14 000 units per month.

Negotiations are presently proceeding with a manufacturer in Hong Kong with a view to importing Doorlarm products made under licence. It is expected that up to 20 000 units could be imported per month once an agreement was reached. This contribution is not expected to begin for at least another four months.

Company financial structure

The ordinary shares of the company are now split according to the details in Table 4.13. The share allocation was adjusted to ensure that the marketing director had a personal stake in the business to motivate and encourage commitment in the company's future.

At the time of writing, the first year's accounts are not yet published but the key points from the anticipated accounts are summarized in Table 4.14.

Table 4.14   Doorlarm Ltd—anticipated end of year accounts

		£
SALES		460 000
Less		
COST OF GOODS SOLD		(160 000)
	Gross profit	300 000
Less		
OVERHEADS		(240 000)
	Profit before tax	60 000
Less		
TAXATION		(18 000)
	Net profit	42 000
	Ord. share capital	(16 000)
		58 000
FIXED ASSETS		24 000
Current assets 80 000		
Current liabilities (46 000)		
Net current assets		34 000
		58 000

Table 4.15   Doorlarm pricing

Product	W/H price	Expected mark-up	Price to retailer (at +20%)	Expected mark-up	Retail (at +40%)	VAT	Recom- mended retail price
Doorlarm 1	£5.17	12½–25%	£6.20	33–50%	£8.69	£1.30	£9.99
Doorlarm 2	£6.72	12½–25%	£8.06	33–50%	£11.29	£1.70	£12.99
Doorlarm 3*	£8.79	12½–25%	£10.55	33–50%	£14.77	£2.22	£16.99

*Expected launch price.

With its successful growth record, the company was favourably placed to raise a substantial sum of further loan capital from three interested Northern entrepreneurs. The sum on offer was £100 000 for a 40 per cent stake in an enlarged company. Otherwise the company could borrow a further £35 000 from the local bank at interest of 16 per cent. None of the current directors could provide further capital to the organization as each had fully mortgaged houses.

Pricing structure

Doorlarm had little information about price sensitivity in its market. What little evidence existed suggested that price sensitivity was fairly low, in the order of 2, which might allow an increase in the retail prices (Table 4.15).

Advertising and other promotional activity

The only paid-for advertising used was an off-the-page campaign to generate direct mail order sales during the first six months. It was moderately successful with a positive return on media expenditure, an improvement in cash flow and a small increase in product awareness.

Local newspapers were used initially, followed by two national campaigns (*Daily Express, Daily Mail*) and the use of specialist magazines such as *Do-it-yourself* and *Home Security and Insurance*.

Currently, an advertisement appears in every issue of *Home Security and Insurance* magazine due to its cost effectiveness.

This medium has not been used to build up general awareness of the products due to the fact that the message that often comes across is one of a more generic nature— that of security products as a whole.

Distribution and initial company progress

Mail order advertisements were used in the first six months to generate cash in advance of orders.

As the only effective sales force in the company was one director and one salesman the coverage and distribution possible was always going to be limited. However, by concentrating on wholesalers in a broad area with a high concentration of wholesalers—Greater Manchester, Liverpool, Birmingham and surrounding districts—they had both achieved considerable success.

To encourage the wholesalers to stock the new products they were offered on a sale or return basis. This proved to be a very good tactic for loading the trade but it has now become the norm for the majority of wholesalers in that region. Sales direct to specialist retailers and independents were achieved in an area only within 40 miles of the factory: chosen to minimize travelling time from base but was not cost effective due to the small order quantities. Attempts by two directors to obtain sales through DIY and hardware multiple retailers were unsuccessful. Most of the problems were due to the directors' inexperience in dealing with buyers representing large accounts. The sales achieved over months 11–16 are in Table 4.16.

The current marketing plan

The current marketing plan was little changed from that given to the bank for the initial funding of the company.

Table 4.16   Doorlarm sales

	Month						Total (past 6 months)
	11	12	13	14	15	16	
Doorlarm 1:							
Mail order	95	90	94	80	65	70	494
Wholesale:							
Sale or return	2200	3000	4100	2000	3600	3600	18500
Outright purchase	300	300	400	200	500	600	2300
Specialist retailer:							
DIY	80	75	40	27	40	37	299
Hardware	50	85	116	30	41	40	362
Multiple retailer	—	—	—	—	—	—	—
TOTAL	2725	3550	4750	2337	4246	4347	21955
Doorlarm 2:							
Mail order	62	49	49	37	35	40	272
Wholesale:							
Sale or return	2400	3800	6000	4500	4800	5200	26700
Outright purchase	100	300	100	200	400	400	1500
Specialist retailer:							
DIY	60	47	40	39	48	29	263
Hardware	32	28	62	75	53	82	332
Multiple retailer	—	—	—	—	—	—	—
TOTAL	2654	4224	6251	4851	5336	5751	29067

Table 4.17   Doorlarm: available distribution channels

	No. of present customers	% of total sales volume
(i) Multiple DIY retailers	—	—
(ii) Multiple hardware retailers	—	—
(iii) Independent DIY retailers	30	2
(iv) Independent hardware retailers	45	3
(v) Specialist security product retailers	—	—
(vi) DIY wholesalers	30	40
(vii) Hardware wholesalers	35	50
(viii) Mail order houses	—	—
(ix) Mail order	—	5

Objectives

To establish a national distribution network enabling maximum exposure of the products to the end user.

Goals

Short-term: To maintain existing accounts profitably and introduce the Doorlarm 3 model to at least 70 per cent of existing customers.

Medium-term: To obtain a national multiple retailer or mail order house account, and accounts with 40 per cent of hardware/DIY wholesalers and 10 per cent of the hardware/DIY/specialist retailers in the UK, selling the full range to all.

Long-term: To achieve sales representing at least 80 per cent of production capacity

Table 4.18   Major UK DIY retailers (multiple)

	Outlets
Magnet & Southerns	250
Jacoa Ltd (Ripolin, Decor 8, Ten Ten)	207
Art Wall Papers (Homecharm)	200
B&Q DIY Supercentres	150
Texas Homecare	127
Payless DIY Ltd	59
Jewson	53
W. H. Smith Do-it-All	45
Timberland Ltd	48
Paul Madeley Ltd	40
Great Mills DIY Superstores	35
Homebase Ltd	14

Source: Retail Directory, Newman Books, 1986.

Table 4.19   Major UK hardware retailers (multiple)

	Outlets
Wilkinson Hardware Stores	40
Knobs & Knockers	45
Carpenter J. W. Ltd (Shergolds)	40
Edmund R. Goodrich Ltd	38
Robert Dyas Ltd	33
Graham Ford Ltd	33
Lawson Fisher	22
Cato Hardware	15

Source: Retail Directory, Newman Books, 1986.

(including imports) in the ratio 30 per cent national accounts, 70 per cent independent accounts.

Hughes considered the available strategic options to achieve these goals. Clearly a distribution oriented strategy is required. Either a 'shotgun' approach is taken, whereby distribution is gained in a broad and relatively uncontrollable manner, through wholesalers for example, or a 'rifled' approach is used, concentrating distribution through selected channels, such as specialist retailers.

The nature of the product dictates that most can be gained from a 'shotgun' approach as it is a relatively simple product needing very little explanation and no after sales service. One strategy therefore will be to obtain new accounts with the channels that offer the widest penetration possible.

A serious problem that could occur, which often affects many small businesses, is that of overtrading—taking on too many orders that cannot be produced and the working capital is not available to finance them.

Table 4.17 outlines the available distribution channels, and Tables 4.18–4.20 contain further details.

Table 4.20   DIY wholesaler independent hardware outlets specialist outlets UK by region

	Wholesaler	Independent	Specialist
Scotland	94	800	64
North West	130	1056	84
North East	114	898	72
Midlands	141	1648	132
East	114	368	29
Greater London	149	2416	193
South East	121	840	67
South West	104	1046	84

Source: Trade estimates.

Factors of particular importance in the market

(1) Multiple retailers and mail order houses

It is dangerous to tie up a lot of production capacity and capital with one buyer as it places the company in a very weak bargaining position and often places a reliance on that one company for business survival.

Negotiations with the buyers of multiples are exhaustive and require skill and authority. It may be too important an account for one salesman to tackle alone and is probably best handled by the directors.

(2) Wholesalers

The products do not have a long sales history, so wholesalers will require inducements to stock the products; sale or return conditions are presently used but increased margins for the wholesalers should be offered.

Pre-selling to the consumer is not expected in this industry where advertising can be counterproductive. The wholesalers' own sales force will not have the time or inclination to promote the new products. The use of wholesalers gives cost savings in invoicing, credit and collection, order processing, delivery and selling costs over the smaller and more diverse retailers but with a reduced margin.

(3) Independent retailers

Although a far greater travelling time is involved covering each retailer, and the order size is normally very small, sales to the retailer enjoy a higher margin. If there is a restriction on productivity, i.e. the number of products that can be sold, then it may be worth spending more time obtaining more 'profitable' sales at the expense of time and its associated cost.

(4) A 'pull' strategy

This is an option but again due to the effect of security product advertising the 'pull' through the trade by consumers would not be expected to be strong. However, by approaching retailers using direct mail (promotional literature) a 'pull' factor may be generated by them against the wholesalers in their area.

(5) A 'push' strategy

This is very feasible as in many ways it is the trade norm. This strategy will of course require a very high degree of personal selling which brings with it further problems.

DISTRIBUTION ASSIGNMENTS

1   Your company is experiencing problems with three channels in different markets. In one, West Germany, the channel members are the main multiple retailers, and market sales account for 20 per cent of total company turnover. In Italy the company employs a distributor and sales account for 5 per cent of total company turnover. In North Africa the company has a commission agent who accounts for 0.5 per cent of total turnover. Up to now the company has only had loose agreements with all these three channels. Suggest what types of motivational mix would be appropriate in your view for each of these channels, and what other action should be taken.

2   Using business journals and library material, analyse the structure of two major industries in the country. What influence is this structure likely to have on the suppliers to this industry? Write a report on one of these chosen industries as a supplier as to how the company should develop its distribution structure.

3   A company has developed a new type of low cost double glazing. You are asked to write a memorandum on the type of channel agreements that would be necessary to replace the current sales policy directed towards independent installers towards an emphasis on:
(a)   franchised outlets,
(b)   major DIY multiple retailers.

4   What type of trade marketing arrangement would the following manufacturers need to establish with their distribution intermediaries:
(a)   A manufacturer of power boats.
(b)   A supplier of hi-fi equipment.
(c)   A travel company.

5   A manufacturer of powered hand tools has asked you to prepare a channel selection profile and motivational mix package for both its industrial and consumer ranges.

Chapter 5

Distribution Channels Outside National Boundaries

When a company expands outside its national boundaries, success in finding a distribution channel appropriate to its targeted market is just as important as it is at home. Often it is more so because a mistaken channel decision can quickly become a drain on resources especially if a company is small. Experience gained in the home market cannot necessarily be successfully transferred to markets overseas and this is the reason for integrating the two in earlier chapters to show that output criteria for distribution channel selection can be applied to decision making in markets at home and overseas. Overall the total distribution concept advises a cautious, systematic approach to both with output criteria indicating that the realistic company makes its decisions on a market by market basis and assumes that no two markets are totally alike.

Caution becomes a virtue in a complex international environment, as this chapter will show. Many of the issues mentioned have been touched upon already, but here we shall undertake a more detailed examination of some specific issues affecting distribution channel decision making for markets outside national boundaries.

EXPANSION OUTSIDE NATIONAL BOUNDARIES—SOME KEY ISSUES

Although companies learn from each other's successes, they are peculiarly resistant to learning the lessons of failure particularly if they relate to mistakes made in expansion outside national boundaries. Acorn Computers, for example, had been one of the UK's most promising computer companies. It faced bankruptcy in early 1985 following a disastrous plan to capture 10 per cent of the US educational market. There were three main problems. The more stringent technical requirements of the American market added to the cost and delayed the launch. Loss-leading by established American companies made the market exceptionally difficult and local educational authorities operated a 'buy American policy'. The company's target was to gain a major presence on the East Coast which made up half the computer market. It was attempting to master the largest computer market in the world within an exceptionally short time, against well-established competition. In contrast Amstrad opted for slower expansion in the US via the major retailer, Sears, which enables it to gain market expertise without major investment in the US. Even companies with experience of the problems of overseas markets often feel obliged to re-invent the wheel; Marks and Spencer, after experiencing many difficult years in Canada with both local Marks and Spencer outlets and its chains of discount clothing stores, has recently spent $750 million on the purchase of Brooks Brothers in the US. This operation is essentially an up-market men's tailor's and has even less in common with Marks and Spencer UK than its Canadian operation.

Let us look at some of the broad questions arising from these examples.

Costs

Since overseas markets involve greater distances physical distribution costs are higher. But the additional costs of servicing overseas markets involve more than those of physical distribution alone. First there is often a substantially increased packaging cost; the requirement to improve either the product packing or the carton strength to withstand the increased physical demands of transport to overseas markets. The increased use of containerization has reduced the need for specialized packing for many markets but there are still some without container facilities. Furthermore, increased overseas sales can also involve the company investing in a greater range of material handling equipment.

Secondly, the costs of administration are substantially higher for overseas orders. Documentation requirements can be considerable; items like certificates of origin, bills of lading, T forms will have to be completed for the majority of overseas shipments and is a time consuming activity for export management. Often documentation is incorrectly completed, leading to a further increase in cost as payment will be delayed until new documents are despatched. It has been estimated that one in six or seven of letters of credit have some error causing some delay in payment. Because of the complexity of documentation, a firm developing overseas sales often has not the necessary expertise to administer the operation and must recruit additional staff. Indeed estimates put the costs of creating an export department for a small company at over £60 000 per annum. Attempts to standardize documentation, such as SITPRO, have recently improved the ability of small companies to handle export trade.

Thirdly, the increased working capital requirements to fund stock in transit from supplier to overseas end user or intermediary have important financial implications, especially if the markets are far from the suppliers' production point. For example, a manufacturer selling £2 million value of goods in the Australian market from a European base would have to increase working capital by £30 000 just to allow for the average six week shipment time from Europe to Australasia. This figure would increase substantially if intermediaries with long credit requirements and/or slow payment systems were involved. Finally, the manufacturer will often need to carry higher levels of stock to supply demands in overseas markets because of a lack of information from the market (see below—'Control'). This too, increases working capital requirements.

Local environment

The potential impact on distribution of the environmental issues examined in Chapter 2 is just as pertinent to markets overseas. First, the legal environment in an overseas market may effectively determine the structure of the distribution system, which may be entirely different from that operating in the home market. Secondly, these legal guidelines may change rapidly, dramatically altering the distribution environment. For example, the increased requirement for local shareholding set by the Nigerian government with a maximum foreign shareholding of 40 per cent had a significant effect on the way in which foreign suppliers organized their distribution system within that country.

In addition to legal constraints, local business practice often influences the way in which a foreign firm can effectively penetrate the market. The Japanese distribution system with a large number of intermediaries is not backed by any legal framework, but no foreign manufacturer could effectively reach the market in any other way unless it were prepared to invest heavily in establishing an alternative distribution system, which, given the vagaries of the Japanese market, might still not be successful.

Control

The combined effect of distance and local market structures can mean that the supplier's control over distribution is more limited than at home. As we saw in Chapter 3 the supplier often lacks the information necessary to formulate a competitive distribution policy—and we shall return to this issue in Chapter 15. The shortage of information also means that the inventory control system for overseas markets is likely to be less effective than in the home market making necessary higher levels of buffer or reserve stock.

Currency

The movement of payment within the distribution channel is complicated in overseas markets by differing currencies and exchange complexities. This will be compounded when the inflation rate in either market is high and there are legal problems in transferring funds, such as foreign exchange controls.

Communication

Distance makes effective communication between supplier and customer more difficult, as we discussed in Chapter 4. This will be particularly important when the product supplied is complex and requires a high level of technical support and spare part provision.

INVESTMENT AND DISTRIBUTION CHANNELS OVERSEAS

As with other distribution decisions, the company is facing a pay-off between the degree of investment, its rate of return and the risk inherent in the investment. This analysis leads to the inevitable conclusion that risk levels are significantly higher overseas. As a result there is a tendency to use distribution channels that require a low level of commitment in many markets with heavy investment only in overseas distribution channels where risk is relatively low. Any discussion of overseas distribution can therefore define a ladder of investment from the lowest—establishing some form of non-contractual relationship with an intermediary generally based in the home market but servicing overseas customers, through a variety of contractual relationships with intermediaries located in the overseas market—to the creation of a totally owned manufacturing facility in an overseas market.

Various aspects of the use of intermediaries for distribution in markets are mentioned in Chapters 3 and 4 as part of an overall discussion of distribution channel selection. Here it should be mentioned that export through intermediaries without a contractual relationship involves the purchase and distribution of product from within the home market to overseas outlets. Ownership of the supplier's products is actually transferred to another organization for overseas despatch normally within the home market of the supplier. There are a number of distinctive types of intermediary operating in export markets which carry out slightly different types of activity.

Export wholesalers buy product on their own behalf, ship overseas and sell on the open market via established outlets. They tend not to maintain a separate sales force to build sales but act as a traditional wholesaler. They may offer a means of developing a particular market area, but distribution is likely to be limited. The company achieves its profit by the mark-up on the goods that it sells in the overseas market. Gibraltar is an example of an overseas market that is mainly supplied by wholesalers operating from the UK.

The confirming house acts on behalf of an overseas buyer, perhaps a store group or government agency. It purchases the goods in the country of origin, arranges shipment and insurance, provides credit for the overseas buyer and receives commission on the total value of the order. Confirming houses will often allow the supplier firm to enter markets where there are particular payment problems. The importance of the confirming house has significantly declined in the 1980s as they have been particularly badly hit by the restricted availability of foreign exchange in Africa.

As retail concentration continues, the buying offices set up by overseas retail outlets become more important to the small firm wishing to find overseas markets. All major Japanese retail outlets have buying offices in Europe. Macy's the well known American store group has them in Paris, Dublin, Florence, Tel Aviv, Copenhagen, Frankfurt, Madrid, Bogota, Lima, Buenos Aires, Sao Paulo, Osaka, Seoul, Manila, Bangkok, Singapore, Hong Kong, Bombay. The buying office is essentially a service organization for the home based retail company. However, on many items they can act in competition with other buying offices of the retail group if it is trying to find a source of international production. As the retail groups grow in size and importance in all major markets, the percentage of outlet own brands that they sell is tending to increase worldwide. This can create difficulty for the exporter trying to establish an own brand but provides opportunities for profitable export activity by manufacturing own brand for these buying offices. Many textile firms in Taiwan and Hong Kong have achieved profitable export activities by providing own label garments for major store groups in Western Europe and the US without ever establishing their own branded product.

The specialist export agency purchases product in the home market and develops sales in specific overseas market(s). The involvement of the export agency varies from a straightforward one—acting as a trading company or providing stock for a range of outlets in overseas markets; to groups that actively plan and promote their suppliers' products in overseas markets. There are a number of advantages associated with using a specialist export agency: in effect, they provide the manufacturer with a ready made export department; they increase the level of control that the manufacturer has by building up distribution and demand in an overseas market; the long-term development of product in the market place is of equal interest to both the specialist export agency and the manufacturer. The Caribbean, for example, poses special problems to many exporting firms. The islands are spread over a wide area—the distance from Trinidad to the Bahamas is over 2500 kilometres—and individually small in population. The use of specialist export firms in this area therefore has many attractions.

However, there are a number of disadvantages associated with specialist export houses. They are often only prepared to accept a global brief or a regional agreement—that the manufacturer agrees to allow the export agency to develop sales within a given area. The nature of the agreement can be too restrictive. Use of a specialist export agency can frequently tie the supplier to one type of distribution system for a long time and this can interfere with the supplier's long-term plans for the market. Furthermore, though export agencies offer a wide ranging service, they may only be especially skilled in one market area.

International trading companies have been particularly important in the development of Japanese and Korean export. They are trade activity co-ordinators having some of the characteristics of the co-operative export venture described later in this section. European international trading companies serve as an important means of establishing an overseas presence. Generally they act as agents for principals in overseas markets, but may pay for the product in the country of origin, as they ship in combined loads to overseas markets. Using international trading companies benefits exporters in various ways: they act as a traditional agent in an overseas market with a long-term interest in product development; they often supply the technical back-up absent in most export agencies; they pay in the country of origin and handle all shipping and documentation. Their major drawback is that as widely spread trading companies they are unlikely to give the individual products the attention a supplier may wish; they will also be carrying a large range of competing products. Here are two examples of international trading companies. UAC, the Unilever subsidiary, has interests in both Africa and the Middle East. It owns retail outlets (Kingsway stores in West Africa) and business equipment manufacture plants and acts as a distributor for a very wide range of European products. Hagemeyer, one of the oldest established European trading companies, has subsidiaries throughout Europe and South America and handles a wide range of industrial and consumer goods.

Co-operative exporting includes three different forms of organization: complementary arrangements, co-operative exporting proper, and export consortia. Complementary arrangements involve a major exporter carrying other lines overseas, a process often known as 'piggy backing', either achieving profit on a commission basis; or buying and re-selling the products. The arrangement provides the minority partner with vastly expanded distribution and market presence at little or no investment, even though the price at which its goods are sold may be below national levels. The majority partner provides additional product lines which may enhance the acceptability of the product; add-ons for sports cars are an example of such activity. The disadvantage is that the small exporting company is heavily dependent on the major and will often have to meet specific pricing and packaging criteria (for example packaging under the major company's logo) which may limit future potential overseas expansion.

In some areas such as toys, individual manufacturers may combine to form co-operative ventures. The co-operative acts as a trading entity operating on behalf of members promoting their goods, paying for the product in the home market and then trading overseas. The development of co-operative ventures have been limited as the interests of the members and their product ranges are continually changing. Brittoys is an example of a British toy consortium established in the US. The advantage for the members has been the co-operative's ability to concentrate on the development of its own products. These make up a comprehensive range and sufficient volume to cover the overheads of a sales operation which would not otherwise have been possible for the member companies on their own.

Where large industrial tenders are involved for the provision of large sites, a consortium will arrange the purchase of the necessary equipment for the entire project. For example, a series of large hospital projects in the Arabian Gulf enabled a manufacturer of pumps for industrial cleaning equipment to become rapidly established in the market. Initial orders enabled them to learn about the market and then to expand into other areas. Consortia are normally companies in their own right, with separate profitability criteria and management staff. Consortia exporting allows a company to gain a foothold overseas without making a long-term commitment. However, the provision of after sales service must be carefully reviewed by the firm entering into such an arrangement.

Where non-contractual intermediaries are most appropriate as export channels

Non-contractual relationships with intermediaries that service overseas markets are valuable as a method of indirect export under certain circumstances. Where a company lacks the resources to establish a long-term overseas operation, they provide an extra source of revenue and win some international exposure for the supplier. For the established company, they provide a means of servicing marginal markets which cannot provide sufficient volume because of economic or political considerations. However, companies will need to continually review their use of indirect methods of export as they have the major drawback that the supplier has no control over the eventual destination of the goods, their pricing and promotion. At best they will remain of marginal importance to the medium to large company in developing overseas sales and be of greatest relevance to the small organization without the resources to fully exploit the international market.

Contractual relationships in overseas markets

The first part of our discussion concerned companies wanting to minimize risk levels; dealing with companies active in overseas markets essentially at arm's length and choosing a distribution method that does not involve any contractual relationship with such channel members. In general terms, however, the distribution opportunities provide an ascending ladder of investment and potential return together with steadily improving control over the market. The level of risk rises with the level of investment and this is one of the reasons why contractual relationships between supplier and channel member are normally a more attractive option to larger, more prosperous companies for whom the benefits of improved market control tend to outweigh the risks associated with higher levels of commitment. Indeed the larger and more complex the company, the more essential the control provided by contractual relationships becomes in overseas markets. A company with a substantial share of its home market must expand in a planned and controlled fashion to minimize conflict between prices and types of promotional expenditure in the different markets. This can only be obtained by a close relationship between the supplier and its representative(s) in overseas markets generally through a formal document assigning duties and responsibilities to the supplier and overseas channel member.

The most important contractual relationships—agents and distributors

Of the various contractual relationships that exist, the one that the majority of companies will choose for some or all of their overseas markets will involve an agent or distributor: over 60 per cent of American companies use distributors or agents for some or all of their export activity; for European firms the figure rises to over 70 per cent. An agent is an individual or organization that acts on behalf of a principal to bring the principal into contact with third parties wanting to buy the principal's products. Agents normally never own the goods which they are selling; they act as a conduit between the supplier and end user. The important point from the aspect of control is that the supplier has a clear agreement defining the agent's authority, and the services that the agent will provide in return.

Agents vary—each type operates in a slightly different manner. The commission agent achieves profit by approaching potential customers on behalf of the principal passing back to the supplier any orders. On each, the agent receives an agreed level of payment. The agent is unlikely to hold any stock, and will not have any responsibility for the credit worthiness of the local firms. Commission agents are particularly suitable in areas where there is no service element, as in consumer goods; where there are particular problems in gaining entry to the market; and where orders are limited and spasmodic. While not holding stock of the finished product, there may be advantages in certain markets in a service or maintenance agency agreement. Here the agent receives a commission on sales as well as providing service or maintenance at an agreed price charged to local customers in the local market. These agents are particularly suitable for industrial products in certain markets as they give the local servicing back-up many firms require. The stocking agent acts as a wholesaler for the overseas principal maintaining buffer stock in a central warehouse for which the principal is charged an agreed rental sum.

Agency agreements are particularly useful to the small or medium sized company building up its presence in overseas markets. They give the supplier company access to an established individual or company in a clearly defined overseas market. This allows the supplier to plan more effectively while limiting the agent's activities to a specific market or market sector and a specific range of competitive product lines. This improves supplier control over where the product is sold, and how it is priced, without having to invest heavily in the market as all sales costs are paid for on a marginal basis when a sale is achieved.

On the other hand, agency agreements tend to result in inadequate coverage and support for large scale market exploitation. They are often also troublesome to administer, producing orders that are small and in inconvenient quantities. Since few carry the credit risk on the customers serviced, they are a source of potential additional risk to the supplier. Agency agreements are therefore most suitable where the market potential is limited, or where orders are likely to be small or spasmodic, or in markets where the company cannot see any long-term potential. But the existence of a single contact in the market with responsibility for company sales development enables the supplier to provide promotional material and carry out market visits to expand the overall level of demand.

Distributors by contrast are customers in an overseas market who have been given the (normally sole) contractual right to purchase and sell on the supplier's goods. They differ from the agent in contracting to maintain stocks of product in the market. They receive income from the difference between the price at which they buy and sell product in the market place. Distributors score over agents as a means of becoming established in overseas markets in a number of ways. They take all the credit risks in the market. They tend to have much better sales forces and support staff than the agent, as they must maintain a high level of volume sales to pay for the high overheads of maintaining stocks. Because they hold stock they can minimize the fluctuations of supply and demand by accepting bulk quantities in 'supplier-convenient' quantities. They can meet special local re-packing requirements should they exist. A further important advantage for the supplier concerns long-term product development overseas. Distributors are frequently sophisticated at planning in-market activities, local sales promotions, exhibitions, which reduce the supplier's workload. As a result of their involvement in these activities, they are more likely to be able to provide the level of information about the market needed by the supplier to accurately plan and develop the product in the overseas market.

Problems of control arise with certain distributors in certain markets. Some can be minimized by well designed contractual agreements, but key areas of conflict will still occur even in the best regulated agreement. Because of their independent position in the market, distributors often have different perceptions of pricing levels, stock holding requirements, promotional expenditure and timing, and specific details of market coverage—whether to concentrate on specialists, generalists, large retailers or small retailers, for example.

Selecting a distributor, like choosing an agent, is part of the firm's strategic development. They are more appropriate than agents in substantial markets with regional or technical problems that the supplier company cannot handle, markets far removed geographically from the supplier's home territory, and markets which, though large, are unlikely to warrant a higher level of investment by the company in the near future. Because distributors achieve higher sales levels than agents, the supplier provides a higher level of support in terms of product modification, promotional expenditure and market visits.

Agreements with manufacturing companies in overseas markets

Up to this point we have been discussing the contractual agreements that suppliers can establish with what are essentially sales organizations in overseas markets. There are, in addition, a number of alternative contractual relationships that manufacturers can establish with other manufacturers in overseas markets. Industrial co-operation ventures are long-term agreements between manufacturers to share industrial expertise. With the steady growth in research and development costs there has been a steady rise in industrial co-operation ventures of different types.

Industrial co-operation agreements involve the sharing of technology, the sharing of manufacture of a particular item, or the combining of two companies to manufacture a joint product range, one item manufactured in its entirety by one company, and sold in the market of another. Zastava and Polmot, vehicle manufacturers in Yugoslavia and Poland, exchange vehicle components with one factory specializing in a range of specific items. These agreements allow manufacturers to share the very high development costs of technical products and provide access to market information on other countries and competitors which would otherwise be unavailable to the individual partners in the agreement. A partner in the venture can develop sales of components or other unrelated technology with the other partner in the venture, while maintaining a low capital involvement in the overseas market—firms only provide their expertise and some form of management presence.

Industrial co-operation agreements have become major distribution channels for East–West trade, as they gain access to large markets which otherwise would be barred by government. A sophisticated manufacturer can use ageing technology in markets where it may be able to get high quality components or raw materials which will support its worldwide manufacturing activity. Industrial co-operation agreements have done much to supplant licensing, once a common distribution agreement between two manufacturing companies. Licensing involves the agreement between two parties whereby one gains access to some form of commercial expertise in return for a payment—which can include a patent covering a product or process, a trademark or brand name, or technical expertise in particular manufacturing areas. Though licensing can provide an avenue to expand the sale of old technology or a brand name in new markets, the problems of maintaining control over the activities of the licencee have made this particular avenue for overseas distribution less popular. The particular problems that licensing companies have encountered include the fact that transferring technology can lead to the creation of a new competitor (as many Western companies have found to their cost in licence arrangements with Japanese companies); that royalty returns from licence arrangements will tend to be low; and that the licence agreement itself may be hostage to changing legal constraints. The creation of the EEC with the stated principle of free movement of goods between countries created substantial difficulties for some overseas firms from countries outside the Community that had licensed manufacturers in some of the member states. Some of the licencees used the Treaty of Rome to expand their sales into other member states.

Because of these problems licence agreements have become restricted to markets where there are high tariff barriers or export quotas; where the product has relatively low added value; where the technology supplied will not pose a threat to the current core businesses of the company; or where the product obtains its market edge from promotional activity—the brand is the most distinctive element of the product. Licensing has proved particularly popular as a spin off to the entertainment business and where there are well-established brand names in one particular business area. The 'Star Wars' films led to a whole range of licensed toys, the stars of 'Dynasty' promote a range of lingerie and perfume, 'Carrington—the essence of a man', and both the Sotheby's and Harrods name have been used to promote a brand of cigarette.

Where the market is particularly attractive but has problems of control, investment in joint venture operations was a common method of establishing distribution arrangements between two manufacturing companies. A joint venture is a project in which two (or occasionally more) parties invest in a jointly owned operation. It normally involves the creation of a new company in which the parties have shares, though neither party has effective control over the decision making process. Scott Industries, an American firm, entered a joint venture with Bowater, a British firm, to form a new company Bowater Scott to develop sales of paper products in the UK, with a 50/50 shared ownership between the two initiating companies. In contrast Levers Nigeria is now termed an associated company within Unilever as the Unilever shareholding has fallen to 40 per cent. As might be expected, joint ventures are particularly well developed in some countries where majority shareholdings of foreign firms in local businesses are either forbidden by law or made difficult by local business structures. Turkey used to forbid foreign firms holding more than 40 per cent of equity in local companies; Japan until the early 1970s restricted foreign ownership of local companies to 50 per cent.

Joint ventures improve the control that the contributing companies exert over the manufacture and distribution of their products in overseas markets; they reduce the level of investment required to set up a production facility; and overcome both legislative problems and any local hostility. As a method of overseas expansion, they have nevertheless fallen into disfavour because of some fundamental shortcomings. Often they are not exactly joint: one company is likely to hold more than 50 per cent of the equity putting the minority partner in the arrangement under pressure to accept the majority partner's decisions. This is accentuated when one partner controls a majority of management with a natural bias in favour of the parent company. It is therefore hardly surprising that an estimated 30 per cent of joint ventures are substantially modified within the first five years of commencement because of factors other than market changes. The schizoid nature of the joint company means that it is often starved of resources by the two parent companies. Scott Industries of the US (see above) has had a successful track record of joint venture operations in overseas markets. It follows the common pattern of having 50 per cent of the total equity, but considers that the key to its success in joint ventures lies in the willingness of both parties to supply equal investments of money and personnel. Finally joint venture arrangements can seriously limit the future development of a successful product concept by the parent company. Xerox formed a joint venture with the Rank Organization which was given the rights, outside the US, to the distribution of photocopiers. This agreement meant that Rank has continued to profit from investment made by Xerox—a total of over $200 million by the early 1970s. With the reduction of trade barriers throughout the industrialized and industrializing world, the markets where joint ventures were most appropriate—those with long-term potential but substantial legal or structural barriers to majority ownership of a manufacturing facility—have declined.

Management expertise transfer

An alternative method of having some form of contractual control over an overseas market is to transfer management expertise. The earliest form of this was the management contract whereby one company agreed to organize some or all of another company's activities by providing experienced staff to run the operation. Management contracts are most common where the management task requires a level of expertise which is lacking in the overseas market: construction projects are an example but international hotel chains like Hilton and Sheraton are the most visible evidence of the spread of management contracts as a means of establishing a worldwide network. They provide a means of acquiring knowledge about a particular market without a significant amount of risk. However, because most of the capital injection is provided by local partners, it is frequently difficult to control the operation sufficiently or guarantee a long-term market presence.

An alternative and increasingly popular means of transferring management expertise is the development of franchising overseas. A franchise is the right to a particular business within a given area. It normally consists of a complete business system developed by a company (the franchiser) which then sells a local franchise—to a franchisee—in return for promotional and managerial assistance. It is estimated that one in three new businesses in the US is a franchised operation and that 10 million people in the developed world are now employed in this sector of the economy. Franchising is broadly a feature of the service economy, including restaurants, transport, household services, retailing. Examples of well known international franchisors are Benetton—retailing; TNT—transport; Dyno Rod—drain clearance; McDonalds—fast food; Kentucky Fried Chicken—fast food; and Budget—car rental.

Franchising allows a firm to achieve rapid international market growth with a new, successful, product concept without major investment as it is the franchisee who makes the financial commitment. Despite this, the more successful franchising companies maintain a considerable level of control over their products because the franchisee contracts to be guided by the company on all matters relating to the product and how it is presented. Franchising can be extremely profitable, often with high royalties on sales (10 per cent or more) paid to the franchiser by the franchisee who frequently contracts to buy all product from the franchiser.

But franchising has its problems too. Firms can perhaps achieve a higher level of profit by running the operations themselves. McDonalds in the UK was originally a totally owned operation, and there are still only two or three franchised outlets because of the high profit potential in the market; by contrast with the position in other European countries where McDonalds outlets are almost totally franchised. It is sometimes difficult to maintain the motivation of the franchisees over a number of years particularly where they are required to maintain a high level of royalty payments. Franchising further requires a high level of commitment to find suitable franchisees and to build up awareness of the franchise operations. It can be difficult to maintain the quality of the franchised operations which can cause an overall deterioration in profitability and long-term potential. Franchises need continual and systematic supervision to ensure that quality is maintained. Many of the retail franchising operations fail to expand effectively overseas because of unwillingness to spend time and money controlling the level of service provided by their overseas outlets. Part of the reason for the successful expansion of the Benetton chain thoughout Europe has been their careful selection and monitoring of franchised outlets. Despite these problems, as living standards improve, franchising will probably become an increasingly attractive common form of contractual relationship for overseas markets, especially in service industries such as retailing and catering where little expertise is required.

The third alternative—company owned operations overseas

The final alternative form of distribution channel in overseas markets is to establish some form of local representation. At the lowest level of investment this means the establishment of a local sales or marketing office, which may manage a local sales force selling the company's product; supervise a number of local sales agents or distributors; act as a holding company for the international company to minimize tax; provide marketing support to a local distributor or joint venture operation; or co-ordinate local contract manufacture. The benefits are largely those of improved control over the market in such areas as market information, market pricing and the timing of promotions. This has to be balanced against the impact of any legislation seeking to control this style of operation in the overseas market; and the overriding issue of cost. A European company would have to consider investing a minimum of £100 000 per annum to establish an expatriate sales manager in Japan. Accommodation would cost at least £20 000, salary and expenses would run at £40 000 and even a small office would cost in the region of £40 000 to establish with secretarial assistance. Paying for such an overhead would require a substantial sales volume, and most companies do not consider this alternative until the current market sales have reached 'critical mass' (see Figure 5.1) where the profitability of the market is sufficient to pay for the costs of the operation.

Local sales offices are most appropriate for the company intent on rapid progress in key overseas markets and for those products with particular technical or service requirements. Generally, the local sales operation acts as an importer of product from the home market, but as the level of sales increases, the company frequently decides to start sourcing product locally, thereby increasing its investment in the local market. Initially the lowest cost alternative is some form of contract manufacture, where a local manufacturing resource makes product for in-market consumption. Contract manufacture is an important option where there are high tariff barriers and the requirement to adapt product to local market conditions. Quality is often difficult to control and it is unlikely to be suitable for products with a technical content—a point considered in the chapter on production location (Chapter 6). When there is a need to improve quality and maintain the advantages of local manufacture, many firms are prepared to invest in some form of assembly—often called 'screwdriver'—operation. Local assembly operations are useful where the company faces tariff barriers which

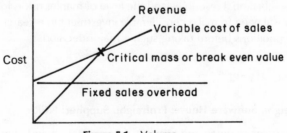

Figure 5.1   Volume

weight the cost of finished goods more highly than components, and where the cost of local labour is lower than the additional cost of assembly. Commodore Computers assembled home computers for the European market at Corby in the UK. The advantages of bringing in the complete circuit boards and assembling locally offered considerable savings over the import of complete units from the US. Many drug companies use local assembly operations because of the low bulk of the active ingredients compared to the finished product, the technology needed for tablet production being relatively simple. Local assembly operations improve the company's acceptability in the local market while retaining the maximum permitted percentage of imported components.

If a company decides that it needs to make a higher level of investment, perhaps because sales of product are booming in an overseas market, this may involve either the purchase of a local company, or the establishment of a fully owned manufacturing facility. Acquisition of overseas companies is currently considered the most cost effective method of overseas expansion where the market is mature; examples include chocolate, soft drinks and building materials. Cadbury Schweppes has expanded into the US by buying a large interest in the Dr Pepper soft drinks company, and Hanson Trust has acquired large numbers of companies in mature industries in the US. Its purchase of the Smith Corona Corporation in 1986 was an example of this acquisition strategy with its interests in the production of industrial raw materials, and food manufacture and distribution. Though a company can gain rapid market share by direct purchases overseas, these new subsidiaries can be notoriously difficult to integrate into the international operation of the firm, due to different management attitudes and operating principles. Many of the many failures of overseas expansion can be ascribed to the inability of the purchasing company to manage the overseas subsidiary effectively: examples include Midland Bank and the Imperial Group with their purchases in the US.

The problems of such integrations suggest that the establishment of a fully owned manufacturing facility would be more logical. Though this offers the best possible control over product, distribution and organization the level of risk is correspondingly high. For example, the disinvestment strategies followed by many overseas companies in the South African market in the 1980s meant many investments being sold for well below their 'book' value. Full scale investment in manufacturing facilities is relevant where the product is complex, the market is large and highly competitive, the parent company has substantial resources and the level of market risk is low—but even so the company will need to make considerable investment in research into the market and market conditions before taking such a major decision.

COMPUTER SOFTWARE

Name: Profreight. Software House: Profreight. Supplier: NCR

Profreight produces shipping and customs documentation and controls all the costs and estimates associated with a job. Full loads and groupage are handled and the system is aligned with SITPRO documentation.

Name: Distribution Expert Inventory. Software House: ASA. System: Digital

Distribution Expert Inventory provides full serialized inventory control with warranty tracking. Users can control orders, receipts, transfers, and physical adjustments to inventory including control logs. The system also handles kit building from individual components.

CASE: DAYGLO LAMPS

Background

The Chairman of Dayglo Lamps had recently attended a conference on appropriate technology and its relevance to small firms. Having been with his company for 30 years he was well aware that its success had heavily depended upon its flexibility in adapting to change. He was eager to discuss the meeting with senior management as part of the process of outlining company distribution priorities over the next five years, and the type of resources that would need to be allocated.

The company

Dayglo Lamps was mainly engaged in exporting paraffin fuelled household lamps to developing countries but had throughout its hundred year history also had a special reputation in manufacturing specialized safety lamps. As a result a small research laboratory had been set up and, influenced by the meeting on appropriate technology, the Chairman began to wonder whether the expertise that had been so successful in the case of the specialized lamps could not be channelled into finding cheaper non-oil fuels for the household lamps in order to further the sale of the lamps overseas, or whether the production technology that they had developed could not be directed into new ventures.

A British company formed during the middle of the nineteenth century, Dayglo had been the first to exploit the market potential of, and acquire a near monopoly in, the sale of oil lamps. It had also quickly recognized the further possibilities offered in the manufacture of the Davy lamps for use in mines so that by the time that twentieth century electrification began to pose a threat to the company's future, there were already two distinct areas of operation: one concerned with the traditional oil lamp, the other involved in the manufacture and development of safety lamps for specialized purposes. The trenches of the First World War had provided the company with additional experience in the development of the latter.

Gas lighting posed the initial threat to the household oil lamp but it was electrification which sounded the final death toll for the British market. The company responded by increasing investment in and upgrading the management of the specialized sector which had until then been a secondary area of activity. To secure its main activity, however, Dayglo sought out overseas markets in what then constituted the British Empire. This was a highly successful decision enabling the company to expand rather than contract.

Electrification in those developing countries to which Dayglo exported did not pose the same sort of threat as it had done in Europe. The process was slower, concentrated on the towns, and frequent power shortages especially in African cities meant that households would still buy standby lamps. The potential of rural markets—areas without electricity—remained largely unexplored because of poor communications. A major problem came, however, with the oil crisis of the early 1970s which meant that those in the Third World who could afford a Dayglo lamp could not afford the fuel for it. Dayglo lamps could still, however, be seen in the majority of small general stores throughout Africa.

Dayglo's specialized safety lamps had not been subjected to the same buffetings of Fate. Initially the company had offered them for export only in response to special orders. But their high quality won them a special reputation and export orders mainly in Europe, North America and the Far East had shown a slow but steady growth.

Dayglo in Africa

Nigeria had been Dayglo's first major export market. Steady growth up to the 1960s had been achieved through a sole agent based in Lagos. Dayglo's London based Africa area manager had kept in close touch with the agency in Nigeria and during trips to the country had been impressed by the good links between the agent and trade distributors which was beginning to penetrate the rural areas around the coastal belt. Events during the civil war had caused the agent to move to Accra, Ghana's capital, where stringent import controls included petrol rationing although the oil lamps were not classified as luxuries!

A few years of stability followed when the agency moved back to Lagos at the end of the war but although sales improved they did not reach pre-civil war levels. With the discovery of oil the prospects for household lamps were better but Dayglo found itself attacked for sticking to its sole agency agreement especially as the agency was owned by an expatriate who was due to retire shortly. This in addition to currency controls imposed as a result of the huge national debt, import restrictions, and continuing political instability meant that the Africa area manager was giving serious thought to the future of the operation.

Kenya was now a more important market than Nigeria. Some increase in prosperity had to an extent offset the rise in oil prices although by the beginning of the 1980s there had been a slight decrease in sales. The Kenyan Government was, however, critical of Dayglo's links with South Africa.

The largest export customer was South Africa. The generally better communications and higher income levels of the poor had given the company some access to the rural areas. Moreover with the ending of the Zimbabwe independence struggle the company had recovered the potential for expansion in Zambia and Zimbabwe itself. So far these two governments had turned a blind eye to the fact that Dayglo's products were sold in their countries through a distributor in South Africa but the Africa area manager was considering appointing distributors in each country on the grounds of political expediency. This was the only area of Africa where sales of household lamps had increased in recent years and where the company also had a market for its specialized lamps. The advantage of the South African market was that they could sell lamps direct to the main mining companies such as Anglo American, companies which operated on a large scale, rather than through government agencies, which was the case in the rest of Africa. Such government agencies required long-term development and could not be handled effectively via the Dayglo UK management.

Dayglo in the Far East

Initially taking only a small share of total company household lamp exports, the size of markets in Malaysia, Indonesia, and the Philippines had grown steadily and the company forecasts suggested that prospects for the market would remain good for some time to come. The cost of oil would not be a problem, incomes were rising and it would be many years before electrification programmes, in Indonesia especially, were completed.

Transport costs had led the company to establish a small assembly plant in Hong Kong. This had been expanded during the early 1970s to keep pace with the demands of the market. There was, however, a substantial amount of controversy in the discussion about the plant's future. If Hong Kong was to be integrated into the People's Republic of China a market containing one-quarter of the human race had its attractions. Moreover Hong Kong also had a level of technical expertise which could be an asset if Dayglo was going to intensify its efforts in the area of specialized lamp manufacture and research. Others pointed to the company's experience in Africa where political uncertainty had cost the company dear. A compromise was being sought in examining the proposal that the factory be relocated in another country whence the potential of the Chinese market could still be explored.

Dayglo had been unable to penetrate the safety market in the Far East which was dominated by large Japanese groups, though it was becoming steadily more lucrative, especially in Australia, Japan, and China.

Dayglo in Europe

The company had used the technology it had acquired in the manufacture of lamps to produce a range of Thermos flasks which were currently sold via some of the main mail order outlets in the UK. With the growth in leisure, the robust Dayglo products had achieved a fairly high level of sale.

A number of general hardware stores had approached the company with an interest in stocking the product. Of these, two major groups, Halfords and Millets, had stated that they could achieve substantial volume—the figures being quoted suggested that UK sales could increase fivefold from their current level.

The company had also been approached by one of the major leisure retailers in West Germany which had indicated that sales levels in that market were also potentially substantial.

During the last two years an experimental production run of sophisticated oil lamps for the UK market had also proved a successful venture with sales in the test region, mainly through gift stores, indicating a substantial market could exist both in the UK and in West Europe.

Dayglo sold its safety equipment to the major nationalized mining companies throughout Europe, but achieved over 80 per cent of its turnover within the UK. Though it continued to receive small orders from France, West Germany, Italy, and Spain it had never succeeded in becoming well established in Continental markets with the exception of Portugal and Belgium.

Dayglo and the US

Dayglo had been approached by one of the leading manufacturers of safety equipment in the US with the aim of manufacturing the current product under licence for the US market. It had been estimated that a likely 5 per cent royalty could be achieved on a turnover of $ 2 million. Dayglo had also had approaches from two independent sales agents in that market who were interested in taking the product for particular areas within the US. No action had yet been taken on any of the proposals.

Dayglo turnover and profit figures

Sales (£ million)

	1984	1985	1986
Africa	22	15	14
Far East	17	19	26
Europe	1	2	3

Per cent profit margin

Africa	31	28	22
Far East	24	26	30
Europe	48	49	51

DISTRIBUTION ASSIGNMENTS

1 Your company selling a highly successful short life cycle product has been approached by a number of companies offering a variety of distribution arrangements:

(a)   Joint venture in Japan.
(b)   Distributor in the US.
(c)   Licensing arrangement for Europe.
What questions would need to be answered on each of the alternatives before a decision could be taken?

2   A small company, based in northern Belgium, producing a range of premium hand carved wooden toys is considering expanding outside the Belgium market. What channels should it consider?

3   Take the published accounts of specific major companies and comment on whether you think they are organizing effective distribution channels for Europe after 1992.

4   You are employed by a manufacturer which produces a range of patented water treatment equipment, which thanks to a stock market flotation has £12 million to invest, half of which has been allocated for overseas expansion. You are provided with the following information about the size of potential markets and their profitability:

Market	Size (£ million)	per cent profit
Europe	35	40
Africa	11	55
North America	50	35
South America	24	45
Asia	88	35

What type of international operation would you recommend, which market area should the company concentrate on and how?

5   A company manufacturing specialist metals for high technology manufacturers has grown significantly over the past three years in its home German market, and has now achieved a 35 per cent market share of a £40 million market. It is considering expansion overseas as the next priority for development. Market estimates were available both for the size of the various markets and their profitability:

Market	Estimated size (£ million)	Profitability
France	30	Low
Italy	20	Medium
Netherlands	15	Low
UK	24	Medium
US	95	Good
Japan	45	Good

What type of market representation should it consider in the chosen markets and why?

Chapter 6

Production—The Interaction with Distribution

We have said that the establishment and management of the correct distribution channel is vital in providing an efficient and cost effective service to the customer or end user and that this is the main objective of the distribution system. The whole question of supply through the distribution channel is part of this process and involves interaction between physical distribution systems, sales force structures, stocks, warehousing, manufacturing facilities and order processing systems. However, many of the decisions on order processing systems, physical distribution systems and stock levels flow from decisions that are taken on the establishment and location of production and warehousing facilities. It is logical therefore to consider the issues involved in the location and organization of production and warehousing before moving on to these other topics.

Take the example of ITT, International Telephone and Telegraph, expanding from its western hemisphere base by establishing local production facilities in all its main European theatres of operation. This meant that a subsidiary like STC, Standard Telephone and Cable, could operate effectively as an independent unit within the UK and provide full back-up for the market there. Indeed the independence of such a company, supported by full manufacturing facilities was such that it was clearly identified as a UK company and not as a subsidiary of an American multinational.

The interaction between investment and distribution decision making is of paramount importance and this theme is emphasized throughout our discussions. Of the range of distribution decisions facing manufacturing companies, the establishment of production facilities is the most resource intensive, then in descending order come stocks, warehousing, investment in physical distribution and finally order processing systems. For a medium to large manufacturing company the scale of the investments required would be of entirely different orders of magnitude (Table 6.1). For small to medium sized companies especially, production and warehousing will be at the same site. Decision making on production facilities and their location automatically determines the siting of the warehouse. However, when the company grows and the geographical area that it services expands, the interrelationships between the warehouses and the production point become more complex. Take the example of the company manufacturing in the centre of a hypothetical country. As demand grows in outlaying areas it must supply greater and greater volume from its manufacturing centre. This may be less economic. Where should it establish new warehouses? Should it close down its central warehouse if other warehouse centres are created in the market?

This chapter will analyse the main components of decision making on the location of production facilities within a particular market, subsequent ones will concentrate on issues of warehouse location and organization.

TO CENTRALIZE OR DECENTRALIZE PRODUCTION FACILITIES?

Influences on production facility location are rarely clear cut, and often decisions are taken for seemingly illogical reasons. Thus the transfer of production facilities by a subsidiary of a multinational from the east of London to south Sussex was inexplicable except that the company's chairman lived by that coast! However, most companies decide on the location of production facilities after weighing up the conflicting demands of the market environment and the needs of the organization. Central to the decision is whether the company should centrally locate production facilities or split them up into a number of autonomous or quasi-autonomous units as a decentralized production resource. The issues that must be considered in such a decision are economies of scale, vulnerability of concentration, political issues, fiscal considerations, flexibility, product issues, transport costs.

Economies of scale

For any particular product there is an element of fixed cost (rent and rates, for example) and costs relating specifically to the manufacture of that item. As volumes increase the percentage of fixed cost relating to each product decreases and, all other factors being equal, the net cost of the individual unit decreases also. These economies of scale suggest that concentration of production in a single unit to service a range of markets or market areas will provide the firm with the maximum production cost benefit. A good example of such a logical concentration is Procter and Gamble producing Head and Shoulders Shampoo at their Newcastle plant for the entire European market. Yet it is the case that economies of scale in this context are most relevant to production processes that require high levels of capital investment, detergents, petrochemicals, and motor car manufacture being good examples. Where fixed costs are low, as in many craft industries, such considerations are less relevant.

Relevant in this whole area is the finding that per unit manufacturing cost decreases as cumulative volume increases. This effect is called the 'learning curve' as it relates to the ability of the manufacturer to find ways of making product more cost effectively at higher volumes. The estimates of cost reduction range from 30 per cent to 6 per cent for every cumulative doubling of production volume (Figure 6.1). This occurs through a whole series of small changes. A motor manufacturer such as Nissan may, for example,

Table 6.1   Orders of magnitude of investment for medium to large manufacturing company

£50–250 million	Manufacturing plant
£2–10 million	Warehousing
£20–80 million	Inventory
£2–3 million	Physical distribution
£0.5–2 million	Order processing

be evaluating over 2000 minor modifications to a model over a one year period, each with an impact on the per unit cost. Whether the Japanese system of quality circles actually increases the effectiveness of the learning curve phenomenon is an issue for debate, but it is apparent that breaking the production units down into a number of independent units reduces the flow of information on production engineering and will as a result reduce the learning curve effect.

Vulnerability

Concentrating all production in one site may make the entire company vulnerable to labour problems or economic upheaval. Multinational car companies like Ford and General Motors initially increasingly moved towards multi-sourcing of components within Europe following the serious problems caused by strikes in the late 1960s and early 1970s, but as the labour environment improved single sourcing became re-established. The Ford strike in 1988 showed that many of the lessons of the 1960s and 1970s were not fully appreciated as plants in Belgium closed down through lack of components. Back-up manufacturing and distribution facilities are crucial for firms with high service commitments. This is another important reason for building a degree of duplication into the production process; insurance may well pay the £3 million loss of a fire-destroyed factory, but the loss of six months' business will be incalculable.

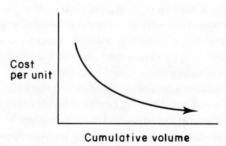

Figure 6.1   Decrease in per unit manufacturing cost with increase in cumulative volume—'the learning curve'

Political factors

For large companies, production decisions involving large investments, often in foreign markets, are frequently heavily influenced by political factors. Particularly relevant are investment grants, tax free periods, and tariff reductions available for investment in particular areas. Companies considering greenfield investments in the UK are often attracted to enterprise zones because of low costs of space and taxation advantages. The decision by Nissan to build its European manufacturing facility at Sunderland was influenced by large subsidies offered to those companies 'investing' in the economically depressed north east of England. Studies on investment decisions tend to indicate that the choice of site, according to the companies concerned, is rarely determined by the level of investment grant available, but rather by other market or strategic elements. Nevertheless, much of the investment activity by UK based firms in enterprise areas where they benefit from lower overheads can be simply regarded as a relocation exercise to take advantage of the grants available.

Financial inducements are not the only method whereby a company can be influenced by political decisions. When a company has a large presence in a particular market, it may prove diplomatic to establish some form of manufacturing presence to reduce resistance among local politicians to foreign investment. Few of the manufacturing facilities operated by Japanese firms overseas are more than assembly plants with a high percentage of components originating from the parent company. There is little attempt to exchange or develop technologies in overseas markets by a process of technology transfer or local research activity.

Legal controls over labour also influence production siting, though this remains a controversial issue, with studies often reflecting the political views of the authors, rather than demonstrating any underlying reality.

Fiscal considerations

Taxation systems may effectively determine the siting of plants. Some countries offer substantial benefits to companies locating production plants within their boundaries. It was claimed that in 1987 the most important single export from the Republic of Ireland was Pepsi-Cola and Coca-Cola—a result of the substantial incentives offered to companies that export the majority of production.

The steady increase in the number of freeports is making an impact on manufacturing policy throughout the world. Freeports allow a company to both import raw materials and export finished material without entering the tariff structure of the country in which the manufacturing unit is geographically situated. The advantages of operating out of a freeport environment sometimes override geographical logic that would suggest location elsewhere.

The ability to locate production facilities in areas where wages are low is important for operations with high labour cost components such as assembly operations. Much of the movement of such companies to the Sun Belt States of the US (Arizona, New Mexico) is a reflection of the 'pro-business climate' of such areas: Arizona restricts union activity by law, and there is a large Hispanic population which will work at the minimum wage levels.

Flexibility

In the 1960s and 1970s the majority of large plants could not easily or cost effect-ively cope with small volume production and needed to concentrate on large pro-duction volume items. In the 1960s Courage—originally part of Imperial Tobacco, then Hanson Trust and in 1987 a subsidiary of Elders IXL the owners of Foster's Lager—deci-ded to invest in large production units to maximize on economies of scale in the beer market making a small range of keg beers for national distribution. But the overall decline in the beer market, matched by the steady switch to real ale and regional beers, increasingly stressed the importance of small run operations unsuitable for the Courage plants.

Increasingly sophisticated computer or numeric control devices in manufacturing allow suppliers to produce smaller quantities of product cost effectively, and large plants are now able to compete with the small in producing limited quantities of products. Hygena, the UK kitchen manufacturer, has managed to decrease the cost effective volume for particular components down from 2000 to around 400 by the effective use of computerization in the manufacturing process and sophisticated stock handling techniques. A company such as Poggenpohl, also operating in the kitchen furniture market, offers tailor made units from a central production point due to massive investment in computer numeric controlled cutting machinery. These examples indicate that the old logic that emphasized the need for decentralized production to meet specific market requirements may be less valid with investment in microprocessor controlled production equipment.

Product issues

The products themselves influence production investment decisions. Often, this can determine whether the company concentrates production resource in a single centre or decentralizes. Here the most important factor is the sophistication of the product. Where a company must guarantee product quality through complex production processes, a logical production decision would be to manufacture for a worldwide market from one production site. The Boeing Aircraft Corporation is an example of the demands of rigid quality control and highly sophisticated product encouraging the concentration of production at one site where the engineering problems of bringing new aircraft into production are less fraught than for the European Airbus, with major components produced by the consortium companies. In contrast, a company like the Bata shoe group operates from a large number of factories throughout the world.

Product sophistication also has an impact on investment levels in research and development. In certain circumstances close links between production and research and development are necessary and therefore emphasize the desirability of centralized production facilities. But many companies do not need a close connection between production and research. Pharmaceutical research can be carried out in any market and at a considerable distance from the production point. The large concentration of research and development activity in the UK by many of the pharmaceutical giants is a result of the control exercised by the DHSS on levels of profitability within the UK market; establishing international research in the UK allows the suppliers to achieve acceptable levels of profit. In contrast, companies such as Motorola, one of the market leaders in the production of silicon chips, must maintain a closer liaison between manufacturing and research and development.

A strong influence on production organization is local involvement in production or the level of specific local demands. Local production having the built-in flexibility to meet local demand will be most effective where there are many local customers with specific regional requirements. Major multinational customers with common product requirements can be supplied from single international production points. Though the investment required to create a detergent factory is substantial, the specific formulation requirements of each European market has encouraged the major multinationals such as Unilever to site production plants in each country.

A product's physical properties affect the choice of production systems. Thus it is logical to locate the production of perishable goods close to their point of final consumption to reduce otherwise high transport costs. The World Health Organization investigates the activities of many multinational companies selling powdered milk for babies in the Third World—shown by medical researchers to cause high levels of infant diarrhoea. Powdered milk, the manufacturers argued, was a better product for Third World conditions because of its storage qualities; and because the problems of producing fresh milk in local markets would mean that they would need to raise the price far beyond that charged for powdered milk. (In the abstract, powdered milk is obviously a better option for markets in the Third World where refrigeration is mainly absent. However, in the case of infant Formula, clean water and adequate sterilization facilities—mainly absent in the Third World—are also essential to produce a safe food for babies.) Where a product is fragile and requires special handling and packaging local production may be more appropriate as this will reduce the amount of damage that may be caused in supplying markets from distant manufacturing points.

Transport costs

Where physical distribution costs are a high proportion of the final product cost, local manufacturer tends to be more appropriate. Bulk products such as animal feed and industrial chemicals are examples. BOCM Silcox, the animal feed subsidiary of Unilever moved from large plants based in dock areas like Liverpool and Avonmouth towards local plants throughout the country. Any losses through declining economies of scale in smaller plants were more than offset by the improvement in transport costs. The cost of transporting raw materials to the plant may also be important in determining the location of production plants in industries where raw materials make

Table 6.2   Heuristic approach to production facility structure

Factor	High	Low
Economies of scale	Central	Localized
Vulnerability	Localized	Central
Commercial issues	Localized	Central
Public relations	Localized	Central
Research and development links with production	Central	Localized
Local market requirements	Localized	Central
Perishability	Localized	Central
Fragility	Localized	Central
Quality control requirements	Central	Localized
Transport costs	Localized	Central

up a large proportion of the final cost: potato based product manufacturers such as Dornay Foods locating close to major areas of potato production, for example.

CHOOSING BETWEEN PRODUCTION ALTERNATIVES

Like the choice between direct and indirect distribution methods, an heuristic approach allows a company to outline the most suitable type of production facility. By considering each of the main issues involved, and assigning a high or low importance to each factor, a decision framework can be established to identify the appropriateness of centralized or localized manufacturing facilities (see Table 6.2).

COMPUTER SOFTWARE

Name: TMS. Software House: UCSS. Supplier: NCR

TMS (Total Manufacturing Solution) contains modules covering production control, master scheduling, capacity requirements running, resource requirements planning, Materials Requirements Planning (MRP), job costing, work in progress, works orders and inventory management.

Name: IMCS II. Software House: NCR. System: NCR

The interactive manufacturing control system provides manufacturers with production planning and control modules for: bill of material, inventory control, MRP, routing, work in progress, capacity planning, order processing and discounting.

DISTRIBUTION ASSIGNMENTS

1   A manufacturer of the basic chemical reagents has steadily expanded sales of its basic product range and is considering producing a new range of colloidal materials for research institutions throughout Europe. How will these changes in the company's production policy affect the distribution strategy it will need to adopt?

2 A small company producing a range of bathroom tiles and ceramic pots, expanding into Europe from its base in the Far East, is considering establishing a manufacture site in France. Consider the advantages and disadvantages of such a course of action and make a recommendation.

3 Take the balance sheets of two high technology companies, two textile companies and two food processing companies all of roughly comparable size and all operating internationally. From these reports derive their manufacturing policy. How can you account for the differences?

4 Textron Ltd currently producing in a central production facility an entire range of industrial clothing—safety harnesses, overalls, protective clothing—is considering producing heavy duty consumer garments. Write a report on how the company, based in Belgium, should consider developing sales in the rest of Europe and where it should manufacture.

5 The company that your company represents currently manufactures its range of children's bicycles for the entire world in the US. Research the local market for bicycles and write a report on the likely benefits of establishing manufacture in Europe.

Warehousing and Location Issues

Investment decisions on production resource allocation fundamentally affect the way a market is served—the existence or lack of a manufacturing resource in a particular market will impact on warehousing policy. Compare two companies with similar sales patterns, one with and one without a production site in a particular market. The company with the local production unit can service the customer more quickly than the one supplying the market at a distance with lower total stock levels in the market. This obviously influences the stock holding requirements and as a result the amount of warehouse space. For some companies the ability of the production source to supply major customers direct—without expensive warehousing, stock holding investment, and intermediary handling charges—is an additional important benefit of local production. This is one of the basic principles of cost effective distribution, to maximize the amount of *direct delivery* within the market that the company services. Direct delivery removes many of the costs associated with distribution, such as warehousing, the costs of delivery into the warehouse, a substantial element of the administrative costs, and much of the financing that maintaining inventory requires. Finally, the location of the first company's production facility will largely determine where other warehouses should be sited in the market, should they be necessary.

ISSUES OF WAREHOUSING POLICY

The investment in production facilities involves a trade-off against company investment in warehousing. Large numbers of separate production points means that intermediate warehousing will be less and less essential. For example, there are 27 Coca-Cola bottling plants throughout the UK allowing the UK distributor, Cadbury Schweppes, to deliver direct from production points to the vast majority of its mainland customers.

Similar trade-offs occur in developing an appropriate warehouse policy. Companies have to decide whether they should invest in a dedicated (company-owned) warehouse system or use third party services; they must determine the numbers of warehouses needed to meet company objectives, their location, and design—including all aspects of automation and layout.

Third party (shared) versus company owned warehouses

For the majority of firms, warehousing investment is the third most capital intensive expenditure in the development of a distribution system. They must consider whether the use of third party warehouse systems might not be a more effective use of scarce resources and some companies, especially multiple retailers, have come to just such a conclusion. Sainsbury's, for example, relies for the bulk of its warehouse management on specialist distribution companies such as the National Freight Corporation to provide an entire distribution service—warehousing, physical distribution and inventory control on a contract basis. This trend is further discussed in Chapter 12. Suffice it to say here that it is set to continue and to become a major part of the distribution environment. When third party warehousing provision is considered for medium to small sized companies, this dedicated contract service is not financially viable and the main option is for them to compare the costs and benefits of using shared third party warehouses.

Direct ownership of warehousing benefits the company through better information flow on the levels of stocks and a greatly improved ability to meet special storage requirements for fragile, hazardous, or perishable products. Most important is the flexibility to organize the despatch of particular orders, and this includes the major advantage of supplying emergency orders. Direct ownership may mean lower unit costs where the firm is shipping large volumes of product. These benefits of direct control over warehouse operations suggest that it is most appropriate where the company has a large and stable demand for product in an area reasonably close to the warehouse site; where there are special product or customer demands involved in the storage and despatch of product; and where physical distribution options are unlikely to change over the planning horizon. It is therefore especially relevant to the large, well established operation with well defined levels of demand.

For smaller companies and those with rapidly changing geographic or product demands, shared warehousing offers a very viable alternative offering a much greater flexibility of location with speed of relocation, avoiding the often lengthy planning procedures that are part and parcel of large warehouse construction. It improves ability to accurately cost the per unit storage overheads—the user will not pay for the inevitable dead space which is part of all owned operations. Even the most efficient warehouses rarely utilize more than 80 per cent of the available space, allowing for aisles, packing and receiving areas and the like. Nor will the user have to bear the variable operating costs of the warehouse itself.

A mix of owned or third party warehouses is the most cost effective option for many companies. Each must carefully evaluate the benefits of the two alternatives and their respective costs. The point at which the cost line of third party warehousing crosses the directly owned operation is given by the following formula:

$$C = (m + c)S + xA + W(L - A)$$

Where:
C = combined annual cost of proposed policy
m = transport cost £ per square foot
c = capital cost £ per square foot in owned warehousing
x = storage cost in owned warehousing £ per square foot
A = square feet in third party warehousing
W = storage cost £ per square foot in third party warehousing
L = total space requirements

However, cost is not always the only criterion used in the final decision between third party and directly owned warehouse operations, and many of the criteria mentioned above may be more important in particular companies and competitive environments.

Warehouse numbers—their cost implications

The number of warehouses—whether owned or third party—required to service a particular market efficiently is an amalgam of factors. Take the example of a company with a single warehouse in a corner of a country 400 miles square. Servicing a customer in the top left hand corner of the market requires a round trip of 1100 miles. That means a very high transport cost, especially if the vehicle could not deliver a full load. Establishing additional warehouses somewhere within the market nearer these distant customers would lower the transport costs but raise other storage costs. The company faces two interacting problems: how many warehouses or storage points should there be within this particular market: and where should they be located. The optimum number of warehouses within the network can be determined by the cost behaviour of all the component parts of the warehouses in the network. The important point to realize is that the optimum point will vary not only from industry to industry, but also within market sectors.

The total costs of maintaining separate warehouses are higher than the cost of one single warehouse but the relationship is unlikely to be strictly linear as there will often be a number of shared costs between owned warehouses. Naturally, the cost component will be greatly influenced by the level of investment that the firm makes in equipment and structures within the warehouse. Where a company is using third party warehouses, costs can be effectively considered as rising in a linear fashion with the total volume stored. Decision making on warehouse numbers involves giving some consideration to the ramifications of various cost factors, summarized in the rest of this section.

Transport costs may not follow a standard pattern as warehouse numbers increase.

There are two main components; inward delivery into the warehouse(s) and outward delivery to the customers. In general terms the increased number of warehouses will decrease the transport distance between store and customer and increase the distance between manufacture point and store. This tends to mean that total unit transport costs initially fall as the additional warehousing means a net reduction in distance travelled. Additional warehouses will then tend to increase the cost as the load factor (percentage vehicle loading) will decrease, raising the unit cost of transport.

Increasing the geographical spread of the warehouses allows the company to take more advantage of supply alternatives to service particular areas of the market. In other words, the company will not have to pay fully double transport costs both into and out of a single warehouse.

The level of safety stock also increases as a function of the numbers of warehouses, which is an important factor when overall stock levels are assessed (discussed further in Chapter 9). It is likely that the levels of obsolescent stock or slow moving stock will also increase as controls over stock utilization become more difficult to implement effectively with the greater number of warehouses.

As the number of warehouses increases so does the ability of the system to supply all customer requirements and the cost of lost orders steadily diminishes. Eventually, however, the cost improvement plateaus as the physical constraints within the system are minimized. Similarly, the cost of supplying emergency orders are highest when the company operates a single warehouse and lowest when there are large numbers of warehouses throughout the market.

With more warehouses in the network, the total costs of controlling the flow of orders within the system will increase, but not necessarily in a linear fashion.

To summarize, we may say that since costs show different rates of increase or decline, there will be a different optimum for each company, which will change with altering levels of volume and modifications to the customer base. Taking a hypothetical example (Table 7.1) illustrates how the combination of rising and falling costs will identify the optimum number of warehouses in one particular case. Here we see that as warehouse numbers increase, warehouse construction and maintenance costs rise

Table 7.1 Changing costs structure with increased warehouse numbers

Factor	Warehouse numbers						
	1	2	3	4	5	6	7
Warehouse costs	10	15	20	25	30	35	40
Transport costs	60	45	35	28	25	22	20
Costs of stock	20	30	35	50	60	70	80
Opportunity cost	17	15	13	11	10	10	10
Emergency supply	12	8	7	8	9	10	11
Supply alternatives	18	14	10	9	7	5	8
Communication cost	2	3	5	5	5	5	5
Totals	139	130	125	136	146	157	174

steadily. Transport costs to individual customers also drop steadily as warehouse numbers expand though not in a purely linear way. Essential stock holding levels rise too, as does the level of slow moving stock. The lost opportunity cost declines and then plateaus. The costs of using differing sources of supply drop at first but then go up with the expansion in the numbers of warehouses. Each additional warehouse will put costs up if a single source of supply is being used; and the costs of administering the receipt and despatch of orders will initially increase and then plateau. For this firm, the current cost environment would suggest that three warehouses would provide the most cost effective solution to its warehouse requirements. Different firms in differing markets with different cost and service criteria would reach other conclusions, and this underlines the importance of continually monitoring this aspect of distribution management.

DEPOT AND PRODUCTION LOCATIONS—MODELS AND SIMULATIONS

Table 7.1 shows how various cost elements change as warehouse numbers increase. However, it presupposes that a decision has already been taken to expand the warehouse network and to position them at certain points within the market. How does a company decide on the best likely locations given the complexity of the interrelationship? It is clear from our discussion that the question of siting and locating warehouses is a complex one requiring detailed analysis and calculation. Much of it is difficult if purely manual methods of calculation are employed as might be expected from the complex way in which costs change as warehouses are added to or removed from the system.

The size of the company largely determines the way in which companies will determine warehouse location. Small companies use rule of thumb methods dictated by the availability of warehouse space—as many opt for shared facilities. For the larger organization the use of some form of linear programming package is more and more important, especially for those companies operating in large single geographic areas such as the US or Europe post 1992.

Depot and production locations in the large company

As both the sophistication of the available software increases and the cost of the available computer hardware decreases, companies are increasingly turning to packages that optimize depot locations via an integration of all the relevant factors. For all practical purposes these are now the sole source of depot location decision making for large companies. Though the complexities of the more recent models lie outside the scope of this book, as they owe an increasing debt to operations research, a brief review of the evolution of model approaches will show how far they have progressed over the last fifteen years.

One of the best known early models is that of Hamburger and Kuehn which was designed to maximize the cost effectiveness of the warehouses in the network. From

Table 7.2   Hamburger and Kuehn model structure

Input:
    Factory locations
    Potential warehouse sites
    Shipping costs between production, storage and customers
    Annual sales levels
    Costs of lost orders due to failure to supply within time limits

Derive number of additional warehouses that would lower total cost compared with current structure

Compare variable cost savings with the additional fixed costs involved in the additional warehouses

a series of inputs the model, through an interactive process, calculated total warehouse numbers and locations. Its key components are summarized in Table 7.2. A shortcoming of the Hamburger and Kuehn model was its failure to consider wider aspects of the distribution environment, such as the interaction of company owned with third party warehouse operations; it also predetermined the possible warehouse locations, and though this is considered to produce functional solutions to the location problem, it tends to be suboptimal. An evolution of this approach, the Displan model, added many of the complexities that were missing from the Hamburger and Kuehn one, calculating the benefits of adding or subtracting warehouses from the network (Table 7.3).

More sophisticated approaches to the problem rely on the development of various simulation systems evaluating the impact of future changes on the distribution network. Systems developed by major companies like Kelloggs, DuPont, ICI and Heinz model the likely changes in the distribution network and the best organizational response for the company. Once these values have been obtained the cost of

Table 7.3   Basic factors in Displan model organization

Input:
    The best way in which product should move from production source to warehouse
    The number and size of the stocking points in the network
    Stock holding requirements by product group and warehouse
    Production volumes
    Costs of transport
    Customer service levels

Identify effects of changing production volumes, customer service, freight costs on warehouse network

Measure the effects of adding or subtracting warehouses to the network
Source: Adapted from Ballow, Business Logistics, Prentice Hall

Table 7.4   Typical components of simulation systems

Customer characteristics
Location
Demand patterns

Warehousing
Fixed investment
Variable costs of operation (and how they are affected by different levels of fixed investment)
Fixed costs of operation
Comparable costs of third party warehousing

Transport costs
Freight and insurance of different product types
Comparison of third party transport systems

Administration costs
The costs of dealing with various sizes of order and delivery costs by product type

Factory
Production and stock availability at factory sites

distribution can be optimized. The most important feature of these simulation models is that they allow a wide range of factors to be integrated, reflecting more accurately the complex business environment faced by such companies (see Table 7.4).

These simulations allow the company to explore the implications of changing the distribution environment at all points of the system, looking at the interactions of customer/product delivery/warehouse/production facilities. They are vital if the company has more than one production point and is attempting to optimize the decisions as to which type of products should be supplied to which territorial areas. The complexities of calculation involved are so large that no manual system could hope to handle the evaluation. The area of complex simulations is a rapidly changing one as the major computer suppliers invest more and more heavily in the development of appropriate software. IBM, one of the major suppliers of both mainframe and minicomputer systems, has made substantial investments in the application of computer technology to the organization and structuring of warehouse systems. As a result, there has been a steady increase in the amount of available software, and Digital, its main competitor in the minicomputer world market, has identified the entire area of distribution as one of the 'focus' areas for future activity.

Site location models for small companies

For the majority of small to medium sized companies the choice of where to site single manufacturing or warehouse facilities has not relied (and indeed still does not rely) on any degree of calculation. The reality of the market infrastructure, access to components or raw materials, labour availability, all impose pragmatic constraints on the final siting of the facility. For example, nuclear power stations need to be sited away from centres of population because of political constraints, regardless of the fact that the demand is in the cities and not in the countryside. Warehouses using road transport are constructed at the intersection of arterial roads close to the main population centres of the country, regardless of the fact that mathematical analysis might suggest that they should be placed on top of an inaccessible range of hills in the centres of the area served. But although most companies take pragmatic decisions on the location of single production or depot facilities, two main models exist to aid in site location, and are most useful where the market area serviced is relatively homogeneous, i.e. an even spread of demand centres and a network of transport facilities offering common transit speeds.

The economic radius of supply—that is, the area that can be effectively serviced from a single depot—is the easiest to calculate among the single site approaches.

$$C = \frac{a + b + c\sqrt{A}}{V}$$

Where:

C = cost per pound of value delivered within the area
V = value of products delivered
A = area serviced by warehouse
a = production cost of products
b = fixed cost of warehouse divided by total units
c = cost of distribution

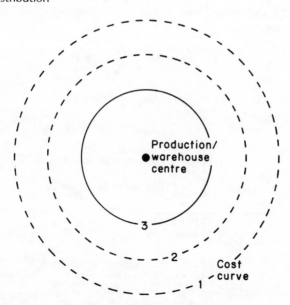

Figure 7.1 Cost contours around a selected production site

From this total cost equation the optimum area under the conditions of a and c can be derived by differentiation:

$$A = \frac{(2b)2/3}{(cK)}$$

Where K the sales density $= V/A$.
As the area derived is spherical, the radius can be calculated as:

$$r = \sqrt{A/3.14}$$

Repeating the calculations produces a series of cost lines or contours surrounding a selected production site. Obviously, this method can be continued from other selected locations, to produce a whole series of interlocking contours, which are technically termed isodapanes, (Figure 7.1).

Another model is the centre of gravity or cost per ton mile. It works back from the demand points or customer locations to establish where, in the current state of demand, the company should locate its warehouse. Thus in a hypothetical instance of a company with its main customers based in the north west corner of a grid and one or two customers in the extreme south east, the gravity model would suggest that not only would it be most economic to locate near the north west, which of course would be common sense, but where in relation to the current customers would be most advisable.

Cost per ton mile methods start by establishing a grid of demand points with X and Y axes (see Figure 7.2). Once these demand points have been identified the optimum value of X and Y—and hence the location of the warehouse—can be calculated with the following equation.

$$X = \sum_{i=1}^{n} (cwdx)i + \sum_{j=1}^{m} (cwdx)j$$

$$Y = \sum_{i=1}^{n} (cwdy)i + \sum_{j=1}^{m} (cwdy)j$$

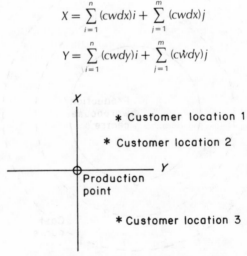

Figure 7.2   Cost per ton mile grid

Where:
w = volume
dx = the vertical axis direction in miles to the supply point
dy = the horizontal axis direction in miles to the supply point
n = number of supply points
m = number of demand points
c = cost per mile of product using current transport system

Because the production site may either be identical with the main warehouse or the factory will supply the warehouse with goods at the most economical freight rates available, the costs of transport between factory and warehouse can often be ignored for the purposes of calculation. Other centre of gravity approaches have been developed to consider such issues as customer service costs, and the effects of delivery time.

All gravity or economic radius models tend to suffer from the same problems. First, the number of calculations required by each approach often presents impossible demands if the customer base or the number of potential sites is high. Secondly, the cost of delivery is assumed to vary in a straight linear fashion between the supply point and the customer, and this is rarely the case. Thirdly, the demand pattern within the area will not be homogeneous—it will fluctuate over time in a varying fashion according to the special demands of particular customers.

Other site location models—methods of defining trading areas

For the retailer, the problem of defining the best area is often more difficult than for the supplier, as the manufacturer is clear as to the demand pattern that exists and the location from which that demand derives. For the retailer, demand derivation is often far more complicated. Take the traditional high street multiple retailer considering expansion outside the main cities where it is currently established and the factors needing evaluation when defining likely potential sites that would yield significant traffic.

First and foremost is the size of the catchment area immediately surrounding the store. Statistics on population densities are available in most industrialized countries, and these can provide a rough overall estimate of the potential of a particular location. The potential attractiveness of an area will have to be related to the number and importance of the potential competitors. One method of approximation used by some retailers is to identify the total market size for a particular area (measured by the total number of consumers and their average expenditure within a particular market sector, figures available from national statistics) and then to measure the likely sales per square foot of the new proposed outlet as a percentage of the total available floor space within the area.

$$\frac{\text{Competitive floor space}}{\text{Potential customers x per capita expenditure}} = \text{turnover per square foot}$$

Should the potential turnover per square foot be greater or equal to the target figure for the company, establishing a branch within the locality will be worth considering.

Within the UK government statistics were collected from the 1950s to define the trade draw area (TDA) for particular regions. Such information will no longer be available from the 1990s, which will complicate many retail planning decisions. The TDA approach and the assessment of area attractiveness by the use of average expenditure, while appropriate for mass market retailers, are often inappropriate for retailers providing specialized products to particular market segments. The development of the ACORN classification system has meant that retailers are better able to identify those areas with appropriate types of expenditure pattern. Socio-economic classifications of such types are important for retail groups serving specific population categories. For example, Marks and Spencer serve a broad spectrum of consumers, whereas companies such as Body Shop in the UK and K-Mart in the US specialize in their consumer target segments.

Such an approximate approach to site location faces a number of complicating factors. Consumers will be influenced to use particular locations by questions such as freedom of access—how good are the roads, how many people have cars, how far are they prepared to drive? Empirical analysis techniques range from fairly unsophisticated approaches like calculating the catchment area of the trading centre from an evaluation of the car licence plates in the parking lots (popular in the US) to some form of heuristic assessment or ranking system. For example, a company selling sophisticated cosmetics might create a grid like the one in Table 7.5 to assess the attractiveness or otherwise of a particular location.

Finally, the surrounding shops will also tend to increase or decrease the attractiveness of the environment to the potential consumer; in other words, improve or worsen the potential 'pull' of the site.

To reduce the uncertainty of demand patterns a number of approaches try to reduce the subjectivity in the choice of retail location. These fall into two broad categories: empirical analyses or mathematical models.

Detailed, empirical analyses require some form of formal questionnaire within the neighbourhood to find out likely shopping patterns. The findings of such research identify a number of broadly similar shopping patterns: that the proportion of

Table 7.5   Empirical approach to define shop location for a cosmetics company

	Weighting	*% fit with ideal site*
High quality shopping environment	10	80
Competitors established locally	5	100
Low rent and property tax levels	3	0
Parking availability	10	80
Restaurants and cafes	5	40
Total suitability of site		75%

customers patronizing a given shopping area varies with the distance from the shopping area; that the proportion of consumers patronizing various shopping areas varies with the width of merchandise on offer; that the distance travelled varies with the type of merchandise purchased; and that the attraction of the shopping centre will be affected by the degree of competition from rival sites.

The results of market research have been used by a number of researchers to develop models that can be used to define the likely structure of the retail environment and where trade is likely to be derived. Of these the most frequently quoted are Reilly's law, the Converse model, and Huff's gravitational model.

Reilly's law states that two cities attract retail trade from any intermediate city or town in direct proportion to the populations of the two cities and in inverse proportion to the square of the distances of these two cities to the intermediate town. The division between the two systems is known as the breaking point, the area in which the effects of the two competing areas will be approximately equidistant.

$$\frac{Ba}{Bb} = \frac{(Pa)\,(Db)2}{Pb\,Da}$$

Where:
Ba is the proportion of the trade from the intermediate city attracted by City A
Bb is the proportion attracted by City B
Pa is the population of City A
Pb is the population of City B
Da is the distance from the intermediate town to City A
Db is the distance from the intermediate town to City B

The breaking point is that point where the trade going out of an intermediate town is divided equally between the two cities, or where $Ba = Bb$.

$$Bp = Dab/1 + \sqrt{\frac{Pa}{Pb}}$$

Where:
Bp = breaking point
Dab is the distance between cities A and B
Pa is population of city A
Pb is population of city B

The Converse model defines the amount of trade that will be retained by the intermediate town, competing with another trading centre. It states that two trading centres will divide the total of business approximately in direct proportion to the population of the two towns and inversely according to the squares of the distance separating the two towns. In addition there will be an inertia factor which will decrease the probability of shoppers moving from one centre to shop in another.

$$\frac{Ba}{Bb} = \frac{(Pa)(4)2}{(Hb)(d)}$$

Where:
Hb = population of the home town
d = distance to the outside town
Pa is population of city A
4 = inertia factor

A major problem with both the Reilly and Converse model is that they do not distinguish between the various types of product and the amount of time that consumers are prepared to spend in shopping. The Huff gravitational model introduced this probabilistic factor and essentially redefines a trading area as a geographically delineated region, containing potential customers for whom there exists a probability greater than zero of their purchasing a given class of products or services offered for sale by a particular firm.

$$Pij = \frac{S\lambda / Tij\lambda}{Sj / Tij\lambda}$$

Where:
Pij is the probability of a consumer at a given point of origin i travelling to a shopping centre j
Sj is the size of the shopping centre in square feet for the relevant product
Tij is the travel time involved in getting from i to j
λ is the parameter estimated empirically to determine the likely effects of various types of product purchase.
The formula can be used to derive the likely total numbers of customers that are likely to be attracted by a particular shopping locality:

$$Eij = Pij + Ci$$

Where:
Eij = the expected number of consumers at i that are likely to travel to shopping centre j
Ci = the number of consumers at i

All of these models face serious limitations and can at best provide only an indication of likely demand within a given area. Geographic features, local customs and local prosperity will all make each trading area a slightly different centre of demand. For the majority of retailers, pragmatic decisions will continue to be more important than the findings of the various mathematical models because they continue to be dependent on a series of assumptions. In the US, the retailer considering the viability of a particular neighbourhood shopping mall will tend to evaluate the total catchment area as being within 35–40 minutes' travel by car. In contrast the catchment of the larger regional malls appears to be determined by a 80–90 minute car radius. Much of the enthusiasm for the development of the out-of-town shopping complexes is associated with the current trend towards lengthy leisure shopping with many shoppers willing to spend long periods of time within the shopping complex and who consider a 90 minute journey as acceptable. Although it is quite clear that this 90 minute journey time is a juxtaposition of American research on the UK, some retailers are acting on the assumption that shoppers are prepared to travel substantial distances, especially where orbital roads such as the M25 provide easier access. Marks and Spencer in the UK, originally a great enthusiast for the high street, is starting to invest in the out-of-town sites in common with other high street 'loyalists', underlining common assumptions (supported by findings at the Metro Centre at Newcastle and Brent Cross in London) that consumers are willing to travel greater distances to shop than they were in the 1970s.

Similar changes in consumer behaviour occurred in France, where the growth in the out-of-town hypermarket was the most important distribution phenomenon in the late 1960s and 1970s. During the late 1970s and 1980s, a swing back towards suburban and city centre shopping occurred, reducing the overall share of the out-of-town complexes. Such differing trends underline the caution with which retail location models need to be treated.

COMPUTER SOFTWARE

Name: TDS. Software House: UCSS. Supplier: NCR

TDS (total distribution solution) provides order processing, inventory management, multi-warehousing, packaging, carriage, home and export documentation, space allocation, order picking, and handles complex pricing structures including discounts.

DISTRIBUTION ASSIGNMENTS

1 Using local directories identify all the companies that have established warehouses in the local area and the types of market sector in which they operate. Why have they located in the area?

2 Make a list of all the shops on the high street. What criteria do you think the companies have used to locate the stores in those sites?

3 A foreign company has, after a substantial sales effort, gained a number of orders from companies A–N on the accompanying chart. You are asked to comment on where the company should locate its warehouse to service these customers.

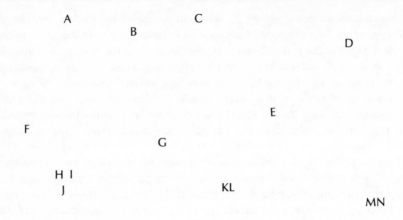

Assume that each customer has an equal demand pattern and that transport costs are directly proportional to distance
1 cm = 10 km

4   The company with which you work, with half of its customers in the North of England and half in the South, has decided to split the current warehouse operation located in the Midlands into two. You are provided with the following information and asked to make estimates as to the likely cost savings of two warehouses.

Turnover	£35 million
Current customers	3500
Average order size	£1000
Standard deviation of orders	+ / − £150
Current percentage split of customers	55 per cent South 45 per cent North
Current level of stocks	£3.5 million
Safety stock	£385000
Obsolescent stock	£150000 (est)
Storage efficient stock	£250 per square foot

Warehouse costs:	Current operation	Northern site
rent	£6 per cent square foot	£3
rates	£2 per cent square foot	£1
labour	£13 per cent square foot	£18

Transport costs: Full load (£10000 of stock) £350 per journey to northern site, otherwise equivalent transport costs within local areas
Emergency deliveries: 3 per cent of turnover in south 8 per cent in north
Out of stock positions: 2 per cent loss in south, 15 per cent loss in north
Order processing: Current costs £35000 per annum—65 per cent system eg (fixed costs). Additional system to be installed at northern site.

Chapter 8

Issues in Warehouse Management

We have examined the implications of company production policy for the warehousing system, the likely cost issues associated with decisions on warehouse numbers and various decision making models and simulations on warehouse numbers and location. Until now we have ignored how warehouse management—that is, the internal structuring and investment within the building—influences the efficiency and cost of the warehouse operations. In the previous chapter, we mentioned that there is a trade-off between investment in production facilities and company investment in warehousing. Here again we have another example of a trade-off within the distribution environment, where different types of investment policy will yield varying unit costs at varying volume levels. Again we are considering another total distribution activity—company policy will affect warehouse management decisions which will affect company policy.

From the analysis of current and future stock holding requirements, discussed in subsequent chapters, the distribution planner can generally calculate the total volume of space occupied by the planned inventory levels. Product properties and warehouse design may both alter the straightforward assessment of space. The most important constraint is planning restrictions on the organization of the storage area especially the height of racking systems or silos; the size of gaps between the racking systems; whether there are any problems caused by the physical product properties, such as safety requirements in the storage of hazardous chemicals. DLW, the leading German carpet manufacturer for example, has specialized storage and handling equipment to deal with the large size and bulk of carpet rolls. Finally the warehouse planner has to evaluate whether adequate mechanical handling systems exist for product in high rise storage areas as this will inevitably act as a restraint to the continuing increase in the height of warehouse construction. Thus the speed and cost effectiveness of the warehouse operation combines investment in fixed storage facilities with that made in other equipment—increased investment in one element, reducing the need for investment in another.

WAREHOUSING: THE PAST TO THE PRESENT

The balance between the level of company investment in fixed and movable equipment is reflected in the volume of stock movements, speed of delivery, the size of the storage area and any special product requirements. In broad terms, high levels of investment in fixed systems are most appropriate where large volumes of product need to be stored and retrieved over short periods of time; investment in other forms of mechanization will be more appropriate where the demands for flexibility and variation are the norm.

Early warehouses relied almost entirely on muscle power for the storage and movement of raw materials and finished goods. For example, film of the Wills cigarette factory operation in Bristol reveals how little equipment of even the most primitive type was employed, and a large labour force man-handled casks of tobacco product and boxes of completed cigarettes, until well after the Second World War. The first important change in the high labour component was the growth in unitized loads based around the concept of the pallet. The pallet in its basic form provided a platform on which goods could be attached and moved with simple equipment around the warehouse and on to transport. Since the late 1960s pallet manufacture has become increasingly standardized and there are now European standards on dimensions allowing pallets to be transferred within a common European pool, even though there has been a slow replacement of the original wooden pallet by metal. Palletization or load unitization has applications in most areas of industrial and consumer goods. There are obviously some large products that cannot be treated in this fashion and these continue to require special packing and handling techniques.

Cartons of product are stacked in a particular pattern on the pallet which is designed to interlock and provide structural strength—the pallet or stacking pattern. The dimensional arrangement of pallet pattern is an important design factor in the creation of any new outer carton design. Production managers must consider how individual packs will fit into the outer carton and how they will combine together on the pallet. A loose configuration will both waste space and lack structural strength, whereas too tight a pallet pattern will have a tendency to topple over. Cartons are attached to the pallet in a number of ways, either by simple banding, some form of plastic wrap cloth (often called 'shrink wrapping'), or vertical tension elements which strap the cartons to the pallet. As containerization became more important pallet sized trailers began to replace pallets because loads can be more quickly and effectively prepacked for container shipment.

With rising costs in the 1950s and 1960s, various mechanical aids were introduced to reduce the labour component further and speed the movement of product within the warehouse. For the majority of warehouses the growth in the use of fork lift trucks to move pallets became the norm, but other investments in mechanization included the introduction of conveyor systems, and methods of automatically attaching loads to pallets. Each of these methods led to increases in warehouse efficiency. For example, in one consumer goods export company the introduction of a shrink wrapping tunnel to attach completed loads automatically to the pallet by a plastic cover not only reduced damaged stock but improved packing efficiency by around 15 per cent.

Fixed storage systems

Generally, the most cost effective warehouses are those that achieve the highest product loading per square metre of floor space—heating, maintenance and other running costs per stock unit will be minimized. However, the delicate balance between product, warehouse equipment and company policy rarely means that the most straightforward stock arrangement, that of simple block storage, is automatically adopted.

Simple block storage—where pallets or individual stock elements are stacked on top of each other in cubes—has the twin advantage of being cheap to install using the most basic of equipment and expertise; and being a highly cost effective method of using warehouse space. Inevitably, with the high weight falling upon the lowest stock, simple block storage causes some damage. And, as it is difficult or impossible to reach the lower tiers of stock in the storage block, it restricts stock rotation—the reduction in the amount of old stock that is held in the warehouse. The way in which the block is built up also prevents warehouse staff stacking product to the maximum possible height as beyond a certain point (for most products around 20 ft) the storage system will become progressively unstable and dangerous to warehouse staff. Because of these constraints simple block storage is most suitable for large quantities of basic, durable material.

Because of these shortcomings, most companies invest in some form of racking system. Pallets or stock units can be fitted into a series of boxes or grids up to the maximum headroom within the warehouse so overcoming many of the problems of simple block storage. Racking systems allow an increased height of stacking, subject of course to the availability of skilled warehouse personnel and suitable equipment; improved stock control and the ability to stock a variety of products. They require, however, skilled handling as well as a sophisticated manual stock control system to identify pallet or stock unit location in often ill-lit warehouse areas. One warehouse manager operating such a system, applied for, and was issued with, a dozen opera glasses to aid warehouse staff in the identification of stock units at the top of 40 ft racking systems! When stock is located high above the floor access to it will be restricted and this will significantly reduce the speed at which stock can be removed from the storage areas and brought to consolidation points (often called stock 'picking').

Automation

The limitations of simple racking systems, especially for companies with a wide product range and high volume sales, led to the development of automated storage systems ranging from powered pallet systems to full warehouse automation. The basic powered pallet is a racking system which moves a pallet from one side of the rack to the other, where the operator is able to remove the pallet or stock unit. More sophisticated systems use conveyor belts to move the product to a centralized collection point. Warehouse manning requirements are lower even though large volumes of incoming and outgoing product are rapidly transferred and control over stock rotation is greatly improved. As these systems become more complex, they require far greater capital investment, management expertise and continuous maintenance support.

Fully automated warehouses are the most demanding of high investment levels. Through the use of computer controlled mobile gantries and robot arms, they can stack and retrieve product from all parts of the warehouse. The high level of fixed investment permits a greater stock density and therefore lower storage costs per unit. The introduction of computer controlled storage allowed Norfolk Farms, the leading supplier of further processed frozen meat products in the UK, to increase the storage efficiency of their main chilled warehouse by 18 per cent with the computer deciding where the pallets of product should be stored. Full automation also minimizes labour costs by reducing the numbers employed in the physical handling process. The Fiat motor car company spare parts warehouse reduced despatch manning levels by more than 80 per cent following its full scale automation. The computer's central role in warehouse management also gives access to much more complete information on stock levels which can lead to substantial improvements in the levels of stocks that are held. One computer manufacturer reported a 40 per cent reduction in the inventory levels held for certain key spare parts following the introduction of computerized warehouse systems.

The picture of the automated warehouse is not, however, entirely rosy and several manufacturers have withdrawn or severely modified their introductory plans. Complete automation severely reduces the ability of the warehouse to deal with non-standard products and loads. Concentrating as it does on the supply of palletized quantities of a limited product range, the capital investment levels and the time required to achieve full operating efficiency can be very considerable. More serious is the spectre of complete breakdown in either the computer or the gantry robot arms. The first may necessitate a complete physical stock check, an awesome task in such warehouses as Lever Brothers at Port Sunlight where over 20 000 pallets may be stored. Secondly, because of the design of automated warehouses it will tend to be difficult or impossible to use manually operated equipment to remove pallets from the racks and this may mean that the entire system grinds to a spectacular halt.

WAREHOUSE DESIGN AND DISTRIBUTION PLANNING

So far, we have been concerned with technical developments in warehouse management as an investment issue. Here we shall take the discussion one step further: any investment in equipment must be related to the warehouse operation itself and the the internal design of the warehouse. There are two issues of overall concern for the distribution planner: deciding on the type of warehouse best suited to a company's operations and then organizing the warehouse itself to meet those requirements. To achieve these broad objectives, specific issues must be examined and evaluated. Each can be regarded as a possible building block which can be combined with others in a variety of ways, to arrive at a configuration special to the circumstances of each company. Some of these are summarized here.

Poor warehouse design can cause sometimes dangerous congestion and delay at the ramp or traffic area (often covered) where goods are received and dispatched. One of the common problems in warehouse management is the confusion inherent in dealing with both incoming and outgoing traffic simultaneously, especially in achieving the maximum efficiency of the conveyor or fork lift trucks, where the problem of the operator carrying out the identical journey firstly to stack product and then to remove it for consolidation is known as 'deadheading'. The design of the warehouse should ideally separate incoming and outgoing traffic. Ideally, a separate access to both the reception and delivery areas will minimize the potential delays that can occur, but planning restrictions will often mean that such a flow cannot be achieved. The type of storage areas will obviously influence the products that can be stored and the way the warehouse will operate. A high rise storage area containing steel shelf units on which pallets of finished goods can be stored will require one type of handling equipment and working method, whereas bulk storage areas with silos or other containers for materials that cannot be palletized, common to chemical or agricultural distribution warehouses for liquids or solids, require different handling and design approaches. Refrigerated and/or chilled storage areas are essential for frozen food storage at below − 18°C; chocolate needs chilled storage in tropical countries or during the UK summer at around 10°C.

The size of load being despatched will also make demands on the design and organization of the warehouse. A picking area may be needed where stocks for orders below pallet size will be supplied. Packing areas for both large and small shipments often include banding or shrink-wrapping machines for completing the final order.

The type of product being stored and the amount of assembly work required largely determine the balance of these areas, and how they are managed. Products like furniture will not be harmed by low temperatures but household liquids must be kept above freezing. As the value of the product stored increases, greater attention to security is required. Though full security systems are expensive to install—£10 000 for a large warehouse—the eventual savings may be substantial. One shared warehouse site, stocking basic electrical components, on the outskirts of a Southern European city was losing an estimated £35 000 per annum through theft, and the cost of introduction of a security system was recovered within four months. Fire control equipment is another vital investment for most companies as the potential damage to the company if inventory should be lost can be irrepairable, though this will depend on the type of fall back planning and production flexibility that the company possesses. It is important for most companies to ensure the safe storage of reserve stocks, minimizing the chances that major holes will be created in the distribution framework. For example, a supplier of electrical cables went out of business in Germany following the total destruction of stocks in the central warehouse. The company could not meet two major contracts and incurred penalty costs which far outstripped the insurance on the fire damage.

The warehouse designer will have to achieve balance between these different types of area and this is largely dependent on the type of warehouse activity involved. Broadly, there are three main types of warehouse. In the storage warehouse, the emphasis is on cost effective long-term storage and ease of movement is not a prime consideration. Assembly and distribution warehouses act as holding areas for goods that are rapidly moving from the point of manufacture to the point of consumption. They receive and store goods, prepare loads and ship them. Ease of access both for loading and unloading is an important design feature for the assembly warehouse. So too is a well designed flow within the building to maximize the efficiency of an operation concentrating on the effective movement of goods. The combination warehouse includes long-term storage with an assembly area.

INVENTORY AND WAREHOUSE ORGANIZATION

Different items of inventory will have varying demand patterns; total volume, order size and seasonality all affect the number of times a product is included in an order. The positioning of stock in the warehouse will have an important effect on the time taken to locate and pack an item for outgoing shipment. Three methods are commonly used to decide how closely the product line should be stored to the picking and final assembly area. The sales volume method places products with the greatest sales volume closest to the picking area to minimize search times. The size method locates the smallest items by cube nearest to the picking area and the compatibility method organizes product by physical characteristics and likely common levels of demand. Soap powder stored near fabrics will taint them with their smell, for example; and products that are often ordered together, like nuts and bolts, should be in the same area. The application of these approaches depends on the products but product demand makes each a possibility under different conditions. Ultimately, analysis of the costs of order collection should be made to define which is the most suitable. The organization of stock will also be affected by the packing routine that is established.

The product and its demand pattern also influence stock collection and movement to the packing area. There are a number of methods in common use. Out and back selection involves collecting a single product and returning to the packing area. It is particularly appropriate for orders that do not involve the breaking down of individual pallets. A second approach is picker routing: organizing a collection journey through the picking area. It is appropriate for companies like publishers filling orders for large numbers of small orders. In automated warehouses conveyor systems are occasionally used to move product from the storage area to the packing point. Many of these problems can be overcome with the installation of the appropriate computer system and software, some of which can identify picking routines and storage locations to maximize warehouse efficiency (see below).

MONITORING WAREHOUSE ACTIVITIES—ESTABLISHING ACTION STANDARDS

The importance of warehousing as a contribution to distribution costs makes the creation of standards and the monitoring of warehouse efficiency particularly important. Although key criteria will vary between companies and market sectors, there are still a number of key ratios which should be established and monitored.

The stock value/base warehouse area ratio calculates the comparative stocking efficiencies of the warehouses in a network by dividing the stock value or stock weight by the total area of the warehouse. It can be used to suggest reorganization or redesign—adding further racking systems, for example, to increase vertical storage space—when there are substantial anomalies between comparable warehouses.

Warehouse productivity can be measured by the stock movement (volume or value) per annum/employees cost ratio. This ratio can also be used to compare the efficiencies of warehouses at different sites. Often such analysis can produce startling anomalies, meaning that either mechanization and skills in specific sites are higher or that working practices need to be substantially improved.

Stocking policy at each individual warehouse will determine how well orders can be filled. Though the completeness of orders/total orders ratio is often part of overall company control systems (see Chapter 15), it is also valuable if carried out on a depot by depot basis as it may suggest improvements in the order processing or restocking procedures.

Security problems vary from depot to depot and it is necessary to identify particular problem locations before effective action can be taken. Similarly, the way in which stock is handled will often vary from depot to depot and this will show up in the analysis of comparative levels of damage. The shrinkage and damaged stock/total value of goods stored ratio will identify problem warehouses.

The ratio stock movement (volume/value) per annum/total warehouse costs evaluates the percentage cost of the annual stock movement contributed by particular sites and will often suggest other areas for improvement—changes in heating methods, for example.

Table 8.1 Optimizing volume and equipment investment interaction

	Option		
Factor	1	2	3
Volume			
Fixed facilities			
Variable investment			
Labour costs			
Order processing costs			
Other overheads			

TRADE-OFFS IN WAREHOUSE MANAGEMENT

Discussion in this chapter has concentrated on the main trade-off in warehouse management: investment versus variable costs. To explore further the costs and benefits at various volume levels, the company will need some form of flexible review procedure to evaluate the main components of the volume/equipment interaction. An example of such an approach is given in Table 8.1.

COMPUTER SOFTWARE

Name: Beta stock. Software House: Systems Technology. Supplier: NCR

Description: A comprehensive stock management system to handle purchase ordering, goods inwards, labelling, stock control, with a full range of management reports.

Name: CWSS. Software House: Litton. System: Digital

CWSS (Conventional Warehouse Software System) allows management to control warehouse activity by directing personnel in receipt, store, audit, pick and consolidation activities.

Name: CDMS. Software House: Cullinet. System: Digital

CDMS (Cullinet Distribution Management System) controls all phases of warehousing from receiving, storing, picking, transport scheduling and shipping. Storage locations are automatically assigned and inventory is tracked by serial number, expiration rate, temperature, size or any other chosen criteria.

Name: Locator. Software House: Synergy Distribution. Supplier: NCR

Locator is a stock location and control system. It incorporates the latest date coding legislation and can cater for many different types of racking material handling systems, and single to multi-site warehouses.

CASE: PARKWAY

Introduction

Parkway, the major Australian brewing group, has succeeded after a long and protracted stock market struggle in acquiring the British brewing business of Hollins and Co, and is reviewing the distribution system that they have acquired. Parkway executives were trying to decide on:

—The correct warehousing numbers and locations.
—The correct choice of physical distribution system.
—The implications of these decisions on the stock holding requirements.
—Production limitations and order scheduling.

Parkway had grown to prominence internationally by the sale of its two lager products Park and Way, which sold throughout the world supported by strong international advertising.

The UK beer market

Prior to 1958 when the UK beers market began to grow at a rate of about 2.5 per cent per annum, the market for beers had fluctuated for a period of about 30 years. In 1959 the excise duty on beer was reduced and this had the effect of reducing the retail price. Many new beers also began to appear on the British market during the 1950s.

Over the next decade other factors boosted beer consumption: the 1960s was a period of major social change and economic growth when, for the first time, young people began to enjoy the benefits of high incomes spent on a wide range of consumer goods, including beer. At the same time, the number of young people had increased as the post-war population boom babies reached drinking age. Certain other factors were not so beneficial to the market: consumers' tastes were changing and beer came under increased competition from wines and spirits. Between 1959 and 1979, beer sales increased by 69 per cent while wine consumption grew by 428 per cent and spirits by 236 per cent.

Economic stagnation during the 1970s meant higher levels of inflation and unemployment. Heavy industry was hardest hit by recession and those who lost their jobs were traditionally good beer drinkers. To make things worse, in May 1979, the taxation on beer was increased when VAT soared from 8 per cent to 15 per cent. Excise duty on beer increased in every subsequent budget so that taxation on beer was actually increasing at twice the annual rate of inflation. This had the inevitable effect on price and volume since the price of beer is 'elastic': the rate of growth of the market therefore slowed in the late 1970s and the downturn in sales of beer by 1980 was expected. There was no evidence that the proposed change in the licensing laws towards an 11 a.m. to 11 p.m. day would have a substantial effect on overall demand, though early indications suggested that it would mean a move towards premium products.

'Going out for a drink'

The phrase 'going out for a drink' highlights some unique aspects of the UK beer market: the importance attached to pubs and clubs, to draught beer and the wide variety of beer available to the consumer. Social pressures such as drink driving

Table 8.2   UK 'tied' houses

Brewer	Outlets
Bass	7500
Allied Lyons	7300
Whitbread	6500
Watney (Grand Met)	6600
Courage	5000
Greenall Whitney	1500
Scottish & Newcastle	1400

legislation and the steadily increasing costs of certain products, especially spirits, were having a significant impact on the amount of drinking at home.

There are an estimated 60 000 public houses in the UK. Of these a considerable proportion are 'tied' to major brewers (Table 8.2).

Though beer has been consumed in the pub, inn or tavern for centuries, over the last 80 years the club has played an increasingly significant role in the pattern of the nation's drinking habits. The club is a peculiarly British institution, particularly the 'workingmen's' clubs, the British Legion clubs and now, more commonly, sports clubs. They are often owned by their members and provide intense competition to pubs in terms of price, flexibility of drinking hours and amenities. There are currently an estimated 33 000 clubs with bars (Table 8.3).

Many clubs are effectively 'tied' to major brewing groups which, in return for the supply of free pub equipment, provide all the beer consumed on the premises. The average investment of the brewers in pub equipment per outlet is estimated at £800 with a payback of around eight to nine months. Estimates vary as to the percentage of outlets tied in this fashion but trade guesstimates would put it at around 50 per cent. Recent changes introduced by the EEC have meant that the ability of the brewers to maintain the 'tied' system in public houses which they do not own or have tenants in, is being replaced with a more informal system.

Distribution is vital to market share as the majority of beer is drunk in pubs (Table 8.4). The pattern emerging in Table 8.4 can be contrasted with the situation in Continental Europe where up to 80 per cent of the beer drunk is at home. Only in Ireland is the figure for home beer consumption lower than the UK's—at less than

Table 8.3   Clubs with bars (main categories, 1986)

Workingmen's	4000
Political	2000
British Legion	3500
Sport	6000

Table 8.4   Beer consumption patterns

88% away from home
62% in pubs
25% in clubs
 1% in hotels and restaurants
12% at home

10 per cent (Table 8.5). Drinking in pubs can be linked to the British love of draught beer. Only Ireland has a higher percentage of draught beer sales than the UK (Table 8.6).

Ownership of outlets is directly related to beer market shares. As might be expected the big breweries dominate the total market (Table 8.7).

A wide choice of draught beer is available in the UK. A pub or club's range will typically include a mild, two bitters, two lagers and a stout—a total of six different beers. Some outlets may offer different portfolios, depending on local drinking habits and tradition: two milds, three or four bitters or three or four lagers. With the decrease in

**Table 8.5   Percentage of beer consumed
in private homes**

UK	12
Austria	40
Belgium	78
Denmark	78
West Germany	40
Netherlands	60
Norway	80
Switzerland	40
Sweden	85

Source: *Brewers Guardian*, June 1983.

Table 8.6   Draught as a percentage of beer sales

UK	79	Japan	8
Australia	40	Mexico	1
Belgium	43	Netherlands	25
Canada	7	Norway	18
Denmark	1	Philippines	1
Ireland	89	Portugal	17
Finland	14	Sweden	10
France	21	Switzerland	30
West Germany	29	US	13

Source: Brewers Society, *International Statistical Handbook*.

Table 8.7   Brewery market shares

Company	Market share (%)
Bass	18
Allied Lyons	16
Courage	12
Watneys	13
Whitbread	13
Scottish & Newcastle	11
Others (regionals)	27

both the number of staff that public houses employed and their expertise at handling beer, the willingness of most landlords to buy stocks of beer and rack them professionally continued to decline during the 1970s and 1980s. The prevailing attitude was one requiring fairly rapid delivery of ready to drink product.

The growing popularity of pubs and clubs during the 1960s led to an increase in demands for draught beer. The quality of beer became more stable due to improvements in brewing technology. New brands appeared in the 1970s, many lagers became available in draught form, giving the consumer an ever widening choice of draught beers. There was therefore a decline in demand for bottled beers with different characteristics—colour, taste and strength—which had nevertheless been complementary to draught beers. Despite the high percentage of beer drunk away from home, the take home market began to experience slow, but steady growth to the benefit of canned beer, though the increasing sophistication and acceptability of plastic bottles made from PET was taking an increasing share of this off-licence market. The off-licence trade demanded heavy investment in both packaging facilities and promotion and was in consequence the preserve of the larger breweries that also owned a substantial proportion of the off-licence specialist outlets. The overwhelming impression of the beer market from the viewpoint of the small producer is that it is extremely competitive mainly as a result of the domination of the big breweries in distribution and continuing investment in high levels of promotion (Table 8.8).

Opportunities for British beer in overseas markets were fairly limited as the majority of other markets were dominated by lager style products. By the mid-1980s the

Table 8.8   Brewery promotional expenditure (1985)

Bass	£15 million
Allied	£11 million
Courage	£8 milion
Whitbread	£4 million
Watneys	£2 million

Table 8.9   Average declared gravity of UK beer

1984	1983	1979	1974
1037.30	1037.50	1037.52	1037.29

Source: The Brewers Society *Beer Facts* 1985.

American market was showing signs of a greater demand for heavier beers but this was still limited to an affluent fringe of the community with over 97 per cent of the beer still sold in lager form (Table 8.9). Some of the major brewing groups were able to take advantage of this slowly developing trend because of their investment in canning and the types of beer that would can effectively.

Current distribution of Hollins

Hollins were an old established company with two breweries near to the centre of Birmingham. From there they serviced their 60 tied houses, and other independent outlets in the Midlands with the two main barrel beers, and three regional distributors that serviced independent pubs in the London, Southern, and Yorkshire areas. The company had invested in bottling and canning plants in both breweries in an attempt to enter the off-trade market which was steadily becoming more and more important, but these were currently under-utilized, and had been one of the attractions of the Hollins operation to the Parkway bid.

The Hollins product range

Hollins produced three types of keg bitter: Hollins Proud, Hollins Extra, and Hollins Mild, from each of the two production sites. Normally all three products were being more or less continuously produced, but the plant could switch between all three over a period of three days allowing full scale production of one line should the market require it. The cost of setting up production was estimated to be around £15000. The company had experimented with the production of lager based products and had invested in the necessary additional equipment to produce it, but had decided that in the short-term it would continue to concentrate on areas in which it had long-term expertise. This was partially because the production of lager would substantially lower the productive capacity of the plant by around 40 per cent, and incur higher set-up and changeover costs estimated to be around £5 000, with a down time of around five days. The keg or pressurized beer that they produced had a viable shelf life when unopened of around a month, beyond which there started to be degradation.

Hollins production capacity

At its two sites, Hollins could produce at full capacity 22 million litres of beer per annum if a single product was being produced. Each plant had a different production

Table 8.10   Hollins production capacity (all in litres)

	Site A	Site B
Production volume	9.8 million	12.4 million
Canning speed/day	50 000	25 000
Bottling speed/day	70 000	12 000

capacity, and the sophistication of the bottling equipment also varied (see table 8.10).

Currently both sites were operating substantially below capacity, a common fact amongst the small independent breweries in the Midlands.

Hollins pricing

Currently, the pricing of the product gave the company a good overall profit margin, when they sold direct to the trade (Table 8.11).

Prices to the distributors were, however, lower, as Hollins' agreements with them stipulated that they would carry out all local promotional activity in return for the extra margin that they would make on or above the wholesale price. This pricing structure also took account of the competitive nature of the market in the various regions. Yorkshire, being the most price competitive market, received the lowest price, whereas the Southern region was the least price sensitive and this was reflected in the charge structure (Table 8.12).

Hollins organized their delivery system into six regions, each of which had particular delivery characteristics. The three Midlands regions were those in which Hollins

Table 8.11   Pricing of Hollins

	Price per litre (wholesale)	% Profit margin
Proud	1.02	35
Extra	1.12	42
Mild	1.08	29

Table 8.12   Distributors pricing structure (pence per litre)

	Yorkshire	London	South
Proud	88	92	95
Extra	90	96	99
Mild	85	90	95

Table 8.13   Delivery timing for Hollins delivery

	Av. time (min.)	Av. distance (per outlet)
Central Midlands	30	4
South Midlands	45	5.3
North Midlands	66	10.8
Yorkshire	400	250
London	250	180
South	600	400

provided direct deliveries to a total of 620 outlets, with about 200 in each area. On average, the delivery time to individual outlets averaged out at 30 minutes and a journey length of 4 miles (including return journeys) in the central core area and slightly longer in the outer Midlands regions. The other three regions, Yorkshire, London, the South, were those in which sole distributors supplied the market and deliveries were direct to their warehouses, which were located close to the railway system in Leeds, Watford, and Southampton. Currently, the company delivered by lorry with a journey time and length of journey described in Table 8.13.

Over the past three years the proportion of sales going to the distributors had tended to increase as shown in Table 8.14.

As might be expected there were considerable variations in the demand pattern throughout the region and the way that Hollins serviced the various areas. Public houses normally carried enough stock for the week and took in beer on a fixed weekly basis at a particular time of the day. The distributors received daily deliveries, because of the significantly higher volumes that they sold.

Hollins operated two types of vehicle for their deliveries. Forty ton lorries had been purchased for the delivery to the wholesalers whereas smaller 20 ton lorries were required for the local Midlands areas as larger lorries were banned from many of the central areas of the large towns.

A 40 ton lorry could carry approximately 35 000 litres of beer in barrel form; 20 ton lorries around 15 000 litres. Hollins currently owned all their own vehicles and estimated that they cost around 50p per mile to run, including all depreciation and

Table 8.14   Percentage of trade via outlet area

	1983	1984	1985
Central Midlands	50	39	32
South Midlands	21	18	17
North Midlands	12	15	17
Yorkshire	10	15	15
London	5	10	15
South	2	3	4

**Table 8.15   Cost per thousand litres
delivered by railway system**

Leeds	£1.80
Watford	£1.20
Southampton	£1.80

drivers' wages. This meant that the return trip to their Southampton distributor cost around £200.

Hollins had considered using rail transport for the delivery to their local distributors, and had received a quotation (Table 8.15) for product leaving Birmingham railway depot to the respective sites.

There would be additional costs involved at either end which were estimated to be of the region of £40 per 60 000 litres.

British Rail estimated that delivery time would be in the region of 48 hours though they would only guarantee delivery within 72 hours, and expected the 90 per cent of the total load would be delivered within 50 hours from time of despatch. Because Hollins sent out the product stored in pressurized kegs, the delay in reaching the customer would not present a problem. However, the keg system did mean that Hollins had to received empty kegs back from the customer, and this was the main convenience of the road transport system. British Rail were prepared to provide a return service for the kegs which would cost 60 per cent of the cost of the outward journey.

Distributors' sales organizations

The distributors serviced a varying number of public houses and clubs within their respective areas; the Yorkshire distributor dealt with 3500 outlets, the London agent around 8000 and the Southern distributor approximately 2500. Not all of the these outlets stocked Hollins as might be expected. The average journey time of the three distributors within their sales area was broadly similar, with lorries having an average 25 minutes between deliveries with 4 miles between deliveries (Table 8.16).

Hollins warehousing

Hollins had maintained over the years warehouses at both of the production points which were ten miles away from each other on either side of Birmingham. These warehouses varied in size and holding capacity. Hollins had considered for many years combining the warehouse function into one new central site of approximately 40 000 square feet which could be run with a slightly greater labour cost and operating cost than those of site B (Table 8.17).

Because of the nature of the kegs, racking systems could not be used to their full effectiveness as the handling characteristics of the kegs only allowed them to be stac-

Table 8.16 Weekly sales patterns for Hollins 1985 (000 litres)

Week	Hollins Proud	Hollins Extra	Hollins Mild
1	165	24	20
2	176	28	32
3	178	22	27
4	183	18	35
5	160	25	18
6	182	26	21
7	176	22	18
8	190	34	15
9	176	14	22
10	156	22	22
11	163	23	35
12	172	29	21
13	143	34	35
14	201	15	17
15	205	18	17
16	132	19	32
17	187	34	33
18	168	28	26
19	159	33	14
20	188	27	38
21	193	32	32
22	207	29	30
23	217	19	26
24	220	25	21
25	216	26	22
26	234	29	33
27	238	27	24
28	214	28	23
29	203	29	31
30	196	32	28
31	194	30	27
32	189	29	25
33	175	23	22
34	177	24	20
35	179	25	19
36	172	22	17
37	167	25	18
38	176	27	22
39	186	29	32
40	192	28	27
41	195	26	22
42	187	22	19
43	176	28	29
44	189	32	33
45	167	30	31
46	176	27	22
47	156	25	19
48	187	45	34
49	172	47	31
50	167	39	32
51	260	65	41
52	189	55	28

Table 8.17   Warehousing of Hollins

	Site A	Site B
Site size (sq ft)	15 000	20 000
Site value (£)	80 000	110 000
Warehouse costs (£ ann.)	45 000	62 000
Labour costs (£ ann.)	38 000	42 000
Admin. costs	12 000	15 000

ked four high in the warehouse. This meant that the average stock levels per square foot worked out at around 150 litres, with a maximum stock holding within the warehouse in the region of 3 million litres of beer, which was rarely required; the Hollins warehouse also operated under capacity.

Parkway

Parkway currently had their two beer products produced via a third party brewer based west of London. Currently, the company did not produce beer for the on-trade and concentrated on the production of bottled and canned beer for the supermarket trade (Table 8.18). They were increasingly aware that to penetrate the UK market effectively they would need to gain access to the much higher volume on-licence trade and this explained much of their interest in the Hollins purchase.

Parkway production process

The third party manufacturer currently produced product in large quantities because of the very high costs of setting up the production run, as they needed to switch from their other products produced mainly for supermarket own labels. The minimum quantity that they were prepared to produce was 1 million litres of either Park or Way lagers which could then be either canned or bottled in the on-site packaging plant. Because of the third party brewer's high volumes, it was able to provide a very high level of throughput for both canning and brewing (Table 8.19). Shelf life for lager both in can and bottle was substantially longer than for the keg beer product produced by Hollins. PET bottles did suffer from slow gas leakage, but the realistic shelf life of both

Table 8.18   Parkway product range

Product	Can	Bottles
Park	400 ml	1.5 litre PET
		2.0 litre PET
Way	440 ml	2.0 litre PET

Table 8.19 Current third party manufacture production speeds

Production	1 200 000 litres/day
Bottling	400 000 litres/day
Canning	550 000 litres/day

cans and bottles was in the region of three months; though sell by dates were substantially in excess of this. This meant that the company was able to build up stocks in advance of periods of major demand such as the summer and Christmas.

Parkway pricing

The off-licence lager market was highly competitive with over 50 brands jostling for position in a growing sector. This competitive market combined with the growing power of the major retailing groups and off-licence chains meant that the prices in the market were exceptionally keen, economies of scale and high volumes being necessary to achieve profitability.

Because of its reliance on third party manufacture, Parkway suffered from low margins on both product lines (Table 8.20), and it was hoped that the purchase of the Hollins plant would enable the company to improve its position in the UK, where, because of low volumes and high advertising investment, the group was running at a loss.

The company sold to the main supermarket groups and into the centralized off-licence chains. This required them to deliver into 55 depots throughout the country, 33 of which serviced supermarkets and 22 the main off-licence groups; a total of 5000 outlets from their single warehouse close to the production point. Supermarket and off-licence chains were able to hold considerably less stock than public houses. With the new centralized control system, the majority of these outlets received deliveries from depots on a daily basis. Parkway was required as a result effectively to deliver to all the central depots on a daily basis. In order to simplify the administration of the ordering and delivery system, Parkway had divided the country into nine regions, some of which were much more important than others, even though each region had a regional sales office and a sales team of at least five sales representatives (Table 8.21).

Within each region there was a substantial difference in the total journey time and

Table 8.20 Current Parkway pricing

Product	Price/litre (wholesale)	Margin
Park	£1.20	19%
Way	£1.40	21%

Table 8.21   Parkway delivery areas and demand pattern
             by percentage of total turnover

	1984	1985
Scotland	8	6
North East	5	5
North West	9	7
Midlands	19	16
Wales	5	7
London	25	26
East	7	10
West	11	19
South	11	14

distance that the transport system needed to cover from the centre of the region from which Parkway calculated all journey distances. (Table 8.22).

As might be expected, lager sales were more seasonal than the traditional bitter, and this was reflected in the week by week sales figures for 1985 (Table 8.23). Sales also showed much greater week by week fluctuations. This was a result of the competitive activity in the off-trade lager market, with large numbers of special promotions appearing on a week by week basis which had the effect of biasing sales and making forecasting especially hazardous, a problem that was far less acute in the on-trade sector of the market. The further complication was that with the heavy promotional investment that Parkway was making in the UK market the underlying consumption trend was steadily upwards over the last three years.

Warehouse costs

The current warehouse occupied 30 000 square feet. Because the company operated on a fully palletized system and did not provide split loads to any destination, the warehouse interior was fully racked and pallets could be stacked four high. This enabled

Table 8.22   Inter-regional average
             journey distance

Scotland	380
North East	320
North West	230
Midlands	190
Wales	290
London	130
East	160
West	140
South	180

Table 8.23 Parkway sales in thousands of litres by week and product

Week	Park can	Park bottle	Way can	Way bottle
1	300	210	150	120
2	220	185	135	105
3	165	190	130	120
4	210	120	120	110
5	110	170	140	120
6	70	220	150	180
7	140	160	170	200
8	170	220	190	220
9	260	230	210	110
10	280	140	220	90
11	250	170	140	120
12	210	190	80	140
13	250	210	160	150
14	270	230	170	160
15	280	130	120	170
16	270	130	130	110
17	250	170	160	130
18	260	190	180	150
19	280	210	200	200
20	320	280	220	170
21	340	290	240	190
22	350	300	180	200
23	360	310	160	140
24	370	320	190	200
25	330	280	170	190
26	380	300	210	130
27	400	240	230	160
28	330	220	210	180
29	350	250	230	210
30	310	270	240	180
31	310	250	220	190
32	290	230	220	200
33	270	230	200	170
34	250	210	210	190
35	260	220	220	190
36	270	210	230	200
37	260	220	220	210
38	270	250	210	170
39	280	270	220	190
40	270	280	260	160
41	260	290	300	210
42	210	270	280	220
43	220	280	270	280
44	250	270	250	200
45	260	240	210	190
46	270	230	250	210
47	280	240	260	220
48	300	210	270	230
49	350	260	280	270
50	380	320	260	260
51	420	350	320	280
52	260	230	240	190

Table 8.24 Current Parkway warehouse costs (£)

Rent	180 000
Rates	15 000
Personnel (3 supervisors	
9 workforce)	75 000
Insurance	10 000
Warehouse equipment rental	15 000
Central admin. expenses	22 000
Order processing	44 000

Parkway to store around 250–300 litres per square foot. The current warehouse costs are detailed in Table 8.24.

Warehouse regional costs

Parkway had considered the possibility of changing the warehouse structure and had managed to complete an investigation for all the nine regions, developing an index of total costs for each of the regions, based on their current warehouse operation (Table 8.25).

The company had also analysed the implications of changing warehouse size upon the total costs and had arrived at the following estimates based on the current warehouse size and operating characteristics (Table 8.26).

Transport costs

Parkway hired vehicles on a contract basis from one of the major rental companies in the UK, which cost around £12 000 per annum. They employed direct the drivers for the lorries at an average cost of £14 000 per annum. Fuel costs per mile worked out at 20p.

Parkway had approached British Rail to see what the potential costs were likely to be

Table 8.25 Regional warehouse costs index

	Warehouse rent	Labour	Equipment
Scotland	20	60	100
North East	45	55	100
North West	40	50	100
Midlands	65	60	100
Wales	35	50	100
London	100	100	100
East	75	85	100
West	70	90	100
South	90	100	100

Table 8.26   Index of warehouse costs by size of operation index

| | Warehouse index size | | | | |
Factor	20	50	100	150	200
Rent	20	50	100	150	200
Rates	20	50	100	150	200
Personnel	40	70	100	100	120
Insurance	20	50	100	150	200
Warehouse equipment rental	50	50	100	120	120
Central admin. expenses	80	80	100	100	100
Order processing	70	80	100	110	110

Table 8.27   Rail freight rates inter-location (£)

	Scotland	NE	NW	Midlands	Wales	London	East	West	South
Scotland	—	20	30	35	45	40	45	50	55
North East	—	—	15	18	25	20	25	35	35
North West	—	—	—	20	25	20	30	30	30
Midlands	—	—	—	—	30	15	25	25	25
Wales	—	—	—	—	—	20	25	15	20
London	—	—	—	—	—	—	15	20	15
East	—	—	—	—	—	—	—	25	20
West	—	—	—	—	—	—	—	—	20
South	—	—	—	—	—	—	—	—	—

Table 8.28   Road distances inter-location (return journey mileage)

	Scotland	NE	NW	Midlands	Wales	London	East	West	South
Scotland	—	400	400	600	600	750	700	850	900
North East	—	—	180	250	300	450	400	650	650
North West	—	—	120	260	220	450	400	500	600
Midlands	—	—	—	—	300	280	300	300	450
Wales	—	—	—	—	—	220	350	250	350
London	—	—	—	—	—	—	200	350	200
East	—	—	—	—	—	—	—	450	350
West	—	—	—	—	—	—	—	—	300
South	—	—	—	—	—	—	—	—	—

for the transport of product from one stock location to another for the transport of 60 tons of product. Additional costs of loading and unloading at the terminals were estimated as £15 per load. As Parkway had no return traffic (all product was sold in disposable containers) there were no return load considerations (Table 8.27).

A similar grid of transport costs had been derived for the distances that lorries would need to travel between current warehouse location and any future site that might be decided upon (Table 8.28).

DISTRIBUTION ASSIGNMENTS

1   Produce a plan of a warehouse for:
(a) A major supplier of agricultural chemicals.
(b) A wholesaler supplying the catering trade.
(c) A manufacturer of consumer kitchen electrical equipment.
What investment in mechanization would you recommend in each case and why?

2   The company that you work for sells products that are almost entirely non-seasonal with an average demand as detailed below + − 20 per cent in weekly sales, which are produced by a third party manufacturer in batches every three months. Each product was sold in a carton 1 ft square, packed onto a pallet configuration 14 × 5 which could be damaged if stacked more than two high. Currently warehouse space cost the company £3.50 per square foot rental per annum, and the current costs of racking which would enable the company to stack up to 40 ft is £5 per square foot. The company currently has two sophisticated fork lift trucks that are substantially under-utilized.

Product	Sales per annum (000 units)
A	398
B	200
C	543
D	128
E	221
F	783
G	245

You are asked to prepare a report on the amount of warehouse space that would be required if the company was trying to provide a 95 per cent service level, and whether you would recommend the installation of a racking system.

3   You are presented with the following information about a warehouse operation. What conclusions would you draw from it, and what improvements do you think the warehouse manager would need to consider?

	1983	1985
Turnover per square foot (£)	55	44
Labour costs/total value shipped (ratio)	0.24	0.32
Packaging/total value (ratio)	2.3	1.6
Total costs/total value shipped (ratio)	4.5	4.4
Total number of lines	200	280

4 You are asked to prepare a report on the likely benefits of containerization to a company producing a range of plastic construction kits which are sold to high street outlets.

5 A company producing a range of canned drinks is considering moving to plastic bottles with a shorter shelf life. What are the packaging and distribution implications of such a change?

Chapter 9

Inventory Control and Effective Distribution Management

Maintaining inventory is a major investment because it ties up large amounts of working capital. For example, a company with a turnover above £10 million might maintain a level of stock (raw materials, work in progress and finished goods) of £2 million, turning that stock over five times a year, a fairly typical figure for industrial goods manufacturers. Higher stock turns are achieved by retailers with stock turns of seventeen per year reported by some companies. The average cost of finance for the company during the 1980s would be in the region of 15–17 per cent per annum, though it should be noted that for small companies costs of borrowing would often be significantly higher. However, even if the lower figure is taken the total finance cost for such working capital would be between £300 000 and £340 000. For each £1 of stock being held by the company there will be a holding cost of 1.2–1.5p per month. One of the major trends during recessions is for companies to reduce the levels of inventories and so reduce the requirements of working capital.

Though working capital requirements are the major element in the total cost of inventory, the effects of stock depreciation should not be ignored. Over time stocks decrease in value partly due to loss, deterioration, and obsolescence—the last being a particularly important issue for companies in fashion related industries with a high rate of new product introduction. High stocks in these circumstances will guarantee a high level of obsolescence. Airfix, the toys and games group, had large quantities of redundant or obsolescent stock at the time of its collapse in 1979 including 750 000 units of one particular Meccano set component, and 8 000 units of a kit featuring Princess Anne and her horse, which six years after production had a limited appeal. In companies with a slower rate of new product introduction like industrial fasteners, 'fashion' depreciation will be a less important factor. Of course, where the product is perishable even more serious losses can occur.

FINANCING INVENTORY

A manufacturing company cannot meet all its customers' demands from current production—demand will never be static and the company cannot maintain continuous production of all products. Stocks must be held to reduce the uncertainty of demand for finished goods and the supply of raw materials. It is therefore possible to classify companies' inventory requirements. A company may hold raw materials; components of the final product required by the production process, stocks or work in progress; the partially finished components of the final product; and finally completed and packed finished stock which may be held at the factory, the warehouse or be in transit between warehouse, manufacturing point, and customer. Across the entire economy 50 per cent of the total inventory value is likely to be in the form of finished goods, 25 per cent as raw materials and 25 per cent as work in progress. These figures depend of course on the state of the economy and vary according to the industry, company and industrial sector.

Finished stock is also obviously the most expensive type of inventory with the most added value —labour and machine time. One of the most effective ways of reducing inventory cost is therefore to maintain stock in an unfinished form. This is the concept of postponement in distribution: the longer the product can be held in an unfinished form the greater the likely benefits. Its feasibility depends on a number of factors. The first concerns the adaptability of the product. Manufacturers of branded goods such as Mazola corn oil cannot in reality modify the product at any stage in the manufacturing process. In contrast, a clothing supplier such as Benetton, can and does hold garments in an undyed form. As fashions change the choice of final colour can be altered, and this policy ensures that Benetton does not carry large inventories of products that are no longer fashionable. Indeed, the company has taken the concept further by ensuring that the majority of this stock is held by the third party manufacturer and not within the company owned network. Similarly, manufacturers of own label products hold unlabelled stock and add the label of the relevant retail chain at the last moment. Savings of this type are, however, only viable if the cost of passing the product through the labelling process is low. Generally postponement is most beneficial in high added value product areas, where the additional costs of labelling or format changing are lower than the finance costs of carrying the stock in its finished form.

Companies can also reduce inventory costs by maximizing standardization of stock holding, using the same basic components in as many parts of the production process as possible. For some companies that survive on variety—makers of baby food, for example—little standardization is possible. In others—like the car industry—substantial standardization is feasible. The original British Leyland group had different product ranges—Rover, Triumph, Austin, Morris and MG—all with different components. Streamlining of components and the creation of a new spare parts group, Unipart, greatly reduced the group's necessary stock holding of components.

Though maintaining a high level of stocks requires substantial funding, the company that can finance them benefits in several ways. The company with a continuing level of stock of all its products can supply all the needs of the market. It will also gain business from competitors unable to offer such a level of supply. During the early 1970s a market panic over a possible shortage of table salt in the UK enabled one manufacturer of sea salt with high stocks to substantially improve profitability and future market share by making product available which competitors could not match. Maintaining stocks also decreases administrative costs—small orders meaning more paperwork—and reduces variability in the quality of the components or materials that are supplied.

Discounts from suppliers may also be an important factor in stock holding decisions. These discounts may not relate solely to reductions in price; they may also include improved credit facilities which may be equally important. Similarly, long production runs reduce unit costs if the costs of initiating production are high. Many executives buying print (posters, leaflets, catalogues, and brochures) are faced with the extremely high set-up costs for colour printing processes compared with the relatively low run-on costs of each additional 1000 units. They must then decide whether it is financially more sensible to buy more than their immediate requirements, and hold over the remaining stock with its lower production cost for future demand.

Production considerations are particularly relevant where demand is highly seasonal, and it may be more cost effective to build up inventories throughout the year to meet a peak selling season rather than have a large manufacturing facility idle for most of the year except during the period of peak demand. Brock's Fireworks build up stocks throughout the year for their highly seasonal sales period that runs from the middle of October to the first week in November. In highly seasonal products where safety of production is not paramount, such as the ski-wear industry, some companies enter into contractual agreements with third party manufacturers to provide additional product over the peak periods.

Stock holding levels also influence the costs of physical distribution, as the larger the loads that the company is able to transport the lower the per unit cost—particularly relevant where the fixed costs of transport per load are relatively high.

STOCK LEVELS

All companies maintain stocks for normal levels of sales activity to ensure that under normal market conditions demand can be met at the determined level of customer service. Thus a firm selling 100 000 units a month of a given product line would have to hold adequate supplies of finished goods as well as sufficient raw materials to meet planned levels of demand. In addition most companies hold safety or buffer stocks surplus to normal stock requirements, especially where there may be substantial month by month fluctuations in demand. For example, across the year demand might average 100 000 units a month, but sales for particular months might vary from 85 000 to 125 000 even if the product did not exhibit a seasonal demand pattern. The problems for companies with highly seasonal and weather influenced demand patterns, like ice cream or sausage manufacturers, are even more extreme. A manufacturer like Heinz finds that sales of tinned soup are much higher in the winter, but a sudden cold spell at any time during the year will drive up demand. The distribution planner will have, in such instances, to keep at least one eye on the weather forecast!

The higher the level of safety stock the greater the ability of the company to meet all potential variations in demand. We have said that as stock levels increase the amount of money that the company ties up in inventories escalates but we can see this as another example of a trade-off in distribution. In rare instances companies may hold 'investment' stocks—substantial quantities of finished goods against possible future market shortage well above any buffer requirement; or raw materials against possible problems in supply. This is particularly important in some commodity markets—tin, coffee, cocoa—that are prone to major changes in cost on a year by year basis. By buying forward or maintaining a high level of stock the company can minimize the problems of rapid changes in the cost of major components. Trading companies are often encouraged to buy large stocks of products on the view that prices will substantially rise in the forthcoming months. This may lead to the sort of major loss carried by a Middle East trading house. It had to dispose of 2000 cases (approximately 100 000 tins) of tinned mackerel after miscalculating movements in mackerel prices which left the firm with slowly decomposing and totally unsaleable fish.

METHODS OF INVENTORY CONTROL

Though each company will need to hold stocks, the amount of money invested will depend on manufacturing flexibility and sophistication, market forces, customer requirements, the physical distribution method chosen, and company strategy.

The manufacturing process itself exerts a fundamental influence on the type of inventory policy followed. Increasingly sophisticated control procedures have reduced the level of stock holding for any particular process—again, a trade-off between increased investment in manufacturing or stock control systems and a decreased requirement for stock holding. There are three main types of computer controlled operation which affect stock holding policy. Materials Requirement Planning (MRP) integrates the forecast level of demand with the production process to ensure that inventory levels are minimized, generally before the production process begins. Savings of 50 per cent of total inventory levels are typical of companies introducing and managing materials requirement planning systems. A modified form of this system has been introduced by major retailers in their attempts to reduce the major cost of inventory in their operations.

Just-in-time inventory control (JIT) involves the manufacturer setting a production schedule and informing the suppliers of exactly what is required and specifically when it should be delivered. This process is already well underway in the US with over 100 companies involved in JIT experiments and some notable car companies such as Chrysler and General Motors achieving reductions in stock holding of up to 80 per cent. However, like fully integrated and automated warehousing it demands high levels of expertise to ensure satisfactory introduction. The Mac truck company, for example, attempted to introduce JIT into its major plant in 1987. Owing to a combination of circumstances—poor supplier support, failures in manufacturing hardware and software—the number of trucks incomplete due to shortage of components rose to over 2000 and weekly production fell from 150 to around 80. Similar problems have been experienced by British Leyland in its attempt to introduce JIT.

Computer integrated manufacture (CIM) can have a substantial effect on inventory requirements by improving product quality and reducing the level of rejects, improving product design using less raw material, and reducing the quantity of product manufactured at any one time by some form of Flexible Manufacturing System (FMS). This provides greater opportunities to reserve unfinished stock ready for completion at the last possible moment—the concept of inventory postponement mentioned in the first section of the chapter.

The increasing investment in the use of bar code systems by retail groups has had a similar effect on the manufacturers supplying the retail sector. These systems, broadly grouped under the title EPOS (electronic point of sale), have been used by some retail groups even to link their sales with computer controlled production within their major suppliers. For the retailer it has been estimated that such systems will improve overall margins by approximately 1 per cent, most of which will be in the area of reducing stock levels within the outlet, though there will be other side benefits (see Table 9.1).

Overall, these high technology stock management systems have reduced the inventory working capital requirement and achieved a much higher stock turnover and therefore return on capital employed. Sophisticated stock control systems can also reduce inventory costs by minimizing substandard components. Thus Statistical Process Control (SPC) helped to revitalize the Jaguar car company. It established clear target specifications and the range of permitted variation of components and manufacturing standards. These procedures ensured an improved quality of final product and fewer rejected components, thereby reducing total inventory costs.

We have seen that stocks are held to supply customers and maximize production efficiencies. The level of stocks held is often crucial in the development of a competitive distribution policy. Though both the speed and reliability of delivery are the central features against which the majority of customers judge a company's distribution system, completeness and information availability are equally important in sectors like high value industrial equipment. To underline the importance of stock availability as a marketing tool, it is interesting to consider two surveys, one on the

Table 9.1 Estimated percentage margin improvement in EPOS systems by cost area

Front end labour savings	0.15
Reductions in stock levels	0.64
Reduction in price marking	0.33
Clerical savings	0.04
Increased maintenance cost	(0.12)
Total savings	1.04

Source: Burns, R., Technology and Retailing, in West, A., (ed.), Handbook of Retailing, Gower, 1988.

Table 9.2   Ranking criteria for expensive technical products

Product reliability
Reliability of delivery
Completeness of delivery
Speed of delivery
Price

Source: Adapted from Hill & Hillier, *Organisational Buying Behaviour*, Macmillan, 1977.

Table 9.3   Key factors in competitive policy of industrial material delivery

Price
Quality
Delivery speed
Information about supply position
Payment terms

Source: Adapted from Hill & Hillier, *Organisational Buying Behaviour*, Macmillan, 1977.

ranking of purchase criteria for high value technical products, and the other relating to the supply of basic raw materials (Tables 9.2 and 9.3). These show that for less technical products, price is more important and the efficiency of the delivery systems less so. This would be expected as the costs of maintaining high stocks of raw materials are substantially less than in situations where a company's operations come to a halt because a piece of technical equipment failed to arrive on time. Even so, product availability still ranks fairly highly in the second survey (Table 9.3). The conclusion is that the delivery criteria of speed, reliability, accuracy and information availability are all very important in achieving a competitive edge via distribution. Most of these depend on the maintenance of effective levels of inventory. We will return to this question of defining the necessary competitive criteria in later chapters, as these factors will be influenced by the type of physical distribution method and the order processing system.

Poor control of inventory levels has significant effects on the costs and management of the order processing system. Long delivery times often lead to the cancellation of orders. This means the loss of the profit from the order and increases the order processing costs as several items of information transfer are involved. Incomplete orders can also cause duplication of paperwork inside and outside the firm, and delays in payment. These may be severe for the firm with overseas customers and paid by some form of documentary credit (such as a letter of credit). A British Overseas Trade Board (BOTB) survey indicated that around one in seven orders suffered from delays in payment due to errors in order completion or documentation. Other commentators from overseas banks in London report a far higher failure rate—anything up to or over 50 per cent of orders may suffer from delay in payment frequently caused by the inability of the supplying company to totally meet the order requirements. Part filled orders also cause confusion at the warehouse—inefficient use of space and labour—and may, when extreme, involve the factory switching between short and uneconomic production runs of product to fill particular orders.

Poor inventory control can also affect the information or forecasting system used for production planning (see below) in a number of ways. It can confuse the pattern of demand as intermittent supply may fail to identify an underlying trend or create a spurious one. For example, the changeover in formulation of an antiseptic soap much in demand in West Africa led to an order backlog of over £1 million, as customers attempted to improve their position in the rationing system that prevailed. Real demand levels for the soap were impossible to predict until the product was again available in adequate quantity.

INVENTORY LEVELS AND PRODUCT REQUIREMENTS

Where the product has a limited shelf life it is essential to ensure that inventory is despatched to the market before it deteriorates. The company will therefore need to develop some system to ensure that specific blocks of stock are rotated. The most common approach is the FIFO method (first in first out), which ensures that the oldest stock will be despatched before more recent production batches.

Potentially obsolescent inventory, however, needs careful monitoring within the system to achieve accurate rotation. Poor stock rotation was claimed to be the cause of a £25 000 write off in a major American meat wholesaler's warehouse after government inspectors condemned large quantities of old meat. With the increased use of bar coding and date stamping for manufacturers of consumer perishables, the control of stock rotation becomes increasingly important. Manufacturers are investing more heavily in control systems to match supply and demand and track products through the production and storage systems to ensure that targets are reached. Makers of yoghurt products, for example, need to liaise closely with their distribution channel members to ensure proper stock rotation to reduce wastage to a minimum. The importance of trade marketing agreements in these particular market segments cannot be understated. As might be expected there tends to be close co-operation between suppliers of perishable goods, such as dairy and meat products, and the main distribution outlets. Computer packages for the control of stock rotation are becoming increasingly important in such areas, especially as hygiene regulations become more and more stringent in the majority of industrialized countries, (see below).

For the producer of durables there is similar need for policies to manage slow moving stock. The company has to evaluate whether there are overriding strategic reasons for maintaining stock—whether the company needs to keep large quantities of spare parts, for example—and the investment criteria for large stock holdings. Once these issues have been explored, a company wanting some form of yardstick for measuring stock against can use the industry average stock turn to identify stock which is clearly slow moving or 'obsolescent'. Introducing an industry norm into the equation allows the company to measure particular stock lines.

$$N \geqslant \frac{C_a}{C_s \times S_i}$$

Where:

N = industry norm (available from annual accounts of publicly quoted companies)
C_a = total costs of forecast annual production
C_s = current cost of stock
S_i = strategic index

The product of the equation should be either greater or equal to the stock turn figure of the main industrial competitors. The value of the strategic index is obviously crucial to the exercise, but its inclusion does enable the firm to define accurately the importance of the product to the company over and above its potential sales value.

FORECASTING

Effective distribution planning will depend to a great extent on the ability of the company to forecast changes both in the environment and in the levels of short-term demand. Should the company fail in doing this it will be less efficient than its competitors in taking the necessary remedial action, and will steadily lose its market position. The extent of the problems depends on the size of the company and the nature of the environment. This can be shown by considering two extremes. In a simple environment of one company supplying a long established loyal customer with a component in short supply, demand is largely predetermined and there is a minimal risk that the environment will change sufficiently to affect the supplier's production. Even if overall demand drops this will be offset by the shortage of supply. A company in this situation could plan with a high degree of confidence for the future, because it would have a clear idea about both the short-term changes in demand and possible long-term fluctuations in requirements. At the other extreme a company with a volatile customer base, a surplus of product available in the market, and a changing market structure faces a very different set of demand problems in both the short- and long-term.

Long-term factors

Earlier chapters commented on how long-term influences will mould the distribution process. Of these the most difficult to quantify can be remembered by the mnemonic

PEST—Political, Economic, Social, Technological factors; as they are the major uncertainties at the heart of many companies' inability to forecast accurately. They are in consequence a major nuisance to the distribution planner.

Political

What happens if a political system collapses or governmental policies alter direction? Changes in the value of the dollar and the level of farm subsidies have had dramatic effects on the fortunes of the US farming community with record levels of bankruptcies. Whether the major debtor nations, Brazil, Argentina and Mexico, would default on their massive debt repayments has overshadowed the planning process in many large banks. Here their ability to act is largely determined by the attitudes of Western governments to Third World debt. A company establishing an overseas distribution network would have to consider carefully the potential effects of political change within particular markets.

Economic

What are the likely changes in economic activity both at home and abroad over the next five years, and how are they likely to affect demand or consumption patterns? For example, commodity prices may have a major impact on certain distribution decisions. The level at which oil prices will stabilize has been a factor of major importance to many companies as fuel costs are obviously important for many distribution decisions. Other costs determined by economic conditions are the level of wage settlements and the costs of land for warehouse development. Rising land prices in the south east of England mean that there is competition for former warehouse space on industrial parks from office and retail developers. The ensuing rises in costs have already started to have a major impact on companies' warehouse location policies. Rent reviews fuelled upwards by such pressures, and the value of the land for redevelopment have been instrumental in companies relocating production and warehousing space into lower cost areas of the country and taking profits on the value of the original site.

Social

What important social changes are likely to take place over the next five years, and how will they affect the pattern of demand for the company? Will shopping favour the out-of-town environment, will mail order re-establish itself as a major distribution channel, or will Prestel or other teletext systems such as the highly successful Minitel in France become a major force in retailing? Will the drift of the American population towards the south west continue at the same speed of the last ten years? Each of these social trends will have a substantial impact on the way in which a manufacturing company organizes its distribution system.

Technological

How will changing technology over the next five years affect the supplier's control of the distribution system and the way the customer buys goods? Technological changes have already dramatically altered the way many companies do business and it will be important for suppliers to be aware of the potential of other likely changes. For example, the introduction of bar code technology by major retailing groups has had a significant effect on their stock ordering pattern; similarly the introduction of just-in-time techniques by large manufacturing units will have a significant impact on their suppliers.

Controlling long-term uncertainty

Some firms consider that analysing these changing trends poses too insurmountable problems, and withdraw from any attempt to determine long-term demand and its investment requirements, or hand over the risk to some third party. The major record companies are an example of the first case. They find it impossible to forecast demand for particular recording artists. Bands surface for six months, a year, and then mysteriously disappear from the public consciousness. The company respond to these extreme fluctuations by keeping as many artists under contract as possible. Record companies producing very high added value products with low fixed production and distribution costs have many advantages that cannot be matched by a company such as the large retailer, Sainsbury. Like many other retailers Sainsbury is turning to third party distribution on a contract basis. By so doing it eliminates much of the uncertainty concerning location, technology and so forth by transferring it to the contract management company. However, many suppliers, particularly those in the manufacture of capital intensive goods where there is requirement for long-term commitment of huge investments, cannot follow either course. For example, the Boeing Aircraft company currently faces the problem of assessing the future replacement of the 747. The investment required will be immense; the pay back period well into the 21st century. Or take the investment by the multinational car firm Nissan in its new plant in north east England at Sunderland. Long-term investment will require the company to have a clear picture of future trends in the market in order to justify the level of expenditure.

Such companies need to develop some system to minimize the risks associated with investment decisions. Any assessment of likely change will inevitably be subjective; in other words the research will be qualitative rather than quantitative, identifying trends rather than actual numbers. A number of methods have evolved to help in the reduction of uncertainty in long-term trends. Of these one of the best known is the Delphi technique. This was developed by the Rand Corporation and attempts to use expert opinion to develop forecasts by an exchange of questionnaires. Members are kept unaware of who else is on the panel and there is no discussion—feedback is maintained by the group leader who analyses the questionnaires and asks individuals who deviate significantly from the group consensus to justify their answers. Companies such as the Lockheed Aircraft Corporation and some of the major car companies have found this a useful technique to attempt to minimize the problems of forecasting in a rapidly changing technological environment and to lay down policy concerning production facilities and market development policies.

Reducing short-term uncertainty

For the distribution planner the ability to identify short-term changes in demand is generally of more importance. They will, for example, be crucial in controlling inventory levels and maintaining an effective use of warehouse space. For the distribution planner the highest level of risk will occur if sales either drop or increase rapidly—known as 'turning points'—because such major changes will mean either a substantial increase in inventory cost or an inability to supply customers, with a consequent decline in the competitiveness of the distribution system. Methods used to forecast short-term trends must be evaluated against their ability to identify possible major changes in the pattern of demand.

The simplest approach is the straightforward historic projection, taking the current level of activity and projecting forward from that base. Being historical and based on a direct extrapolation of recent market activities, this will be unlikely to identify major changes in the environment as it will be heavily affected by short-term fluctuations. However, where the firm has close links with a limited number of customers direct contact with them over likely future demand will often provide a highly accurate forecasting system. Customer contact is fundamental to the development of trade marketing or distribution agreements between major channel members and the supplier (see Chapter 4). Where they operate they can have a substantial effect of reducing the degree of uncertainty in the level of future demand.

For most companies the percentage of trade marketing agreements, though growing, only reduces rather than removes the need to cope effectively with such problems as fluctuations and underlying changes in demand. A method of removing fluctuations, such as those caused by high seasonal sales, is to combine the sales for the year or two years adding current months and removing sales which occur outside the time period. This system, known as moving totals, is extremely easy to apply and fairly accurate as a short-term indication of likely trends being particularly suitable where the change in sales levels is fairly gradual (Table 9.4).

Where there are rapid changes in the sales history, recent events will be far more important in explaining the near future than sales of one or two years ago. Introducing a smoothing constant which gives greater importance to more recent sales is one way of overcoming this problem.

New forecast = actual demand + (1 − smoothing factor) × previous sales

Obviously the choice of smoothing factor is fairly crucial, and there is a tendency in

Table 9.4 Moving totals—an example of how its application can reduce the effects of seasonality

Months	1	2	3	4	5	6	7	8	9	10	11	12	13	14	15	16	17	18
Sales:																		
Year 1	10	10	10	15	17	18	19	20	21	22	21	15						
Year 2													15	16	17	18	19	22
Moving annual total												198	203	209	216	219	221	223

many projections to choose the smoothing factor that best fits the data, which tends to be self defeating. Such exponential smoothing methods will be most valuable where the environment is changing rapidly.

More sophisticated analyses, such as the Box-Jenkins method, attempt to take a number of elements of the company sales record and produce a model to explain the underlying trends. Both this system and the more complicated X-11 system produced by the US Weather Bureau require computer assistance and a degree of statistical expertise. Both systems do, however, reduce the element of risk in the forecast process by more accurately identifying possible turning points within a one year projection period. The underlying logic of such time series analyses is that they combine the various types of sales variation to produce a model of the underlying sales trend (Table 9.5).

The main shortcoming in all time series analyses is the fact that the information used to develop the forecast is internal. The company will not be able to rapidly relate violent change in the external environment to the effect on demand. To do this the firm will need to determine a factor in the external environment causally related to the demand for the company's products. Unilever's detergent policy, relating on a worldwide basis the amount of detergent consumption to gross national product (GNP) per head, is one such relationship. Rising GNP appears to have an effect on the overall consumption of detergents.

Other relationships identified by companies include the level of consumption of consumer durables (on fast food consumption in the US), the level of unemployment (on demand for holidays in the UK). Such causal systems allow the firm to predict demand patterns more accurately. The main problem in using them is the complexity of data analysis required, the removal of spurious interrelationships, and critical

Table 9.5 Time series analysis

$$D = T \times S \times C \times R$$

where:
D = demand levels
T = sales trend
S = seasonal index
C = long-term (cyclical factors)
R = residual index

assessment of what are in fact independent rather than dependent variables. For example, there might be a relationship between the numbers of miles of motorway and overall ice-cream consumption; the real underlying factor would perhaps be increases in GNP. Secondly there would be a clear relation between the number of new cars and demand for number plates; one would be a dependent variable on the other.

At its simplest level regression analysis of a single factor against another will yield information about underlying demand trends. Often more than one factor will be important in influencing demand and therefore multiple regression techniques will be important for complex sales relationships. In many large companies this is built up into an econometric model which attempts to provide an explanation or a simulation of all the main external factors affecting sales. Bowater Scott and Beechams are two companies that have developed sophisticated models to explain the effects of environmental factors upon their leading brands. The logic underlying the model suggested to Bowater Scott that continuous advertising would be highly profitable for the Andrex brand; Beechams that increasing price along with extra promotional expenditure would be the most profitable route for Dettol.

These econometric or causal models at their most sophisticated simulate the external environment; they enable firms to test out hypotheses such as the effects of increasing distribution, lowering price, and raising promotional expenditure on the total market sales. Where they are regularly employed such advanced forecasting systems are invaluable in determining the overall production and stock holding requirements for the distribution planner.

Though econometric models are too expensive to establish and maintain for the majority of medium or small companies, the availability of a wide range of low cost forecasting systems on personal computers makes effective demand analysis far easier to achieve. Distribution planners are able to receive assessments of likely future demand and the degree and uncertainty associated with the projection.

THE COMPANY AND ITS FORECASTING REQUIREMENTS

Each forecast system will have a degree of error associated with it. The more exact the forecasting system, the lower the degree of error. As might be expected, the more sophisticated the forecasting method, the greater the investment that will be required. But as risk increases, the need for forecasting investment will grow. Various investment issues exert a crucial influence on the type of forecasting system chosen, especially the level of investment involved in the particular company strategy, the speed of return on that investment, and the uncertainty in the environment. Higher levels of investment will mean more risk, as do longer and longer pay back periods, with the consequent need to increase the sophistication of the forecasting systems that are available.

Regardless of the level of investment several problems will still confront the distribution planner, the most important being the forecast demand for new products. As we have seen, the basis of all forecasting is the ability to extrapolate the past into the future but a new product will often mean that the company lacks information to

Table 9.6 **Percentage variation of forecasts with actual out-turns**

Factor	Forecast	Actual result	% variance
Sales of A	200	250	25
Sales of B	350	300	(14)

handle the demand forecast effectively. Where the product is introduced into an established market, the company can either rely on previous experience of products in that market, or the performance of competitors. Where the company is involved with totally new products in market sectors about which it has little knowledge, forecasts will be most prone to error. A classical example of such a forecasting problem was shown by IBM during the launch of their new personal computer, the PC. Because of the novelty of the product and the inexperience in the market, delivery dates for equipment lengthened to over six months during the worst period of over demand. The result of their inability to supply the market was that competitors such as Olivetti and Compaq were able to become firmly established.

MONITORING THE FORECASTING SYSTEM

Once the forecasting system has been established, it is important that the distribution planner is able to measure the degree of confidence that can be placed in the results that it provides. Fortunately, maintaining records of forecasts and the eventual actual out-turn will establish such benchmarks of reliability (see Table 9.6). From such tables the distribution planner will be able to identify those forecasts that are most subject to error and take the required action to improve the method of measurement, by investment in improved data collection or more efficient analysis.

CASE: OFFICEQ

Introduction

The managers of Officeq, a small office equipment wholesaler, specializing in the supply of accessories for information technology in London and the Home Counties, were meeting to review their stock holding policy in the face of declining sales and the continuing loss of customers.

The market

The office equipment market is highly competitive. There is, in addition to the large number of regional and national wholesalers selling via catalogues, a broadly based retail sector, consisting mainly of small independent outlets though there were a growing number of retail chains such as Wilding Office Equipment.

The market is characterized by low barriers to entry and high service costs which are balanced by the high levels of margin that companies are able to achieve on individual product lines—average gross margins varied between 33 and 40 per cent on all the items stocked. Large customers could negotiate substantial discounts from the manufacturers, but for the small to medium sized company the best option was generally to buy either from the wholesaler or retailer. Of the two, many companies preferred to deal with the wholesaler because of the more rapid service and higher level of stock holding.

For the majority of wholesalers selling a standard range of widely available products, the main differentiation that they could achieve was on service rather than on price. Whilst not insisting on price regulation, the majority of manufacturers were less than enthusiastic in supplying product to discount operations as this damaged their market sales, relying as they did on a large number of retailers and wholesalers.

This trend towards standardization in price was also encouraged by the fact that there was low price elasticity in the office equipment market. Companies tended to buy on guarantees of performance, continued supply of accessories and where relevant technical support, rather than on price, though this varied from product category to product category, with furniture tending to be more price sensitive than accessories or computer peripherals.

With the emphasis on service as a means of competitive differentiation, which tended to take the form of offering immediate (or very rapid) delivery on the majority of their product range, wholesalers faced the necessity of holding high stocks of product to meet delivery requirements. High levels of stock holding thus became one of the major cost centres of each operation, and meant that such companies depended on high sales volumes to achieve profitability, a problem exacerbated by the significant office management and promotional costs that were involved in servicing their customer base.

Officeq sales progress

Started in 1981, Officeq had initially grown rapidly over the first two years, achieving a turnover of £555 000 in 1983. Since 1983 sales had stagnated, and the company had even shown a slight decrease in the customer base over the period up to 1987 (Table

Table 9.7 Officeq sales progress

	1983	1984	1985	1986	1987
Sales £000	555	568	620	662	598
Gross profit £000	55	60	75	55	55
Promotional cost	20	28	38	35	38
Profit (loss) £000	30	32	37	20	17
Customers	360	430	450	350	320
Average sale	£100	£110	£120	£105	£98

Table 9.8 Percentage contribution to Officeq sales by sector

Sector	1983	1987
Small office	82	67
Medium office	5	8
Large office	3	5
Education	10	20

9.7). Since they had started operation, the competitive environment in the area had changed considerably, with the opening of several computer retailers in the catchment area and the entry into the market of a further four national and two regional catalogue suppliers. The result of this activity had been that Officeq had seen their market share slip even though the market continued to expand at about 20 per cent per annum.

Customer base

All the customers serviced by Officeq were within a 100 mile radius of their base in Orpington, Kent. Turnover contribution came mainly from the small office sector, though over the five year period there had been a slow increase in the importance of the education sector (Table 9.8).

Each sector had a different ordering pattern. The education sector tended to order in two periods—when budgets became available. In the area serviced by Officeq this meant September, and then in another peak to ensure that budgets had been fully spent, around March/April. The office sector showed less dramatic seasonal trends, very little was purchased from July to early September, which coincided with the holiday season.

Officeq, in common with many of its competitors, found that the length of effective credit that it offered to its customers had increased over the five year period, even though the official period of credit, 30 days, had not changed over the period. Since 1983 the average credit period had increased from 33 days to a worrying 55 days, slightly higher than that of its competitors which tended to receive payment within 40 days. This worsening profit trend was creating further problems for the company as the cash flow declined with the drop in sales. Recently Officeq had also had to increase the level of discount—up from an average 10 per cent to nearer 20 per cent—that it offered its major customers with a further drop in overall profitability.

Officeq operation

The firm followed the policy of maintaining stocks of all their product lines, so that they could be immediately delivered. This meant that in contrast to their competition, their product range was relatively limited, carrying a mere 250 product lines in contrast to their competitors that offered a lower guaranteed delivery but a far wider range of available products—generally over 1000. This high level of inventory meant that a major part of the costs of the company were tied up in the level of borrowing that was necessary to maintain high stock levels. In 1987 this amounted to £150 000. Such a high level of stock holding meant that the stock turn ratio of Officeq when compared with the competition was extremely poor—most national wholesalers were, it was claimed by industry sources, able to achieve a seven or eightfold stock turn in the year. The cost of financing this high level of stocks was estimated to be around £20 000 per annum.

Another continuing expense was the updating of the catalogue, which took place every six months, and was then mailed to a list of 3000 local companies. The total cost of the catalogues had grown to nearly £40 000 by 1987. Most of the sales achieved by Officeq were achieved as the result of its mailings to local companies and the company employed three telephone sales operatives to take details of orders. In 1986, Officeq had recruited its first sales representative to develop sales with major customers, and the early indications were that this was proving a success. Total salaries of the office, warehouse and management were £90 000 in 1987, up 15 per cent on 1986.

The company's headquarters, a converted warehouse on an industrial estate, cost the company an annual rental of £45 000 for the 10 000 square feet that the company occupied.

Service offered

Officeq offered two types of delivery service: a 24 hour guaranteed delivery which cost an extra £5.00 per order and a two day service which was included in the order price. Officeq used a third party, Worldwide carriers, to provide transport except for small items that were despatched by Datapost. The relevant price lists for the two day

Table 9.9 Distribution costs by weight (single consignment) in £/kilo

Weight (kg)	Worldwide carriers	Datapost
1	4.50	0.75
2	5.00	1.5
3	5.50	2.0
5	7.00	4.50
7.5	8.50	6.50
10	10.00	9.5
15	12.00	15.0
20	15.00	20.0
25	17.50	25.0
30	18.00	30.0
35	18.50	35.0

Table 9.10   Top selling lines, retail prices, weight and sales value (£000—1987)

Product	Price (£)	Weight (kilos)	Sales value
Computer discs (packs of ten)			
$3\frac{1}{2}$ inch	21.60	0.3	45
5.25 inch			
(single sided)	18.50	0.35	25
(double sided)	23.40	0.35	30
Cartridge			
(5 mb)	62.00	1.5	22
(20 mb)	127.50	2.5	18
(60 mb)	172.00	3.0	25
(80 mb)	173.00	3.5	17
(200 mb)	420.00	4.5	11
Tape leaders	2.00	0.1	12
Cassette tape	13.00	0.1	14
Streamer tape	105.00	2.5	16
Data cartridge (packs of five)	85.00	1.5	14
Computer software storage			
small	650	22.5	11
large	750	34.0	12
Computer filing boxes			
$3\frac{1}{2}$ inch	25.00	1.2	8
5.25	21.00	1.2	6
VDU screens			
small	35.00	0.5	3
medium	55.00	0.5	3
large	95.00	1.0	2
Computer accessories			
connector cable	4.00	0.5	2
adaptor plug	4.00	0.5	2
dual port cable	25	1.5	2
modem cable	92	2.0	3
networking cable kit	205	3.5	5
trunk cable	55	1.5	3
drop cable	89.50	2.0	2
transceiver	365	3.5	5
Furniture			
desk	190	15.0	6
desk and drawers	260	17.5	8
executive desk	520	35.0	4
lockable unit	220	18.0	7
printer stand	150	18.0	11
basic chair	100	13.0	15
adjustable chair	165	13.0	4
meeting table	305	32.0	3
Acoustic printer hoods			
small	280	8.0	3
medium	350	11.0	2
large	400	15.0	2
freestanding	550	21.0	3

Table 9.10 (*Contd.*)

Product	Price (£)	Weight (kilos)	Sales value
Printer feeders			
single sheet	250	7.0	3
multiple	400	9.0	2
tractor feed	460	10.0	3
Printer heads			
Type 1	18	0.1	3
2	18	0.1	2
3	18	0.1	1
4	18	0.1	2
5	18	0.1	2
6	18	0.1	3
7	18	0.1	4
8	18	0.1	2
Computer paper filing systems			
small	105	8	3
medium	168	12	4
large	190	15	3
Paper			
thermal	35	3	12
standard	11	3	8
premium	11	3	3
Printer ribbon			
Type 1	6	0.1	3
2	5	0.1	4
3	8	0.1	3
4	5	0.1	2
5	7	0.1	3
6	8	0.1	5
7	10	0.1	7
8	11	0.1	3
Printer and computer security system			
basic locks	20	0.2	5
integrated locks	55	1.0	4
electronic system	125	1.5	3

service provided by both organizations is shown in Table 9.9. Worldwide carriers became increasingly cost effective when a large order was received from an individual customer.

Product range, pricing, weight and sales volume by product line

Along with many other companies Officeq found that the majority of their sales were achieved with a limited number of items in their total range. These key items which made up the substantial proportion of total sales are shown in Table 9.10.

In order to help the company determine whether a new stocking policy would improve the profitability of the company and end the continuing sales decline, the management had analysed the five weeks sales pattern for March 1987, a period which had historically provided the peak sales activity in the office equipment market (Table 9.11).

Table 9.11 Weekly sales patterns for March and average stock value 1987 (in £000)

Product	1	2	3	4	5	Stock value (£)
Computer discs (packs of ten)						
$3\frac{1}{2}$ inch	0.5	0.5	0.5	0.8	0.9	8
5.25 inch						
(single sided)	0.3	0.2	0.7	0.4	0.3	6
(double sided)	0.4	0.1	0.1	0.2	0.2	5
Cartridge						
(5 mb)	0.1	0.1	—	—	0.2	2
(20 mb)	0.2	0.2	0.3	1	0.1	3
(60 mb)	0.5	0.3	—	—	—	3
(80 mb)	0.3	0.2	—	—	—	4
(200 mb)	—	—	—	—	0.5	4
Tape leaders	0.1	0.1	0.1	—	—	3
Cassette tape	—	0.2	0.1	0.1	—	4
Streamer tape	0.3	1.5	0.4	0.5	0.7	8
Data cartridge (packs of five)	—	0.3	—	—	—	1
Computer software storage						
small	—	0.1	0.3	0.2	—	3
large	—	1.5	—	—	—	4
Computer filing boxes						
$3\frac{1}{2}$ inch	0.1	0.1	0.2	0.2	0.1	2
5.25	0.3	0.1	0.2	0.2	0.1	3
VDU screens						
small	—	—	0.1	—	—	1
medium	0.1	0.2	—	—	—	1
large	—	—	0.2	0.1	—	1
Computer accessories						
connector cable	0.1	0.1	0.1	0.1	0.1	0.5
adaptor plug	0.1	0.2	0.15	0.15	0.1	0.5
dual port cable	0.2	0.05	0.1	0.05	0.1	0.6
modem cable	0.1	—	—	—	0.1	0.2
networking cable kit	—	0.3	—	—	—	0.2
trunk cable	0.1	—	0.2	—	—	0.4
drop cable	—	—	—	—	—	0.6
transceiver	—	—	—	—	0.5	1
Furniture						
desk	0.2	0.2	—	—	0.2	3
desk and drawers	—	0.2	—	—	0.4	4

Table 9.11 (Contd.)

Product	1	2	3	4	5	Stock value (£)
executive desk	—	—	—	0.4	—	4
lockable unit	—	—	0.2	0.2	0.2	5
printer stand	0.1	0.3	0.2	0.3	0.2	4
basic chair	0.2	0.3	—	—	0.2	4
adjustable chair	0.1	—	—	—	0.2	2
meeting table	—	—	0.2	—	—	2
Acoustic printer hoods						
small	—	0.2	—	—	—	1
medium	—	—	—	—	0.2	1
large	—	0.2	—	—	—	1
freestanding	—	—	—	—	0.5	1
Printer feeders						
single sheet	0.2	0.2	—	0.2	—	2
multiple	—	—	—	—	—	—
tractor feed	—	—	—	—	—	—
Printer heads						
Type 1	0.1	0.1	0.1	0.1	0.1	0.5
2	0.1	0.1	—	—	0.1	0.4
3	—	0.1	0.1	—	—	0.2
4	—	—	—	0.1	—	0.2
5	0.2	0.1	0.2	—	—	0.3
6	—	—	0.3	0.2	—	0.5
7	0.2	0.1	0.2	0.1	0.2	0.8
8	0.3	0.2	—	—	—	0.6
Computer paper filing systems						
small	0.1	—	—	0.1	—	0.5
medium	—	0.3	0.1	0.1	0.1	0.8
large	—	0.2	0.3	—	0.2	0.6
Paper						
thermal	0.1	0.3	0.2	0.4	0.2	5
standard	0.2	0.1	0.1	0.1	0.1	1
premium	—	0.2	0.2	—	—	1
Printer ribbon						
Type 1	0.5	0.2	0.1	0.1	—	1
2	0.1	0.1	0.1	0.1	—	1
3	0.2	—	—	—	0.2	1
4	0.1	0.1	0.1	0.1	0.1	1
5	0.1	0.1	—	—	—	1
6	—	—	0.3	0.1	0.1	2
7	0.1	0.1	0.1	0.1	0.1	1
8	0.1	—	—	—	0.1	1
Printer and computer security system						
basic locks	0.2	0.1	0.1	0.1	0.1	1
integrated locks	0.1	—	0.2	—	0.1	1
electronic system	0.2	0.2	0.3	0.1	—	1

Supplier lead times

The majority of the products could be obtained from the manufacturer within a week, or if Officeq were prepared to pay a delivery premium—normally in the region of £15 per order—within two days. The exception to this was in the supply of office furniture where six week lead times were the norm. There were no effective minimum orders.

DISTRIBUTION ASSIGNMENTS

1 You are asked to categorize the following products according to their annual sales pattern. The company's total sales during the period were 1200 units.

Product	1	2	3	4	5	6	7	8	9	10	11	12
A	12	8	2	1	10	1	1	3	5	8	9	2
B	5	8	5	4	5	6	4	5	8	4	5	4
C	11	13	15	17	19	22	10	9	7	16	12	11
D	2	—	—	—	5	—	1	3	—	2	—	—
E	7	3	3	4	11	4	5	10	5	5	4	6
F	21	18	15	23	15	14	17	11	8	7	6	18

How should your categorization affect the stock levels that the company needs to maintain for individual products and what additional information would you require?

2 You are asked to forecast demand for the following products for the next six time periods which had sales records over the last 13 sales periods as follows:

Product	1	2	3	4	5	6	7	8	9	10	11	12	13
A	12	25	34	26	31	16	17	27	29	38	22	15	14
B	5	7	9	15	18	21	22	21	28	32	35	38	35
C	65	67	61	59	59	50	45	43	48	43	45	59	42
D	11	15	16	17	17	14	15	18	17	21	22	27	29

3 A manufacturer has a wildly changing sales pattern for a range of industrial protective clothing, which is produced in batches of 500. Suggest methods by which stock control could be improved, with the production lead time of two sales periods for the details of the products supplied below.

Product	1	2	3	4	5	6	7	8	Current stock (units)
A	200	102	55	34	26	120	250	25	450
B	110	670	120	55	66	102	110	260	105
C	25	24	225	115	120	140	150	240	340
D	305	320	15	10	120	110	280	420	—
E	160	115	85	40	230	210	190	150	90
F	35	55	140	180	65	80	170	160	420

4   A manufacturer is continually failing to forecast demand accurately, in a growing market. Create a new forecast for each of the product lines using a variety of forecasting techniques. Which are most appropriate for the different product lines and why?

Product	1	2	3	4	5	6	7	8	9	10	11	12	13	Forecast 14
A	23	33	45	32	45	46	55	66	56	78	88	98	102	55
B	15	23	45	56	56	89	98	120	134	100	65	56	43	88
C	12	41	23	65	9	73	11	18	77	45	21	89	41	33
D	9	5	3	1	—	15	19	28	2	—	26	23	18	12
E	210	134	154	165	131	148	126	119	134	109	89	132	103	120

Decisions on Inventory Levels

The previous chapter considered some of the broad investment implications of inventory policy emphasizing various trade-offs. These suggest broad guidelines for the distribution planner concerned with minimizing the costs of inventory while maximizing market opportunities from the maintenance of stocks. This then is the trade-off function—as stocks increase, the cost grows but so does the market opportunity. Where should the level of stocks be held to maximize the market opportunity, while minimizing the cost? This chapter will outline some of the approaches to decision making on inventory levels using a step by step approach.

IDENTIFYING PRODUCT CONTRIBUTION

Before taking any decisions on inventory levels a distribution planner must evaluate a product's importance to the company. This is not as simple as it first appears. The easiest to identify are products with an 'objective' measurement standard like sales value, or sales frequency, or profit contribution to the company. These measures aid decisions on how much of the product should be stocked, and where the product should be made available—either throughout the warehouse system or only at a certain percentage of the depots. An example of this approach is given in Table 10.1. Though straightforward it misses two vital issues of accurate stock management. Firstly, profit contribution is rarely the sole criterion for company stock holding; secondly, it is not the most sensible approach for technical companies supplying complex, high value added equipment to demanding customers whose needs are paramount. Here it will be essential for the firm to evaluate the customer/product interaction.

An illustration based on a small plastics company will clarify the point. During the 1970s the company was forced to call in outside assistance to reorganize its approach to the market. Part of the rationalization involved a rigorous assessment of the necessary stock levels and a subsequent dramatic reduction in overall stock holdings. Unfortunately, its major customer used the firm partially because it maintained stock of a whole range of specialized accessories unavailable with ease elsewhere. These

Table 10.1   Product line availability and depot location analysis

Product line	% total profit contribution	Inventory criteria	Depots
A	55	continual availability	all
B	15	out of stock acceptable	some
C	15	50–60% stock holding	few
D	15	30–50% stock holding	one

specialized items had made only small contributions to overall profitability and were run down with the reduction in stock levels. The inability of the 'rationalized' company to supply these items almost led to the loss of this major account and over 30 per cent of its total turnover, until it was realized that many of the slower selling lines were providing a vital 'service' function. This example shows that the definition of important stock often requires judgement on behalf of the supplier company and is not always identifiable purely in terms of pounds, dollars of Deutschmarks.

For suppliers of technical equipment, adequate stocks of spare parts are crucial to inventory management. Neither will the consideration of single products be of great importance to companies supplying a range of fairly low added value products where the sharing of cost across the product range will be an important issue in cost effective distribution. For example, a company's most profitable product line might be product A, but major company X only orders small quantities. In conjunction with products B, C, D, and E, the company is able to achieve cost effective distribution. These products though they may not be major profit earners for the company often have a valuable role in spreading both the manufacturing and the distribution overhead, and are in fact occasionally and conveniently classified as 'overhead lines'.

Furthermore, the evaluation of profitability is obviously historical and denies the existence of future profitability: it reduces the potential importance of new products that are the future bread and butter for the company. As the speed of product change increases, the importance of new product lines to overall turnover and profitability will continue to grow and this must be recognized by any stock control system.

Finally, the firm must consider the 'worst' case stock requirements and what should happen if there were major failures in production or individual warehouse systems.

Table 10.2   Product range categorization

Category A: major profit earners
Category B: essential service products
Category C: new products
Category D: minor profit earners
Category E: non-essential service products
Category F: overhead lines

This issue of contingency planning and its effects on the entire distribution system will be further discussed in Chapter 15.

Once consideration has been given to the various contribution of items in the product range to the overall strength of the firm, some form of ranking system can be introduced (Table 10.2).

DEMAND, PRODUCTION AND SETTING STOCK LEVELS

Having ranked the relative importance of products, the company is in a position to set targets on type or range of stock availability. Here it is necessary to understand the nature of demand, and how stock levels move over time. These can be regarded as cyclical: a peak following replenishment, followed by decline as the product is sold or moves through to other parts of the distribution system (see Figure 10.1), and then a further quantity of replacement stock is received. There are three stock levels of particular interest to the company in this cyclical pattern: the minimum stock level or safety stock; the maximum stock level; the stock level at which reordering should occur.

On paper stock cycles appear neat and tidy. Unfortunately orders from the market do not always appear in an ordered fashion, neither does the production process always manage to produce the right quantities at the right time. As a result, there is substantial uncertainty about the entire stock cycle—what minimum levels of stock should be maintained and where the stock reordering should occur. Further complications arise because loss of orders does not necessarily follow from lack of stock: within many industries with long delivery times, like the furniture sector, many orders are not filled from current stock—there is a considerable amount of 'back' ordering, and manufacture of stock after the order has been received. The calculation of stock levels where there are multiple stock locations means that allowance must be made for the additional stock requirements of the depots. The equation involved is fairly simple.

$$SS_n = SS_1(n)/\sqrt{n}$$

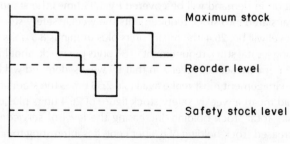

Figure 10.1 Changes in stock level

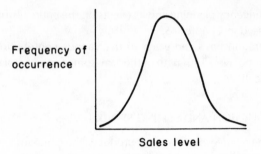

Figure 10.2 Normal distribution curve of sales

Where:

SS_n = safety stock at n locations

SS_1 = safety stock at one location

n = number of locations

No inventory system can provide total or 100 per cent stock availability: demand will vary from day to day and week to week over what is in the long term a normal distribution of demand. This is shown in Figure 10.2. For the majority of firms most sales variation occurs in a fairly clearly defined range, on either side of the mean, making up the central portion of the classic normal distribution curve. There are occasions, uncommon though they may be, when demand will either be significantly larger or smaller than the average level of demand. An understanding of the way demand spreads around the mean demand level enables a firm to set its minimum stock level. The issue of safety stock is further complicated by particular seasonal or trade cycles involving sudden increases in demand. Understanding them is an important contribution of forecasting systems.

Predicting the demand pattern and the production lead time (see below) allows a company to set the level of safety stock; demonstrated in the following example. A company has a weekly sales pattern as follows: 20, 24, 25, 28, 32, 22, 28, 27, 26, 35, 24, 29, 31, 19. The mean is: 26.4, with a standard deviation of 4.36. Management has decided that it wishes to ensure that in 95 out of 100 weeks stock meets the likely level of demand. Applying traditional statistical theory, it can be shown that 95 per cent of the likely variation in demand will be covered by 1.95 times the standard deviation. When this is translated into stock requirements the weekly safety stock requirement at the service level will be: 26.4 (the mean) units plus or minus 8.5 units (1.95 standard deviations), giving a total stock requirement of 35 units per week. Should the firm want to provide a 99 per cent service level—in that 99 weeks' demand will be met by the stocks held—management must make available 2.58 times the standard deviation of sales. This would mean a weekly safety stock figure of 26.4 units plus or minus 11.24 units or 38 units total stock holding. Increasing the level of service by 4 per cent requires an increased stock holding of 8.5 per cent. It is interesting to note that in this example a 95 per cent service level copes adequately with the vast majority of

Table 10.3 An example of setting service levels for product categories

Category	Service level (%)
A	95
B	99
C	95
D	65
E	55
F	55

demand patterns, and for the majority of firms in competitive markets, 95 per cent service levels will be more than acceptable. This is particularly true where a degree of back ordering—where companies are able to supply customers from current production—is possible.

For companies supplying a wide range of products, customers look for a joint level of service rather than one relating to particular single products. This underlines the importance of continually reappraising the product ranking system determining service levels, because understanding the customer requirements allows the company to set the service levels for particular categories of product (see Table 10.3). The actual total stock requirements for the warehouse as represented in the percentage figures in Table 10.3 can be simply calculated once the lead time of production has been established. For straightforward production processes the lead time can be calculated as follows:

$$O = S + T + Q/P$$

Where:
O = operating days in advance of requirement
S = set-up time at supplier
T = transit time
Q = quantity
P = production rate per operating day

Where a company has a widely dispersed warehouse network and is using physical distribution methods given to wide variations in the service provided, the distribution planner must not only confront this uncertainty but also may be unable to guarantee the timing of production. Manufacturing lead times in these instances are also being subject to a degree of variation which will need to be quantified in much the same way as the variation in demand. Where the production process is dependent on a large number of factors sophisticated planning systems such as PERT (Programme Evaluation Review Technique) must be employed. PERT was one of the many

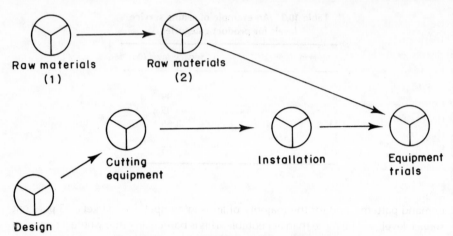

Figure 10.3   Use of PERT in widget manufacture

techniques originally developed by operations research to cope with the uncertainties of processes with many component parts, each subject to delay.

   PERT involves the creation of a network of interrelated activities, an example of which might be the manufacture of a complicated form of widget (Figure 10.3). Like other examples of networks, the production process is dependent on the completion of each individual state in sequence. For each event there will be a degree of variation in the completion time between the fastest possible, slowest and most likely. Standard deviations can be used to estimate the likely probability of the production process achieving the most likely production time and the range of variation from this most likely time. From these estimates the total completion time can be estimated using the following equation.

$$T = 1/3\,(2m + M)$$

$$= 1/3\left(2m + \frac{o+p}{2}\right)$$

$$= \frac{o + 4m + p}{6}$$

Where:
T = total time
o = optimistic time
m = most probable time
p = pessimistic (worst case)
M = mid-range value

   Calculating stock levels in more complicated factory environments requires more sophisticated techniques, including such approaches as queuing theory, as there may be limitations imposed on the manufacture process at a single point. Even these techniques will not be adequate if arrivals are abnormal and do not follow a standard distribution pattern (which is often the case in the real world) or there are a large number of interacting factors.

Reduced data processing costs have led a large number of companies to introduce computer aided techniques to organize the correct flow of material through the distribution process. This allows evaluation of all the various pay-offs more effectively than was previously possible. Readers, however, should be aware that many of the techniques developed by mathematicians are slowly being applied to the complex needs of manufacturers of wide varieties of products using a single production site to service a network of warehouses; and to the even more complex interrelationships of multiple production sites and multiple warehouses where each can draw product from any of the production sites in the network.

These techniques are applied to resolve the basic underlying problem of production processes subject to considerable variation in timing where the combined uncertainties of production and demand necessitates the holding of very high, and often uneconomic, levels of stock. This is indeed one of the major problems of the just-in-time (JIT) concept for a supplier company as it must hold extensive stocks to meet a likely wide ranging demand pattern which will need to be rapidly met (see Chapter 9). Scheduling problems also arise when the company is having to meet direct deliveries from production site to customer, though such problems will be minimized with the establishment of trade marketing agreements which allow the distribution planner to forecast demand more accurately.

Reorder policies

Our discussion to this point has concentrated on calculating stock levels. Every order has administrative and often considerable set-up costs to initiate production. The main reorder policies recognize that it is possible to establish an economic order quantity (EOQ) based on profitability of the particular item, the cost of maintaining stock, and the start up costs of initiating production.

There are basically two alternative approaches—though there are methods derived from them—to reordering either at a particular fixed volume or at a particular fixed time. Fixed reorder point policies (often termed 'Q' policies) are characterized by a constant order quantity, a variable reorder period, and a constant volume reorder point. A variation of the Q policy is min–max reorder policies which accept that the constant order quantity will often need to be increased because of the lag time between the receipt of the stock level information and the decision to reorder. Under these conditions, the EOQ is calculated as the point at which the benefits of ordering a larger quantity of stock due to decreased set-up or manufacturing processing costs will be offset by higher inventory charges.

$$EOQ = \sqrt{2(DS)/IC}$$

Where:

EOQ = Economic or optimum order quantity
D = annual demand
S = cost to place order (set-up costs for manufacture)
I = annual stock holding cost as a percentage of unit cost
C = price per unit

The alternative reorder approach is to order at fixed time periods (often termed 'P' policies). Such systems are characterized by a constant order quantity, and a fixed reorder time period. The T, R, M systems derive from this approach and combine P policies with a min–max approach by reviewing stock requirements on a fixed time basis to ascertain whether the volume has dropped to reorder levels. Volumes ordered will be subject to similar variations to those in the min–max system.

The optimum length of the order interval for any item in an inventory will be a function of the demand rate, ordering cost and inventory holding costs for the product.

$$T = \sqrt{\frac{DIC}{2S}}$$

Where:

T = Optimum order interval
D = annual demand
I = annual stock holding cost as a percentage of unit cost
C = price per unit
S = set-up costs

For the majority of companies, the fixed order Q policies will be the most appropriate, having the greatest level of flexibility. However, fixed time reorder policies will be necessary when the supplier must conform with some demand of the production line or when orders need to be consolidated for shipment. The greater demands that P systems place upon the organization can be seen in Table 10.4.

Table 10.4   Demands of two main reorder policies on company

Factor	Fixed order Q	Fixed time P
Forecasting demands	Less accurate	More accurate
Inventory levels	Generally lower	Generally higher
Effects of seasonal demand	Higher stocks	Generally lower
Ease of vehicle scheduling	Better	Worse
Control demands	Lower	Higher

Backorder conditions

The previous equations refer to a simple situation where a company unable to fill an order due to shortage of stock loses the order. For many industries this rarely occurs; in others it is only relevant for some of the key product lines which therefore require higher service levels. The furniture industry, for example, rarely if ever supplies product ex-stock. Orders are met several months later against established demand. Thus in many situations it may be possible to meet an element of the orders by future production, though there is obviously a risk that a part of these orders will be cancelled because of the inability of the distribution system to meet deadlines. As a result the calculation of optimum order quantities in these circumstances is often referred to as ordering under risk.

$$EOQ = \sqrt{\frac{2D[S + \pi E(u > R)]}{IC}}$$

Where:
D = Annual demand
S = Set-up costs
I = Annual stock holding cost
C = Price per unit
π = 3.14
$E(u > R)$ = the sum of the excess of demand u over the reorder point R

The problem of multiple products

Though individual items in a large product range can be controlled using the EOQ formula, there can be substantial complications especially in the previously mentioned circumstances where a large number of items carried by the company only contribute a small percentage of total sales. Because the annual demand pattern, production lead times and costs of production initiation will often be rapidly changing, stock controllers cannot use previous reorder quantities. This further increases the work load involved. Companies with manual stock control systems will be faced with splitting stocks into categories and applying different control methods to each category.

Obviously, the stock categories requiring the most efficient control are those that are most profitable. Table 10.5 shows the ranking of the main profit earners, listed in descending order of importance, of a hypothetical company. Because of the importance of the top seven product lines to the total company sales, it is worth controlling them individually. This process has become far less complex with the advent of the computer, as even the smallest business can establish the reorder levels for the top selling lines with industry standard software such as spreadsheets, applying the basic formulae to the control of important lines.

Where a large number of minor product lines make an important contribution to total turnover and expertise is limited, effective stock management requires some

Table 10.5   Ranking of main profit earners for a hypothetical company

Product	Sales	%
A	36	18
B	28	14
C	22	11
D	18	9
E	14	7
F	10	5
G	8	4
H	6	3
I	4	2
J	2	1

form of simple, easy-to-follow system which can be used by all stock and warehouse personnel in calculating the reordering requirements of particular product lines. The most common manual method is the bin system where the reorder level is set to be the moment at which the reserve bin of stock is entered. When this occurs, the reorder is placed and while it is awaited stock is despatched from the reserve bin or holding area. When the new stock is received, a new reserve bin is created; this ensures that stock rotation is maximized. Another simple approach to coping with a large range of products is the use of nomographs. Here, the distribution planner can use a graphical relationship between annual demand, order quantity, inventory carrying cost, and the cost of ordering, with interrelating logarithmic scales also called the nomograph. In the example (Figure 10.4) provided, connecting inventory cost (IC) with the ordering cost figure (S) will provide a line which cuts the reference scale at a certain point. Projecting

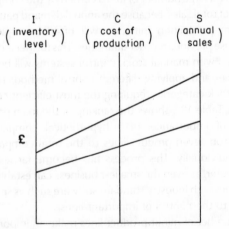

Figure 10.4   Nomograph method of establishing inventory level

this line back to the annual demand will identify the ordering quantity where it cuts the Q line. Though such a system can take time to establish, once set up it can provide rapid stock control within a multiproduct system.

With the reduction in cost of the processing power of computers, primarily manual card methods of keeping track of stock, such as Kardex systems, are being replaced by computer based methods. Even small companies will often find that the use of a personal computer and an integrated accounting and inventory software package such as Pegasus to analyse and control stock will be far more effective and efficient than manual methods.

MONITORING THE EFFICIENCY OF THE INVENTORY SYSTEM

There are a number of useful methods for evaluating the efficiency of stock control.

By product line:

$$\frac{\text{Total number of times products delivered}}{\text{Total number of times products ordered}}$$

The product line method divides individual product deliveries by the number of times that they have been ordered. Though it provides a measure of stock holding effectiveness across the entire product range it cannot deal with situations where there are split deliveries or where there is a conscious policy to maintain low stocks. It will be most appropriate for companies such as wholesalers holding high stocks of all the product lines in their range.

By turnover:

$$\frac{\text{Total value of deliveries}}{\text{Total value of orders}}$$

The turnover system has the merit of being simple to calculate and is appropriate where a product mix has fairly similar levels of profitability. However, where the profitability varies considerably it will be inappropriate; for example, a company supplying a wide range of petroleum and oil based products would find that the bulk product made up a significant proportion of total turnover but a limited amount of profitability.

By profit:

$$\frac{\text{Total profit of deliveries}}{\text{Total (estimated) profit of orders}}$$

Profitability analyses will often be difficult to carry out in a complex product range, but give the best indication of the overall importance of the product and its inventory level to the company.

The efficiency of an inventory system should be constantly monitored to ensure that the objectives set in the overall distribution plan continue to be met. The integration of this information in the control and monitoring system will be an essential part of the effective development of a distribution system (see Chapter 15).

COMPUTER SOFTWARE

Name: Stock Control. Software House: Skytronics. System: NCR

Stock Control maintains a master file of all stock with an alphanumeric code and a product group code, as well as stock location and product type if required. Facilities catered for include minimum stock levels, stock movements, preferred and alternative suppliers, multiple price bands and updates, parts description, stock enquiry and transfer to invoicing.

Name: IDCS. Software House: NCR. System: NCR

IDCS (Interactive Distribution Control System) is an order processing and stock control system for the distribution industry, including stock control, order processing and sales reporting.

CASE: GOLDY TOYS

Introduction

In September 1985 the board of Goldy Toys were reviewing the production and stock holding requirements for their company to meet the demands of customers over the forthcoming Christmas period.

Goldy Toys was a small toy company which had been founded in the late 1970s to produce a range of adult and children's board games. The company had grown throughout the 1980s and by 1985 employed several people in a small factory based in North Wales. As the games market had become steadily more quality conscious, the company had invested in its own printing and packaging plant as third party manufacture had been subject to considerable fluctuations in quality which had caused some of the major retail customers to stop stocking particular lines. In common with most printing processes the majority of the cost of manufacture was in the high set-up charges that each production run incurred. Goldy's printing plant was capable of handling all the lines that it currently sold, but because of the high costs of the new machinery Goldy management could not afford to carry high stocks of any particular line. Goldy's sales force of five covered the entire UK and sold both to national chains and local toy outlets.

By 1985 its product range consisted of five items each of which sold to different sectors of the market, though often through similar outlets, with a concentration on the major retailers (Table 10.6). The details of the product range follow.

Table 10.6 Main distributors for Goldy games and 1984 sales levels

Outlets	Game of Life	Dark Side	Kung Master	Emergency	Blitzkrieg
Woolworths	3000	5500	4000	1500	750
Argos	4500	2500	6000	—	—
Specialists	2800	1500	700	1100	1200
Tesco	2200	1200	800	—	—
Debenhams	3000	3200	1100	800	—
Zodiac Toys	2100	1100	700	500	—
Toys R Us	800	500	300	600	550

The Game of Life. This expensively packaged game was designed for the adult market and was the most profitable item that Goldy produced, retailing for £25.00. The average retail margin of 40 per cent meant that Goldy's average selling price was £15.00. The product itself cost £5.00 to manufacture, and £0.50 to distribute. This product had now been on the market for three years.

The Dark Side. This game of ghosts and magic had been designed for the teenage market and sold at £15.00. This product had been introduced in the previous season and had received substantial media attention which had a significant effect on sales. The product cost £3.50 to manufacture and £0.40 to distribute.

Kung Master. Kung Master was the oldest product in the Goldy range and had been the game on which the firm had built its initial reputation. It was aimed primarily at the 6–10 year old market. It was priced at £9.50, cost £2.50 to make, and £0.50 to distribute.

Emergency. This game had been produced as a spin off to a television series, and was aimed at the female 10–15 year market. Costing £3.50 to produce because of a number of expensive bought in components, it retailed for £10.50. In addition to the retail margin, Goldy had to pay the copyright holders of the television series a 15 per cent royalty, based on their selling price, for each of the kits sold.

Blitzkrieg. Blitzkrieg had been the second game that Goldy had produced, and had been only moderately successful, aimed at the 8–15 year audience with a retail price of £8.95 and a manufacturing cost of £2.00. Both Blitzkrieg and Emergency cost £0.40 to distribute.

Retail margins were on average 25 per cent of the gross retail price, though chains such as Argos accepted lower margins for higher volumes.

These groups of retailers made up 80 per cent of the total sales of the company. In addition, the company made occasional sales to mail order firms and had a steady sale to companies overseas, especially in West Germany and France.

Ordering pattern for Goldy products

As might be expected the vast bulk of the game sales occurred during the Christmas period, though there were steady sales of most of the product lines throughout the year, especially at Easter. The details of monthly sales are provided in Table 10.7.

Table 10.7   Seasonal sales pattern—per cent sales by month (1984)

						Month						
	1	2	3	4	5	6	7	8	9	10	11	12
Game of Life	2	3	4	9	3	2	2	4	2	15	35	19
Dark Side	3	5	8	10	6	5	3	2	10	10	25	18
Kung Master	3	5	4	3	3	3	2	3	14	20	20	20
Emergency	3	6	17	15	12	5	5	3	14	10	6	6
Blitzkrieg	2	2	1	2	2	3	4	5	3	25	35	16

The outlets varied as to insistence on exact delivery dates and the quantities delivered. Woolworths was prepared to accept split delivery with half the stock ordered for mid-November being delivered in early December. Tesco and Argos were far more demanding and any failure to deliver the entire quantity by the specified date might lead to future order cancellation. There were additional uncertainties in the ordering pattern because one of the mail order companies tended to order between 8000 and 10 000 units of games in mid-October for delivery by mid-December for their spring catalogues. Previously, Goldy had managed to meet these orders from stocks that had been on hand, but this year with the launch of the new games line, the board was unsure of whether the stocks should be held or built up against the eventuality. Should the company be unable to deliver on time it would lose the mail order business which had been the original life blood of Goldy in its early days.

The production plant

The printing press that Goldy had bought was capable of producing 50 board games per hour. The cost of setting up the production process of each game varied considerably from product to product:

Game of Life:	£1500
The Dark Side:	£750
Kung Master:	£550
Emergency:	£600
Blitzkrieg:	£300

It generally took three to four hours to change over from one production run to another, a time that included the necessary checks on print quality and the like. The factory normally worked a standard eight hour shift during which 400 games could be produced. Adding a further eight hour shift was possible with extra labour that could be hired from outside. The addition of the extra shift would mean that production costs would increase by around 30 per cent. The directors had decided that on no

Table 10.8   Seasonal sales pattern (1983)

	Month											
	1	*2*	*3*	*4*	*5*	*6*	*7*	*8*	*9*	*10*	*11*	*12*
Game of Life	2	3	5	5	4	5	4	11	15	23	11	14
Dark Side	8	5	3	6	4	3	12	10	11	18	15	15
Kung Master	3	7	6	5	7	3	4	3	15	18	18	11
Emergency												
Blitzkrieg	2	2	2	2	1	2	3	5	17	19	30	14

account would production be extended to a third shift, and neither would weekend working be considered. The directors had always felt strongly that part of the success of Goldy Toys had been in their insistence on quality and ensuring that all the product was produced in-house. After two poor experiences with using outside printers, one of which had lost them a prestige export order with the American giant, J.C. Penney, they had decided as a policy issue to manufacture only in-house.

The toy market ordering pattern

The toy and games market was, as might be expected, highly seasonal. The majority of the products were sold during the Christmas period and ordered by the multiples in mid-October for delivery by the middle of November. As a result the five year sales pattern for the product range (see below) showed considerable seasonal variations. See Tables 10.7 and 10.8.

The tendency of the multiple chains had been to delay their ordering until the last possible moment, a trend which had moved away from the previous practice in the industry of the retailers indicating to the suppliers in the early part of the year what the likely demand for particular product lines was likely to be. In contrast the specialist retailers were much more co-operative.

The games market is subject to substantial fluctuations and changes of consumer taste. The game of one year may not be the most popular of the next, even though there are standard games that sell from year to year such as Monopoly and Cluedo.

Table 10.9   Index sales levels by year

	1980	*1981*	*1982*	*1983*	*1984*
Game of Life		100	92	88	73
Dark Side			100	72	53
Kung Master	100	83	72	66	59
Emergency					100
Blitzkrieg	100	78	75	72	66

Goldy had seen the sales of some of its lines follow a similar pattern since their introduction, that of steady decline from their initial launch. Based on an index figure of 100, no game ever rose above the sales level achieved in the first year (Table 10.9).

The new product

Every year, Goldy tried to introduce one new games concept. For the 1985 season it had presented the game Millionaire to the trade early on in the year. Millionaire was aimed at the young adult market, was to be priced at £14.95, and would cost around £3.85 to produce. Initial trade response was enthusiastic and the major buyers of all the main stores had indicated that they would be placing orders for the product around the end of September or the beginning of October for delivery by the end of October or the first week in November.

Volume demand was uncertain in September but it was felt likely that the company would be able to sell around 20 000–25 000 units as the recent rise in the stock markets had made the game topical and a potentially entertaining gift for the affluent gift market.

Current stocks

Because of the needs of working capital, the Goldy directors had tried to keep the stocks of products down to a minimum before the heavy Christmas period, so that the factory could work efficiently through the run up to Christmas.

Kung Master:	1200
Dark Side:	800
Game of Life:	300
Emergency:	250
Blitzkrieg:	200
Millionaire:	2500

DISTRIBUTION ASSIGNMENTS

1   Devise P and Q reorder systems for the following products.

Factor	A	B
Annual demand (units)	200 000	250 000
Production time (weeks)	2.0	3.5
Stock costs (per cent per annum)	20	35
Purchase price (£ per unit)	15	25
Initiation cost (£ per order)	2000	300

2   Decide on the level of safety stock for the following products, which together comprise 30 per cent of the total company sales.

Product	1	2	3	4	5	6	7	8	9	10	Reorder time (periods)
A	35	26	35	56	55	56	67	45	36	27	0.5
B	210	230	205	194	168	176	210	235	245	267	1.0
C	178	123	167	154	132	173	165	165	154	154	1.5
D	98	65	77	88	84	67	83	91	80	73	1.0
E	143	178	142	165	156	102	65	210	267	56	1.5
F	167	34	21	16	219	310	245	123	78	278	1.0

3 A company with the following sales pattern is thinking of increasing the current stock safety levels from 80 to 95 per cent. Analyse the cost implications of such a move and make your recommendation as to whether you consider this a sensible proposal.

Product	1	2	3	4	5	6	7	8	9	10	11	12	Reorder time	Value (£/unit)
A	15	34	43	25	36	66	36	31	37	45	48	30	1.5	23
B	21	56	67	62	59	53	54	21	28	29	38	48	1.9	120
C	58	98	90	92	78	79	81	81	72	66	56	83	1.8	155

4 Your manager has asked you to evaluate whether the following products that comprise only 0.5 per cent of total company sales should be considered obsolescent. The costs of storage of each £1000 of stock is £15 per annum, the gross margin on all of them around 30 percent, and the likely residual value, if sold off, would be 20 per cent of face value. The industry stock turn norm is eight times per annum, (all figures in £).

Product	1	2	3	4	5	6	7	8	9	10	11	12	Stock value
A	210	215	225	167	254	214	251	267	187	198	205	206	12045
B	589	563	529	503	462	480	367	405	345	362	364	367	11000
C	109	99	55	37	62	65	87	77	62	128	156	178	3000
D	116	56	45	54	46	48	67	36	38	178	256	323	8000

5 A supplier of ice-cream has to decide each year what numbers of cabinets it needs to order to service its market. The state of the market is dependent on the weather, the level of disposable income, the state of repair of current equipment and the underlying trend towards a greater consumption of frozen food. Because the order has to be placed with an overseas manufacturer the supplier cannot reorder once the season has started. It estimates the probability of demand to be as follows:

Number	Probability
200	0.1
300	0.2
400	0.3
500	0.2
600	0.1
700	0.6
800	0.4

Each unit costs the company £200, the company accepting a loss on each unit in return for guaranteed placement of its product. The minimum order is 250 units, with additional units being available in 50 unit lots. What size order should the company place? Assuming that the company can borrow money at nil interest from the manufacturing company to finance the stock until it is sold, what level of order should then be placed?

Chapter 11

Physical Distribution

Discussion at the beginning of this book identified transport decisions as one of the more visible aspects of distribution. Lorries emblazoned with famous company names pass by on the motorways, and rail tankers lie in railway sidings and become identified as synonymous with the whole range of distribution activities.

Road and rail transport are the two most commonly used alternatives in the UK distribution environment, but it should be realized that different markets display a great deal of variation in their use of the transport systems available: road, rail, air, water and pipeline. Furthermore, the contribution of each is ever changing and physical distribution systems that work well in one market may be totally inappropriate for another. Awareness of the influences on the development of transport systems is important to the distribution planner who will also have to consider how they are likely to change in the longer term.

Geography, or more accurately topography, is obviously of paramount importance. Thus landlocked countries like Switzerland cannot make extensive use of water based transport but where there are major river systems, as the Rhine in Germany, they become integral to the transport network playing a key role in overall freight movements. Topographical features influence the transport system too. The complexities of the construction of the Tanzan railway in East Africa during the 1970s clearly show this with the Rift valley mountains effectively acting as a block to the cost effective introduction of a railway network. Geography can also influence the distribution infrastructure indirectly: Peru's Lima airport being 16 000 ft above sea level cannot be used effectively for air-freight. At this height only smaller loads are feasible in the thinner air.

Investment in a country's transport infrastructure changes over time and has a major influence on trends in transport system utilization in the country. There was an impressive development of the UK canal network during the early Industrial Revolution when much freight travelled by canal. This wave of investment was followed by concentration on the rail network which began to contract during the 1960s when a considerable expansion of the motorway network began. We touched upon the Channel Tunnel project in Chapter 1 and mentioned its likely impact on transport

Table 11.1   Percentage of (internal) freight movements by country

	US	UK	FRG
Rail	62	12	25
Road	25	85	60
Air	5	2	3
Water	8	—	11

Source: Adapted from BOTB (British Overseas Trade Board) Reports, 1985.

systems but the implications for the UK rail network will be marginal unless supported by investment in other sections of the national system. Where there has been little, insufficient or no investment in distribution infrastructure as in the Third World, distribution tends to rely on river and seas.

Official attitudes in a country make a very important contribution to the balance between different methods of transport. Massive government expenditure on the railway system in France has, for example, seen it maintain its share of freight movements. Rail investment and the role of river transport in Germany means that with the same mileage of roads and the same population the roads are half as congested as those in the UK. Lack of investment, as is the case in Ethiopia, limits the available transport options and has been seen throughout the mid-1980s to seriously interfere with famine relief management. Concern about the quality of the environment has also started to impinge on the acceptability of types of transport and this is also becoming evident in governmental investment plans—legislation controlling the use of various transport systems becomes an increasingly important factor in long-term development. In the EEC, the legislative emphasis has been on the control of road freight with restrictions on the total daily hours a driver can spend behind the wheel, monitored by the tachometer or 'spy in the cab'. In addition, regional or national governments restrict the total loads carried by road—40 tons in the case of the UK; or limit access of road freight to particular areas, as the now defunct Greater London Council restricted road access to London during night-time.

Geography and investment patterns do much to explain the differences between industrialized countries in the pattern of freight movements (Table 11.1). High levels of investment in the road network have meant that this is of overriding importance in the UK, large river systems in both the US and West Germany explaining their continuing importance as a method of physical distribution.

CHARACTERISTICS OF THE MAIN TRANSPORT TYPES

The distribution planner is concerned to identify those special characteristics of each transport system which make it most suitable for particular products, customers and market conditions. Understanding these characteristics will enable the planner to identify those transport systems which may possibly be used, and exclude those which are automatically inappropriate.

Rail

Railway systems are fixed line networks mainly operated by government backed organizations servicing both passenger and freight transport. As railway systems are state owned (with rare exceptions) they provide a shared service to all the manufacturers within a particular market. Though railway operators have very high fixed costs but low variable costs per mile, how they charge for freight movement will depend on how the government sets the profitability/return on capital employed and any special concessions for freight. The result is considerable variation in the costs of rail transport from market to market and little relation to the underlying cost of operation. For example, how British Rail allocates its £900 million per annum government subsidy can have a significant effect on freight costing. The railways offer the manufacturer a range of options of vehicle types including bulk liquid containers, flatcars and refrigerated containers. The more specialized the freight requirement the greater the need to invest in the purchase of specialized dedicated railway rolling stock. British Petroleum owns and maintains a stock of several thousand bulk liquid containers for moving oil within the UK. In the US General Motors owns a large number of car transporting railway stock to move new cars between manufacturing points and dealer outlets. Investment in such specialized railway stock often involves a major capital investment by the manufacturer, and is appropriate where large volumes are carried.

Many railway systems in the world have attempted to improve efficiency and load carrying capacity by introducing large scale electrification throughout the network. This permits systems such as the French network to offer a competitive passenger service to airways between Paris and Geneva by the TGV (Train de Grand Vitesse) and loads of over 2500 tons per train with improved reliability and speed. Freight transport in electrified systems often achieves an average of 40–50 mph throughout the journey, though heavy loads will be carried much more slowly. As might be expected, the type of freight carried by rail systems is primarily bulk product—industrial feedstocks and raw materials.

Water

There had been clear distinctions between inland water transport and sea freight systems. These are now becoming blurred with developments such as lighter aboard ship (LASH) systems providing rapid transfer of freight from ocean going vessel to estuarine delivery system. The majority of inland water transport is still carried by barges of various types, either self propelled or towed with up to 30 others by tugboat. The capacity of barges is substantial and one large barge can often carry the same volume as an entire train. However, in Europe and the US they normally carry around 1200 tons per barge. The total volume of product carried by 20 or 30 towed barges therefore rivals the load carrying ability of large ocean going ships.

The ocean going freight transport market has altered considerably since the 1960s. Large bulk dry cargo carriers, oil tankers, and liquid gas ships have all grown steadily larger with smaller and smaller crews in proportion to their size. By the mid-1980s they had on average one-sixth the numbers of crew that earlier ships had employed. With the decline of small general cargo ships, the majority of deep water (long distance) cargo is carried by container vessels, achieving a similarly high productivity with low crew levels and high levels of mechanization and automation. Whereas a general cargo ship in the 1950s and 1960s spent up to eight days in port discharging and then loading cargo, the large container ports like Rotterdam, Hong Kong and Singapore are achieving turnrounds of larger boats in less than a day—Hong Kong reported a fourteen hour target performance in 1987.

Until the middle of the 1970s freight carriers between certain points were almost all included in some form of trade association, or shipping conference; for example, the North Atlantic Conference dealing with Europe, which set common rates. The system is similar to that organized by IATA (International Air Transport Association) for international air travel. With the expansion of trade carried by the Comecon countries and the growth of Far Eastern lines, these conferences have become less important and the freight environment has become increasingly competitive.

Shallow water or short sea crossings have grown in importance as a way of speeding transport; special areas of importance include the Baltic, North Sea and Mediterranean. RORO vessels (roll on, roll off) allow the rapid transfer of freight from one road system to another. By the mid-1980s there were over three hundred operating throughout the world, though fears over their safety, especially during collision, may reduce their continuing use.

The speed of cargo boats varies considerably. In inland waters they are practically universally restricted by law to 5–6 knots maximum (and less in narrow waterways) because of the damage they may cause to the river banks. Commercial deep water voyages will average anything between 15 and 18 knots, though this speed will be maintained throughout 24 hours.

Road systems

The share of road transport as a percentage of the total freight moved has increased throughout the industrialized world for a number of reasons. For many countries, road networks absorbed most of the investment in infrastructure throughout the 1960s and 1970s and national networks of high speed often toll-free roads were created. Fixed costs are very low and the market highly competitive. A wide variety of third parties offer the full range of service from small parcel delivery to the transport of bulk products.

Road transport involves the widest range of vehicle types from small van operations to the large refrigerated or liquid containers and loads run from 100 to 200 kilos up to the maximum legally permissible weight. In the US, the move towards double units (double bottoms) is growing with total weights of 60 tons; EEC legislation currently restricts the weight limit to 40 tons. Typical road speeds vary enormously; UK studies suggest average outer London area road speeds around 15–20 mph; with inner

London road speeds often below 10 mph, a consequence of both the large number of road users and the inadequate trunk road system. Speeds outside urban areas are considerably higher, especially where road users have access to the trunk network. An example of how road systems can limit a company operation is clearly shown by the two Birds Eye frozen pea plants, one located in East Anglia and the other in the Midlands. With a limit of two hours from picking to freezing the area serviced by the East Anglia plant is restricted due to the inadequate and slow road network; in contrast the Midlands plant situated close to motorways can draw product from a much wider area. Road transport provides the greatest flexibility in size and type of load and destination, but has the disadvantage of high cost and slow speed over long distances. Long journeys suffer from additional problems of driver fatigue and legislative control.

Air-freight

Air-freight expansion owes much to the increase in total capacity with the advent of the larger aircraft introduced in the late 1960s. Freight capacities in the largest are up to 150 tons. With the de-regulation of more and more air routes, air transport has started to offer the sort of opportunity that motorway expansion provided for the small operator in the 1960s and 1970s. A wide range of freight services have therefore become available and range from regular domestic and international main line carriers which also carry freight—Pan Am, KLM, British Airways; to local service airlines, air freight specialists, to the smaller air taxi services. Many of the major international parcel operators are beginning to invest in their own aircraft and are becoming major competitors. Federal Express provides a nightly trans-Atlantic flight to Germany from the US, and TNT the Australian parcels company announced the purchase of a large fleet of aircraft in 1987. Air offers by far the quickest transport method with commercial jets in the 1980s achieving speeds in excess of 550 mph. The growth in the use of air-freight has been particularly marked with perishable, high value items. Thus tomatoes, flowers and shellfish are all extensively air freighted.

Pipeline and conveyor systems

Pipeline and conveyor systems were developed for specific transport requirements where large volumes of product need to be moved, often over long distances. The Siberian pipeline project is one of the largest civil construction projects of all time, involving as it does several thousand miles of complicated construction and pumping stations across central Russia. Pipelines tend to be product specific, that is they will be used for only one particular type of liquid throughout their design life. Though slow—speeds of around 3–4 mph are common—pipelines can operate 24 hours a day, seven days a week and as a result move vast quantities of material cost effectively.

TRENDS IN TRANSPORT SYSTEMS

Overall, there has been a common and steady rise in load carrying capacity for all physical distribution systems. Lorries, ships and aeroplanes are all carrying larger loads

**Table 11.2   Relative costs of freight systems
for the US 1975/1980**

System	1975	1980
Air	100	100
Road	30	33
Rail	6	7
Water	2	2
Pipe	1	1

Source: Adapted from US Department of Trade Analysis of
Freight Costs 1989.

than they were ten years ago. Planes such as the Lockheed Galaxy offer an effective payload of 200 tons in the 1990s, a tenfold increase over that possible with earlier generations of civil jets. This improvement in the load bearing capacity of aircraft has meant that the cost of air-freight has tended to decrease in relative terms, even though it continues to be the most expensive transport method and pipeline the least. The comparative cost trends for the US are shown in Table 11.2. It should be noted that because of air traffic de-regulation in the US the cost profile is different from that of Europe. However, the underlying conclusion that the cost of air-freight will continue to fall in relative terms in the 1980s and 1990s is still valid.

Containerization

The steady growth of containerized traffic is perhaps the single most important influence on the way companies organize physical distribution of their products. It affects not only the physical distribution systems, and how they interact, but has also had far ranging implications for warehouse management and product management. The container in itself is somewhat unexciting. It is simply a box 8 ft high by 8 ft wide and 10, 20, 30, or 40 ft long. The normal shell construction is of steel but other materials used include aluminium, reinforced plastics or even in certain circumstances plywood. Special containers have been developed to handle specific loads, for example frozen food, and reinforced containers are available to handle heavy items. The importance is in the concept—containers are not just loads protected by the external steel shell, they are also unitized and sealed.

These characteristics of containers mean that they speed many aspects of the distribution process and reduce costs. Containerization has achieved impressive improvements in labour productivity, made mechanization more effective, reduced handling time at the docks and within the warehouse, and the strength of the container allows an entire 40 ton load to be moved in perfect safety by one operator. Sealing the load has dramatically reduced documentation costs and increased speed of clearance at intermediate custom points and reduced losses due to pilferage and other damage. Insurance premiums charged for the loads are therefore lower. External carton or fiberite cost can be substantially reduced as the container itself provides the additional packaging strength necessary for long distance transport—companies often use home trade packaging for overseas. Though this may seem a minor point, it can in reality reduce inventories by half, as companies no longer have to maintain stocks of specially strengthened export packs for overseas customers.

The large sizes of containers do, however, mean that companies often have to ship larger quantities of stock than would otherwise be the case. This problem has been reduced by the growth in the number of firms that can provide shared or 'groupage' consolidation services for overseas markets. Warehouse organization and equipment will also have to be substantially altered to handle container traffic. Occasionally this may lead to duplication of warehouse systems where there is continued involvement in standard packing operations and so warehouse space utilization will be less efficient. Warehouse staff must be trained to ensure that containers are properly filled or 'stuffed' so the skilled labour required is higher than in the traditional warehouse operation. Indeed, the correct packing of the container remains a problem for fragile goods as loose space within the container leads to damage as the load shifts during transport. In the age of the computer, various software research projects are focusing into designing systems that will 'pack' the container by determining which carton should be placed where to maximize the efficiency of the container operation.

Because the container is a standard size and configuration, regardless of its contents, its widespread use has been accompanied by interest in the development of integrated transport systems which allow the transfer of goods from one physical transport system to another. This is called *multi-modal* physical transport and allows the transport user to mix a variety of physical distribution methods to achieve cost effectiveness. The most common development has been the rail and road mix, with the road trailer (not normally the tractor unit which supplies the motive power) being carried on a railway flatcar, a system known as piggyback. Containerization has also allowed considerable interactions between road and water—the growth of RORO being an example—see above. The road and air mix is limited by the need for specialized packaging for aircraft transport, though there have been developments of specialized road transport containers that are internally modified to carry the air cargo.

Identifying the savings of introducing a container policy

The substantial investment required by containerization is cost effective when the various associated costs are lower than for a non-container.

$$C_p + C_m + C_s + C_r + C_p + C_i + C_h < K$$

Where:

C_p = Initial cost of purchase of containers
C_m = Maintenance and repair of containers
C_s = Cost of container storage

C_r = Cost of returning containers to initial despatch point when there is no return load
C_p = Cost of packaging using container methods
C_h = Cost of container handling
C_i = Cost of inventory
K = Current cost structure

Many companies lease rather than own containers and it is estimated that around 80 per cent of world container freight is carried in leased units. The use of leased containers will obviously reduce the initial start-up costs and lower the point at which the introduction of container systems become viable.

PACKAGING AND THE PHYSICAL DISTRIBUTION POLICY

Extensive use of containers means often substantial savings in the material cost of packaging. Because packaging fulfils a variety of other roles there is inevitably a limit to how far material costs can in fact be reduced. Packaging must protect the product from external damage and deterioration (physical requirements of the package), which will be reduced by containerization. It must also supply a surface to promote the product and the company, and provide information to the end user—promotional requirements of the package. It has to allow the product to pass safely and cheaply through the manufacturing process—production requirements. Finally packaging must meet the demands of the intermediaries or end user who handle the product— the specific channel requirements.

Channel requirements will be particularly important in defining how resistant the package will need to be. Japanese durable products have successfully developed international high street non-specialist sales by providing products completely sealed and protected. Such products can be sold in a boxed state by the retailer who does not have to unpack and carry out modifications to the product for the particular market. The needs of distribution channel members also make demands on product packaging. The milk bottle is one casualty of the demands of the channel members on suppliers to improve storage. Retailers faced with the poor shelf stacking properties of bottles and the damage that could be caused by broken bottles, wanted milk (and many other liquids) supplied in cardboard containers though this is a more expensive packaging material. Another issue is the information required by the channel member and incorporated by the supplier on the pack—not only bar code information on the product itself, but storage identification on the outer carton to ensure that the product can be identified in store. There is wider use of bar code systems in retail outlets as well as in warehouses to locate products. For example, a jeans manufacturer uses bar code information on the computer to help in load planning. When the cartons come into the warehouse the bar codes are read and stored on the computer, and when specific products are required their locations within the warehouse are automatically available. Such a system is of immense benefit for companies producing a wide range of a standard product—in this case separated by size.

In addition to these distribution channel considerations, the channel member in the consumer sector also has a major interest in the display or 'marketing' components of the packaging—to ensure that the product is visible, that the information on the package contains sufficient information for the end user and so on. The development of packaging concepts and their implementation will as a result form part of most trade marketing agreements (see Chapter 4). Certain major hypermarket groups in France are insisting that product comes ready packed for end of aisle display in special cages, and such trends are likely to become more important as the multiples gain increasing market share.

FINAL APPRAISAL OF THE PHYSICAL DISTRIBUTION SYSTEM

Cost evaluation of the alternatives will suggest the most logical physical distribution system available. Once this has been established the distribution planner will be able to consider some of the trade-offs that may exist within the system.

(a) Capital versus labour. It will often be cost effective to increase the level of investment in the physical distribution system chosen to minimize the labour content, especially in high labour cost areas.

(b) Capital versus cash flow. Will it be more effective to lease or use third parties rather than invest company assets into the distribution process?

(c) Own capital rather than intermediaries. Taking advantage of third parties to hold stock or handle elements of the physical distribution can again provide valuable improvements to the overall cost of physical distribution.

DECISION CRITERIA FOR PHYSICAL DISTRIBUTION SYSTEMS

So far we have concentrated on the mechanics of physical distribution: the characteristics of transport methods available and the trends occurring. For the distribution planner concerned with decisions about cost effectiveness, it is particularly important to know what each system offers in performance terms. This section will give special attention to these matters always bearing in mind the lessons of the total distribution concept: that physical distribution decisions will interact with such aspects of distribution policy as production and warehousing. Thus one will not be faced with the straightforward issue of supplying a customer from a distant production

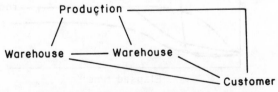

Figure 11.1 The physical distribution system

point, but with a multiplicity of physical distribution elements—production point to warehouse transfers, warehouse to warehouse movements on occasion, production point direct to customer, and warehouse to customer (see Figure 11.1). Where there is this degree of complexity, different types of physical distribution system will often be appropriate to meet the different requirements. To clarify what is appropriate for each type of movement the distribution planner will need to apply particular output criteria for the options available to help to identify trade-offs at various volumes and delivery speeds.

Specific output criteria

As with other distribution issues, each of the available physical distribution alternatives is especially suited to particular types of company policy, sales volumes and customer and product requirements. The planner must identify from the performance criteria of the various channels in a particular market which of the alternatives best meets the company objectives—as these may not, as shown in earlier chapters, be solely concerned with cost effective distribution, but be directed towards gaining competitive advantage. The output criteria for the company's physical distribution management will be based on the ranking of factors essential to meeting the customer's requirements.

Scheduling

The first group of factors needing evaluation concern scheduling: how can the available physical distribution systems meet particular delivery requirements, ensuring that the order reaches the customer within the specified order cycle time (see Chapter 13). The main issue here is obviously the *speed* of the available systems. As stated ear-

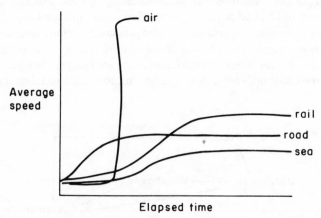

Figure 11.2   Average speed overtime of different transport systems

lier, transport systems vary considerably and speed over the ground, in isolation, is not of much use to the planner as it ignores the often considerable loading and unloading dead time—particularly important in both water and rail transport. As the distance travelled by the load increases, the waiting time tends to become a steadily smaller proportion of the total time taken (see Figure 11.2), and average speed increases. Average speeds will thus vary considerably, and this will be further complicated when problems such as inner city congestion are added—for example, it has been estimated that inner London deliveries will take up to five times as long as similar deliveries in the suburbs—and the uncertainties of cross border delays when transport across national boundaries is necessary. Delays at particular borders within the EEC are always of concern to lorry haulage firms as they may on occasion double the effective time of the the journey. A manufacturer based at Lyons in France, for example, may find that customs clearance at the Italian border takes longer than the total time on the road between Lyons and a northern Italian town such as Turin.

For the distribution planner, therefore, each particular market sector serviced by the company will have different delivery speed profiles for each of the alternative physical distribution systems that are available (see Figure 11.2). Though these remain fixed in the short term, over the longer term they will be continually changing, due to the introduction of new roads, rail networks, alterations in material handling systems, and changes in customs procedures. Total delivery times are also affected by the type of materials handling system at both ends of the journey—the impact of containerization in this respect has already been discussed.

The spread of journey times to a particular location or the *reliability* of the delivery method is as important as average speed to the distribution planner—how effective is the transport system in reaching the customer within a given period? Each market varies on the reliability of a particular physical distribution system, and the actual out-turn for the newly established company will be very hard to predict. However, experience of using different type of transport allows the distribution planner to establish some form of pattern for particular transport types, a typical example of which is given in Figure 11.3. Here we can see that the air-freight and pipeline systems are the most reliable with little variation from the central mean, whereas road freight

Table 11.3   Example of physical distribution grid to particular market areas

	Transport mode & speed (hrs)			
	Road	*Rail*	*Air*	*Water*
Market area A	8.2	12.6	N/A	N/A
Market area B	15.6	13.2	N/A	N/A
Market area C	18.2	13.6	2.1	N/A
Market area D	21.5	15.2	2.3	46.2
Market area E	31.7	18.2	2.5	57.3
Market area F	33.6	19.6	2.3	71.2

shows the greatest spread. But this pattern can rapidly change and will need to be continually re-evaluated. During the 1970s the port of Lagos became overstretched with the arrival of large numbers of freighters carrying material for the construction industry. At one stage over 300 ships were at anchor. Suppliers were forced to alter their physical distribution methods to the Nigerian market by concentrating on trans-Saharan lorry transport because of the decreased reliability of sea freight to that market.

A physical distribution system that is *flexible* in destination may also be of great importance in maximizing the efficiency of the scheduling process. Pipelines, for example, are totally inflexible in operation, whereas road transport offers the most flexible system in terms of destinations and adaptability to changing market conditions.

The other criterion for scheduling decision making is the possible *frequency* of the distribution method. In general, the pipeline will offer the greatest frequency of delivery as the system is always in operation, and in most markets, sea or water borne transport the least. For example, the steady decline in trade between Australia and the UK has been matched by the decrease in the availability of shipping to Australian ports, and companies may now have to wait up to three weeks for a suitable sailing.

Product requirements

It is self evident that not all products can be handled in the same way, and the distribution planner's main concern is to identify factors that are likely to favour or disqualify particular types of physical distribution. The *mass* of the product (size × weight) often excludes types of transport limited by their load carrying capacity or size. For example, even with major road networks, it is very difficult to transport large generators by road, because of their weight and dimensions, whereas transporting similar loads, often over 100 tons, is far less of a problem by sea. Similarly the *perishability* and *fragility* of products make specific demands upon the physical distribution method. Thus tomatoes are often air-freighted within the EEC, for instance from the Channel Islands to the UK, because of time constraints in supplying the market with a fresh product, though this transport method will generally be more expensive than alternative RORO and truck methods. Whether or not the distribution system is sufficiently *secure* may also be an important consideration. Road transport is often considered the least secure method of physical transport with greater opportunities for pilferage and robbery than the more secure air-freight and rail systems. The fact that the majority of radioactive waste is now carried by rail rather than road reflects this. The specialized containers are more easily transported on the rail system which also has a far lower rate of accidents (a lower accident per mile ratio than road).

In certain circumstances the distribution planner may evaluate the *vulnerability* of the physical distribution system: strikes within the postal system were partially responsible for mail order companies developing their own distribution network since a long postal dispute could force them out of business. Part of the development of the contingency or fall back distribution plan which should be part of every company's strategic evaluation (see Chapter 15) will revolve around the question of delivery system vulnerability. What will the effects on the distribution process be if the chosen physical distribution system is no longer available due to weather, strikes or other problems? The 1988 postal strike led to the reappraisal by the Littlewoods mail order group of their distribution arrangements as they had lost substantially during this period in contrast to other groups that had used different distribution methods (independent carriers or collection from retail outlets).

Customer requirements

Though a particular delivery system meets a majority of output criteria, the distribution planner cannot ignore constraints placed upon the system by the customer. After all, it is the customer that the system is being designed to service. The location of customers may in certain instances determine the effectiveness of certain types of physical distribution system in servicing them. Proximity to the sea, for example, may mean that the convenience of shipping out or in will outweigh the overall cost considerations. Rowntree Mackintosh, situated on one of the main railway systems in the UK at York, was ideally placed to continue, by rail, to service customers located in the centre of towns throughout the UK. The reduction in the railway network in the 1960s and the gradual movement of both wholesalers and retailers to suburban or out-of-town locations made rail less viable.

More important is the customers' ability to receive goods from a certain type of distribution system—whether or not they have adequate materials handling equipment. Retailers' centralized depots are constructed to receive palletized loads via road haulage, and other transport alternatives will be unacceptable. Such considerations can also influence the type of transport in overseas markets. For example, there is no facility in the Seychelles to handle container traffic and the only option is small freighters specializing in general cargo.

Analysing distribution criteria

A firm can use a heuristic process similar to those employed in decision making in other areas of distribution to help define the best options for transport (Table 11.4). Where a company splits its physical distribution systems each element may yield different results. For example, analysing the supply criteria direct from production point to customer, and from warehouse to customer might suggest that road transport would be most appropriate, whereas transfers from production point to warehouse have to meet different criteria and therefore different transportation systems might be appropriate. Such considerations led Taunton Cider to reappraise its production to warehouse transport system, replacing road with rail for this part of their distribution network with an estimated saving of £250 000 per annum. Having established the likely candidates that best meet customer, scheduling and product requirements, the

Table 11.4

	Weighting				
Factor	Air	Road	Rail	Pipeline	Water
Speed					
Reliability					
Frequency					
Security					
Flexibility					
Mass					
Perishability					
Fragility					
Vulnerability					
Material handling					
Location					

final choice will obviously have to rest with the most cost effective option. The way the company transports its product inevitably has implications in other areas, and to arrive at a final decision certain trade-offs must be evaluated.

Trade-offs within the physical distribution environment

Certain important trade-offs affect the final choice of the distribution method. First, the faster the system operates the lower the stock holding requirement. The company can finance less stock between production point and customer, and there will be a pay-off between the costs of the faster transport system and the effect on the reduced stock holding.

Cost cross over = transport cost + inventory storage (carrying) cost + receiver's inventory storage cost + ordering cost

$$C = rD + utD + a/s + wsD/2 + wk[(s + t + k)D]\tfrac{1}{2}$$

Where:
C = cost
D = total annual demand
r = transport cost
t = average delivery time
s = average time between shipments
u = carrying cost of shipment inventory
w = carrying cost of receiver's stock
a = set-up costs of production
k = cost of stock

Though for many planners the choice of distribution channel is self evident, the analysis of cost systems indicates where, in high value manufacturing companies, air transport may be far more viable than had previously been considered. Digital, the American computer manufacturer, found that using air-freight to supply Europe from American manufacturing facilities substantially improved profitability. Decisions on the most cost effective system greatly depend on the volumes that the company is transporting. Each available method varies with respect to the point at which higher fixed costs are offset by lower variable costs, and vice versa. The volume being transported within the system is crucial in determining pay-off levels and it is important for the company to monitor the various alternative systems. The point at which transport systems should be reassessed can be provided by the following equation.

$$C = \frac{F_1 - V_1}{F_2 - V_2}$$

Where:

F_1, F_2 are fixed costs of the alternative systems
V_1, V_2 are variable costs of the alternative systems

When volumes increase it becomes commercially more sensible to reduce variable costs by higher levels of fixed investment. This calculation is especially important for oil companies when they consider the viability of particular oil fields. At a certain volume level, the installation of pipeline systems will be commercially far more viable than alternative transport methods.

MONITORING THE PHYSICAL DISTRIBUTION SYSTEM

As physical transport makes such a substantial contribution to the total distribution cost, monitoring of the chosen system is vital to ensure its continuing viability or to allow different options to be evaluated.

Percentage load used. The ability of the distribution system to utilize fully the physical distribution facility used is an important matter in evaluating its cost effectiveness. For example, the cost of a road trailer remains absolute regardless of the volume it transports. The nearer the distribution system is operating to 100 per cent of the available load, the lower the likely costs. Should the load factor drop significantly, the distribution planner must re-evaluate either the way that loads are consolidated, such as by altering the level of the minimum drop (see Chapter 15), or by changing the type of physical distribution system used.

Transport cost/area revenue. A major problem of physical distribution for the distribution planner is controlling the overall level of cost while servicing different market sectors. Using sales areas as a basis for calculation, it is possible to rapidly acquire information about whether particular regions are costing the company more in percentage terms, and from that review the physical distribution method for that specific region. It will also isolate areas in which distribution costs are particularly low, from which lessons may be drawn for other areas.

Planned delivery time/actual delivery time. Where it is important that the company achieves delivery on time, the monitoring of the actual out-turn of the delivery system against that which is initially planned is necessary to ensure that the distribution planner can continue to meet delivery deadlines accurately.

CASE: TECHNOCHEM

Introduction

The Technochem Inc board was reviewing the performance of the company's European operations, which still lagged significantly behind the rest of the group in such key performance criteria as total sales, market share and profitability.

Technochem had headquarters in downtown Burbank, California and was founded at the turn of the century by a colourful ex-rodeo showman Max Klei, who had identified the growing need for both diagnostic equipment and high grade reagents in the developing manufacturing sector of the East Coast. The move to California had occurred during the Second World War with the tremendous growth in electronic manufacture in nearby states and the demands of the Manhattan project in New Mexico with which Technochem had been closely involved.

The company grew throughout the 1960s and 1970s by concentrating on areas of specialization and by a judicious mix of manufacturing in-house and buying in components. Historically, the company had concentrated on the US for the bulk of its business though the overseas expansion of American manufacturing activity had meant that there had been a rapid growth of demand for Technochem products from the overseas subsidiaries of American companies.

By the early 1980s the senior management of the company were more aware of the need to develop some form of strategy towards overseas expansion as the world market was increasingly dominated by a small number of large companies with integrated production and supply facilities and would eventually be able to out-compete companies such as Technochem.

The company operated in three sectors by 1984. Each was regarded as an independent profit centre with its own management and sales teams within the US though there was a degree of overlap in some small overseas markets.

Technochem structure

The *Electronics Division* produced laboratory diagnostic equipment primarily for the education sector, a second most important sector being both industrial and government research laboratories. The product range was currently assembled at the company plant at La Jolla, California using semi-skilled labour from south of the Mexican border. Worldwide the market was increasingly competitive particularly on product/technical quality and to a certain extent on price, though this was less of a worry in the majority of markets. Because most sales were to research type institutions the competitive advantage of fast delivery times was minimal.

The *Reagents Division* manufactured a range of basic industrial materials such as alcohols, aldehydes, and ketones used in a variety of organic syntheses. Recently the company had become more and more involved in the manufacture of pure energy sources for the rapidly expanding bio-technology sector. By 1984 two sophisticated integrated manufacturing sites both costing around $200 million were producing the range of company products, one on the West Coast not far from the Electronics Division plant and the other near the coast in Virginia. The reagents market was highly price competitive throughout the world because it was in the main perceived as a range of commodity products. In general it was very demanding on delivery schedules, as many of the major buyers in the world manufacturing sector had moved over to Japanese just-in-time material-ordering patterns.

The *Resins Division* had initially formed part of the Reagents Division but now traded separately. It was involved in the manufacture of the increasingly complex resin products required by the manufacturers of composite materials such as glass and carbon fibre. The initial plant purchased by Technochem and then extensively modified and extended was on the outskirts of Chicago from where the company serviced its entire US and European operations. In contrast to the Reagents Division, where the manufacturing plants were operating slightly below capacity, the Chicago plant was already at breaking point due to the rapid growth of sales even though continual improvements and modifications kept the operation running. Company executives were in the process of deciding on where a new $150 million plant should be located. Resins were tailor made for particular applications; Technochem worked closely in conjunction with the OEM design teams to determine the loads and stresses that would be involved in a particular application. Because of the specificity of the product, the market was not price sensitive, but very concerned about the reliability of

Table 11.5   Company sales ($ millions)

	1978	1979	1980	1981	1982	1983	1984
Total sales	450	520	630	800	890	1190	1300
Total profit	32	56	80	100	130	170	200
Division (sales):							
Electronic	250	260	280	290	300	310	320
Reagents	160	190	250	290	310	450	520
Resins	40	70	100	220	280	430	460
Division (profit):							
Electronic	21	26	32	30	35	60	65
Reagents	10	15	20	26	30	42	49
Resins	1	11	28	44	65	68	86

Table 11.6   Sales by market ($ millions)

	1978	1979	1980	1981	1982	1983	1984
Total sales	450	520	630	800	890	1190	1300
US	360	380	420	450	480	550	640
Europe	90	140	210	350	410	640	660
Total profit	32	56	80	100	130	170	200
US	27	45	50	67	88	97	115
Europe	5	11	30	33	42	73	85

delivery schedules because of the expensive manufacturing processes involving the resins.

The company had concentrated on two markets: the US, where Technochem was particularly strong on the Western seaboard; and Europe. Over the seven year period both sales and profit had grown at a more rapid rate in Europe than in the US and at current rates of progress the European activities would be providing the bulk of company profits within the next three years. The worrying feature was that the European operations still yielded lower levels of gross margin. This was a result partly of the competitive environment in Europe but mainly as a result of high distribution costs in the electronic and reagent businesses (Tables 11.5 and 11.6).

In Europe during the mid-1970s, Technochem was split into the three divisions of the parent company each acting as a profit centre within the organization though there was a degree of overlap in manufacturing.

Products and markets

Electronics Division

The Electronics Division concentrated on the design and final assembly of diagnostic equipment for manufacturing industry and research laboratories. Its main products were: oscilloscopes, fluoroscopes and chromatographs. They were assembled in Arizona, from components made to the company's design by a range of sub-manufacturers both within the US and increasingly, from overseas. During the early 1980s Technochem began to develop a range of products for the hospital sector, dialysis machines and portable X-ray equipment being most important.

The use of sub-manufacturers allowed Technochem to continually upgrade its products at negligible cost. Technochem was at a competitive disadvantage in a situation where the integrated companies could gain economies of scale from the manufacture of the components and the finished products. The market environment was changing rapidly as the major manufacturers in the sector invested heavily to produce new sophisticated multi-function measuring equipment. The level of invest-ment that the competition envisaged necessary for the new generation of equipment

Table 11.7 Electronic division production costs

	Circuit board	Outer casing	Assembly
Oscilloscope	$25	$12	$15
Fluoroscope	$30	$10	$25
Chromatograph	$68	$12	$40

was around $200 million, including the creation of an integrated manufacturing plant.

For Technochem, the production process of the three main types of equipment could be separated into the preparation of the circuit boards, the production of the outer casing, and the final assembly which involved the addition of various other sub-components such as screens and leads. The circuit boards were currently bought from the best suppliers within the Pacific basin and imported into the US; both the assembly and the production of the outer casing were in-house. Technochem had considered having the entire production subcontracted overseas, and although this would decrease the cost per unit by around $5, this would tend to reduce the advantages of the current manufacturing process that could with ease, slightly modify products for specific overseas markets.

The costs involved in production processes for the main product lines sold through each sector are shown in Table 11.7. Included in the cost of the circuit board was the $2 duty payable into the US; freight for such a small high value item was relatively negligible.

The freight cost between the US and mainland Europe was on average $3 per unit. The company tried to ship in container load quantities to each of its main European

Table 11.8 Duty and transport costs within Europe

	Average trade price ($)	Import duty (%)	Cost of internal distribution ($)
Austria	130	15	3.0
Belgium	110	8	1.5
Switzerland	180	35	1.5
UK	100	8	2.5
West Germany	180	8	2.0
Italy	120	8	1.5
France	140	8	3.0
Scandinavia	190	27	2.0
Iberia	85	32	4.0
Greece	90	25	4.0

NB: Greece though in the EEC had yet to harmonize duties on the import of electronic components. (The electronics division in contrast to the two others had no representation in Iberia or Greece. This had been a decision of a previous Vice President of the division who was no longer with the organization.)

Table 11.9   Technochem annual country review—electronics division

Country	Market size ($ millions)	Sales ($ millions)	Average % margin	Relative market price av: 100
Austria	28	4	40	125
Belgium	35	6	55	112
Switzerland	27	3	45	160
UK	110	26	37	98
West Germany	150	34	42	102
Italy	115	22	32	88
France	130	18	28	85
Scandinavia	45	7	45	132
Iberia	25	5	23	145
Greece	18	2	22	176

markets; shipments to smaller markets had to be grouped with other American products. Because of the large volume of shipping between continental US and Europe the speed of delivery was generally good; a delivery period of four weeks from date of order could generally be maintained though this varied with product type and the availability of shipping to small markets.

The cost of shipment to the various European markets varied slightly, but the overall average was around $2 per unit; duties, however, varied considerably (Table 11.8).

Import duties for components as opposed to finished goods varied slightly from market to market. There were exceptions to this general rule; component import into the UK was significantly higher at 25 per cent than for finished goods, whereas the duty on the importation of components into Austria was 5 per cent lower.

Technochem carried out a review of each of its major markets every year to determine future marketing tactics. Table 11.9 reports the most recent.

The Electronics Division in Europe did not handle any of the hospital range which accounted for over 30 per cent of total world divisional turnover. As a result, the European contribution to total turnover was more limited than for the other two divisions.

Each of the main European operations varied since each had grown up as an independent unit as Technochem had set up new subsidiary companies, appointed agents or had bought distributors in other markets. The law relating to agency termination varied throughout Europe and would also be subject to individual court rulings. One of the main competitors to Technochem in the reagents sector had carried out a realignment of its distribution structure, and had on average ended up paying compensation of three years market revenue to each of the dismissed local company representatives.

Austria. The Austrian market was serviced by a distributor based in the Austrian capital Vienna. The distributor, with a sales force of five and two qualified service engineers, supplied local services for Technochem products which were used by around 350 customers throughout Austria. Stock with an average value of $200 000 was held in the Vienna warehouse.

Belgium. The Belgian market was serviced by a commission agent that was one of the first companies to handle Technochem products overseas. It employed seven sales representatives and serviced approximately 400 customers throughout Belgium and Luxembourg. A major problem for Technochem in the Belgian market was that the agent found the level of service support difficult to maintain. Another difficulty was that the lack of holding stock in the market meant that orders were taking more than three months to meet, a slowness of response that could only be offset by the competitiveness of the pricing policy that the company followed.

Switzerland. The Swiss market was also serviced by a local commission agent with three sales representatives servicing 200 clients. The Swiss market was relatively large because of the large number of research laboratories established there. However, the market demanded sophisticated products and a large amount of technical back-up and Technochem was slowly losing market share as a result. The Swiss agent held stock to an average value of $300 000.

UK. In the UK Technochem had bought, in 1972, an industrial wholesaler specializing in the distribution of analytical equipment. The company now employed 25 staff and a sales force of ten calling on around 600 customers. Holding stock included all the major lines (on average $600 000 in value) and full service back-up throughout the country.

West Germany. In West Germany Technochem used the same distribution arrangements as the Reagents Division, with a sales force of 20 (shared across the product lines) calling on around 300 industrial customers. The company held stock to the value of $250 000 on average but found it difficult to provide a full service and technical back-up, generally relying on third parties to carry out the necessary technical work.

Italy. In Italy, Technochem had one of the most successful distributors throughout Europe. The company also distributed technical glassware to industrial customers. It had followed a policy of only maintaining small stocks of the Technochem range but paying the premium for air-freighting the product in from the US when required. This meant that it could keep the level of stocks down to around $50 000, while being prepared to pay the extra $10–15 per unit for air-freight charges. The distributor was able to provide a full technical service to customers in the industrial north, while using third parties south of Rome.

France. In France, the Electronics Division operated through a totally owned local subsidiary with a staff of 28 and was able to provide a full technical service throughout the French market calling on approximately 1100 customers. The sales subsidiary held stock of around $400 000.

Scandinavia. The Scandinavian market was serviced by a commission agent with five sales representatives calling on around 450 major customers throughout the market. Both market sales and share had been declining due to the inability of the commission agent to provide customers with the high level of service demanded, and the slow delivery of equipment which often took three months to arrive.

Iberia/Greece. Both the Iberian and Greek markets were serviced via distributors. The Iberian market was supplied by a company with headquarters in Madrid, calling on around 250 customers in Portugal and Spain, with a sales force of five. The company had been unable to provide effective service back-up, losing market share as a result. A similar process was occurring in Greece, where Technochem was badly under-represented with only 50 long-term customers. Both distributors carried small stocks of around $100 000 in value.

Reagents Division

The Reagents Division in Europe had developed differently from Electronics. The management team saw themselves as operating in the chemical industry and had concentrated on the problems of moving bulk material within the European land mass. The market was increasingly dominated by the industry majors—Hoechst and Bayer in Germany, ICI in the UK, Montedison in Italy and Rhone Poulenc in France. Overcapacity in all markets meant that the sector was highly price competitive with the inevitable effects on profit margins.

Duty costs were significantly lower than for the Electronics Division but the group faced much higher transport costs from the US and internal distribution within the European market. The average costs of transport by sea from the US worked out at $40 a ton of product. Transport costs within Europe were also extremely high, most of the product being moved by road. Because of the high freight costs, Technochem tried always to ship by bulk carrier. This requirement and the problems of manufacture of a wide product range meant that the delivery time from receipt of order would be in the region of eight to ten weeks; this required the European distributors to carry higher stock than the Electronic Division (Table 11.10).

In contrast to the Electronics Division, there were only three operating units in Europe: in France, Italy and West Germany. The French company serviced the markets of France, UK, Belgium, Spain, Portugal and Switzerland; the German company

Table 11.10   Duty and transport costs within Europe—reagents division

	Average trade price/ton ($)	Duty (%)	Cost of internal distribution ($)
Austria	880	3	45
Belgium	760	3	30
Switzerland	900	15	27
UK	740	3	35
West Germany	800	3	30
Italy	880	8	25
France	720	3	42
Scandinavia	900	12	38

Table 11.11   Annual market share estimate—reagents division

Country	Market size ($ millions)	Sales ($ millions)	Average % margin	Relative market price av: 100
Austria	350	22	15	95
Belgium	280	18	12	90
Switzerland	180	24	16	110
UK	600	49	18	102
West Germany	780	82	22	110
Italy	380	15	14	102
France	550	34	18	95
Scandinavia	295	22	20	110

Germany, Austria, the Netherlands and Scandinavia; the Italian company Italy and Greece.

The best established company in the distribution network in Europe was in France. This was a totally owned subsidiary of the parent company, Technochem. It employed a sales staff of 45 and maintained substantial stocks of speciality products (around $10 million) at the Le Havre warehouse and headquarters. From there the product was transported by truck to the 1200 customers.

In Germany, Technochem had established a joint venture with one of the smaller German manufacturing companies to distribute products of both the Electronics Division (only in the German market) and Reagents Division. The 20 strong sales force called on the main 350 customers in the market. The company held a large stock valued at around $5 million in their warehouse near Frankfurt.

The Italian company was far the smallest of the three European operations. Technochem had appointed a distributor in 1975 to handle this market. This company held stocks of all the main product lines valued at around $500 000 and called on 120 major customers in the north with a sales force of five.

Like the Electronics Division, the Reagents Division produced an annual market share estimate for all the major European markets (Table 11.11).

Resins Division

The Resins Division as a new and specialized product sector had followed a separate course from the other two Divisions. It had established a single company subsidiary located in Brussels to service the entire European market. Within each country there was a sales office but all the European technical staff were based in Brussels and would travel from there to hold discussions with individual client companies.

Because of the high margins in the sector, the company held reserve stocks of all customer product ranges, to the value of $15 million in the Brussels headquarters even though the majority of product was air-freighted from the Chicago factory to individual customers. The resulting freight costs were high, but relatively low as a

Table 11.12   Duty and transport costs within Europe—resins division

	Average price/kilo ($)	Import duty (%)	Cost of internal distribution ($)
Austria	34	2	2
Belgium	32	2	—
Switzerland	40	10	2
UK	36	2	3.5
West Germany	40	2	3.5
Italy	42	2	3.5
France	38	6	4
Scandinavia	52	5	3
Iberia	55	12	5
Greece	45	15	3

proportion of the total value of the product—the average cost per kilo from the US was $2, because of extremely favourable rates that the company had negotiated with several of the trans-Atlantic carriers. As a high proportion of product was air-freighted to national airports direct from the US, internal distribution costs were negligible, but when product was shipped from the Brussels warehouse by road they tended to be high by contrast (Table 11.12). Because of the use of air transport Technochem Europe could manage to meet the demanding supply requirements of the major customers.

As the market was growing rapidly and there was a general lack of production capacity able to supply the highly complex resin material to individual customers' specifications, prices were high and margins satisfactory throughout Europe (Table 11.13).

Management

The three Technochem Divisions were organized in a similar fashion.

Table 11.13   Annual market share estimate—resins division

Country	Market size ($ millions)	Sales ($ millions)	Average % margin	Relative market price av: 100
Austria	230	45	65	130
Belgium	300	70	55	102
Switzerland	130	30	56	140
UK	200	25	45	120
West Germany	380	45	45	115
Italy	260	22	48	135
France	330	27	34	98
Scandinavia	270	3	45	120
Iberia	120	—	—	—
Greece	95	—	—	—

The main board

In the main board of the company located at its headquarters in Los Angeles, there were the six executive officers:

William Dougall. Chief Executive
Michael Zabronski. Finance Director
Daniel Cohen. Communications Director
Toby Anderson. Head of the Electronics Division
Simon Parker. Head of the Reagents Division
Michael Giorgiou. Head of Resins Division

The operating divisional structure

Reporting to the divisional heads, at the divisional headquarters, each of which was based in the US were subsidiary boards consisting of:

Production Director
Research Director
Finance Director
Sales and Marketing Director

Within each department, each director had two regionally based teams, one for the US and the other for Europe.

DISTRIBUTION ASSIGNMENTS

1   Deepcut discount stores sells only private (own label) products from its 100 outlets nationwide. Each store has a $2 million turnover and is supplied from 5 company owned warehouses which each cost £250 000 a year to run. Write a report analysing the likely benefits of this to the company and any alternative arrangements that they might adopt, and the information that it would need to come to a decision.

2   A company has the following information about the various physical distribution options that are available to it to reach a particular market area distant from the production point. The company supplies bulk frozen food to a variety of catering establishments. Discuss the advantages and disadvantages of the various options open to the company and which would appear to provide the best solution to their transport problem.

	Time (days)	Variation (days)
Air	1	0.2
Road	3	2
Rail	2	1
Water	4	1

3   You are asked to prepare a report for the new national canal authority on the possibility of developing the freight carrying business on the canal network. Which areas of freight should the authority concentrate on, and why?

4   Evaluate the options available for transport of product from the North of England to Vienna. What type would be most appropriate for large quantities of: (a) computer printers, (b) tinned potatoes, (c) frozen sausages, and why?

Managing Physical Distribution

Having selected the transport system best suited to its strategic and market needs, a company must then effectively manage and control it. The main management issues can be summarized as a series of questions. Whether to use some form of third party transport—either a shared distribution arrangement or contracting out the physical distribution process—or to rely entirely on company owned vehicles? How should transport systems be purchased? How should the maintenance and replacement of the vehicle fleet be planned and organized? How to plan the delivery cycle effectively—load planning?

THIRD PARTY DISTRIBUTION

Suppliers have been forced to re-evaluate their approaches to physical distribution management owing to the impact of the demands placed on the distribution network. There has been a significant shift away from company owned and managed distribution systems towards the involvement of some form of third party. A survey in the mid-1980s in the UK showed that both manufacturers and retailers were moving towards the use of third party distribution (Table 12.1).

Types of third party distribution

Historically, third party distribution was usually shared: an independent third party rented either warehousing (see Chapter 7) and/or vehicle facilities to manufacturers. From this, shared distribution developed to offer such specialized distribution services as refrigerated transport, international haulage, and services in the transfer of delicate equipment such as computers. By the mid-1980s there were three main types of shared distribution. The most important are major national companies offering common user distribution services and which frequently focus on a particular market niche. Federal Express is one of the leading branded distribution companies in the US and has during the mid-1980s begun a major expansion into Europe. Christian Salvesen in the UK provides specialized food distribution services; another firm Tibbet

Table 12.1   Types of physical distribution by operation

Retailers
23% run their own operation
15% use distribution contractors
54% run their own operation and also use distribution contractors
 8% have no distribution system

Manufacturers
29% have retained an in-house operation
42% operate a mixed in-house third party distribution system
29% contract out all work to the third party distributors

Source: KAE, 1985.

and Brittan delivers clothes; Securicor initially specialized in the transport of cash and securities and now offers document delivery, while the Unilever subsidiary, SPD, has a division which provides secure delivery of delicate computer equipment.

These national shared distribution operations have many similar advantages to the shared warehouses mentioned in an earlier chapter. These are essentially those of greatly improved flexibility, though for large volumes it significantly raises distribution costs. A small printing company in East London found that it was not viable to employ a driver and own a van before turnover had passed £100 000, even though the majority of deliveries were within a narrow geographical area.

The second most important shared transport operation involves manufacturing companies with an already established national distribution network. They offer companies with complementary products access to their distribution network to reduce overall distribution costs. Milk and dairy suppliers have spearheaded this approach, selling space in their distribution network to companies requiring chilled distribution. It reduces transport costs and also often improves the positioning of the complementary product within the retail outlets. But there are major problems especially the relative inflexibility of the operation and the special demands placed upon the user to meet the organizing manufacturer's requirements on special handling, speed or volume.

Finally there are a large number of independent local companies servicing localized markets, such as large metropolitan areas throughout the world: New York, Paris or London. But the main growth area of shared distribution throughout the 1980s has been in the delivery of small parcels, with a number of firms competing with the postal services to offer more effective services. Typical services operating in the UK and the US are shown in Table 12.2.

Contract distribution

Contract distribution is the supply of all the transport requirements by a third party. The service offered is a dedicated one and can range from transport through to

Table 12.2   Small parcel delivery specialists—UK and US

UK	US
National Carriers (LYNX)	United Parcel
Federal Express	Federal Express
Securicor	Greyhound Package
TNT	

complete warehousing and stock control provision. The involvement of a third party in the distribution system has a number of significant advantages for the manufacturer.

Contract distribution reduces the manufacturer's capital investment requirements in the physical distribution system, even to the extent of the contracter building warehousing and installing the necessary computer systems to run the service. The contract agreement also allows the company to have an accurate costing structure on which to base forward pricing as is the case with third party warehousing, discussed in Chapter 7. Any problems that the supplier may encounter in labour or restrictive practices operating within the distribution environment are reduced since it is the contract distributor's responsibility.

As distribution makes increasingly sophisticated demands of management, the use of a specialized distribution contractor gives the manufacturer access to these highly specialized distribution skills, albeit on a 'loaned' basis, without extensive training and retraining in-house. Contract hire will also allow the firm to rapidly change the method of operating its distribution network without the major upheavals that might be caused if it was running a totally company owned operation.

There are some disadvantages to contract distribution that deserve thought. The contract relationship ties a manufacturer into a long-term relationship with an outside organization. Should the manufacturer wish to withdraw from a particular market, for example, it would frequently be costlier with a contract distribution agreement. Moreover there are penalties for the manufacturer if volumes significantly drop below expectations. Control of the distribution process by third parties can mean that the management lose touch with an important element of the marketing function and fail to respond effectively to changes in the service demanded by customers, insulated as they are by a distribution intermediary.

FINANCING COMPANY TRANSPORT

Where a company is organizing its own road transport fleet it must decide whether long- or short-term use of vehicles is required, how the purchase should be financed, and how the investment will be maximized by effective replacement and maintenance policies.

With the escalating cost of road transport vehicles (large articulated vehicles cost over £40 000) many companies looked to methods of financing vehicles other than straightforward purchase, and the majority of methods available reduce the capital commitment of the firm to vehicle purchase. Hire purchase first provided partial finance from the vehicle supplier or a financial intermediary. The purchaser pays back both the remaining capital cost and the finance charges over a fixed period. At the end of the contract period the vehicle becomes the property of the purchaser. Hire purchase does not have a great deal of attraction to the majority of companies in the UK because of taxation regulations and the inability to depreciate vehicles quickly enough. In markets where the taxation allowances are different it is often the main method of purchase. In contrast, in leasing agreements the customer pays a fixed monthly sum to the supplier of the vehicle but ownership is not transferred. Such an agreement has a number of attractions: lease charges can be offset against tax; leasing reduces the capital employed in the business. Leasing, however, means the user company maintains the vehicles and this can lead to an unacceptably high level of overheads. Because of these shortcomings in leasing arrangements, contract hire has become more popular. It differs from the leasing arrangement in that all maintenance is the responsibility of the leaser. Furthermore, the agreements tend to include provision of replacement vehicles. Contract vehicle hire may also include the costs of the driver who will be employed by the leaser rather than the lessee.

The final option available is for the company to enter into a series of short-term hire agreements to meet specific freight requirements. Short-term hire is less feasible when the company is involved in the continual transport of large volumes of stock. Comparing the fixed costs of maintaining a vehicle with the variable costs of hiring can provide the company with the point at which it will be more economic to enter into a long-term vehicle purchase agreement rather than use short-term hire.

$$PY > F(VY)$$

Where:
P = Hiring cost
Y = Days used
F = Fixed annual cost for leased or purchased vehicle
V = Variable cost per day

Table 12.3   Key features of leasing or contract hire agreements

The period of the contract, and the amount of notice required on either side.
What replacement vehicles will be made available and under what conditions.
The details concerning the exact equipment provided with the vehicles (an especially important point when the company has particular materials handling requirements that will need to be met by the vehicles).
The exact duties of drivers under contract and the roles of their replacements if necessary.
What annual or weekly mileage is permitted under the terms of the contract or lease.
The exact payment terms and conditions, (especially insurance).
A detailed analysis of the required maintenance schedule and what responsibilities are incurred through vehicle breakdown.

The nature of company operations influences the feasibility of various purchase methods. Where specialized vehicles are required the most common purchase methods will be leasing as contract hire companies concentrate on standard products. The smaller the vehicle fleet required, the greater the attractions of contract hire as the supplier will not have to carry any maintenance personnel. Though the graph of vehicle numbers against maintenance cost will be slightly different for each vehicle operator, the underlying trend has been steadily upwards since the 1970s, company owned or leased fleets only being economic if there is need of a substantial number of vehicles. Because of the long-term commitment in leasing or contract hire the distribution planner must analyse any agreement with care (Table 12.3).

VEHICLE REPLACEMENT POLICY

A company managing its own fleet will have to establish some form of vehicle replacement and maintenance policy. Vehicles have to be replaced if they become obsolescent, or if they fail to meet the changing payload and speed requirements of the company's distribution plans, or become too expensive to maintain. There is a point at which these variable costs will be far higher than the fixed costs of re-financing a new vehicle though this will vary according to the distance travelled (Table 12.4). In this example the vehicle initially costing £25 000 depreciates at 30 per cent per annum. This depreciation may not be allowable under existing taxation but accurately reflects the decline in the market value of the vehicle. Tax and insurance are assumed to remain constant during the five year period; diesel consumption and tyres to increase slightly in real terms for the same mileage over the five years due to heavier consumption in the ageing vehicle. Maintenance charges will substantially increase towards the end of the effective life of the vehicle. This particular example indicates that the company will need to consider replacing the vehicle at around 3 to 4 years where the cost curve starts to rise steeply. Beyond 5 years keeping the vehicle in the fleet will be extremely costly. One of the more recent developments in maintenance has therefore been the introduction of planned replacement policies to identify possible component failure and to replace them before it happens. A policy might, for example, produce the analysis in Table 12.5.

Because the interaction of the various components is often complex, computer

Table 12.4 Example of cross over points in maintenance

	1	2	3	4	5
Depreciation	7500	5250	3675	2575	2000
Tax/insurance	1000	1000	1000	1000	1000
Diesel/tyres	12000	12250	12500	13500	14000
Maintenance	500	1500	2800	5500	7400
Total	21000	20000	19975	22575	24400

Table 12.5   Planned maintenance component forecast

Component	Likely failure (miles)	Replacement (miles)
Alternator	60 000	55 000
Camshaft	75 000	68 000

programs have been developed to enable the transport manager to maximize efficiency at the lowest cost (see below).

LOAD PLANNING

Once a company has opted to own its physical resources and has acquired a fleet of vehicles, it is faced with the task of managing and organizing its delivery process. The job is a complex one. Customers—or demand centres in load planning jargon—will be situated in different places; often they will only accept loads at certain times, sometimes called the 'delivery window'; they will want different levels of service. The supplier must consider in addition the total delivery time available which is limited by the working day; the speed at which the transport system operates between the delivery points and any restrictions that may exist; any delays that may occur at the customer; the speed at which the customer can offload the goods. All these demands must be evaluated against the cost of the physical distribution system chosen.

One of the guiding principles of effective distribution management is *consolidation:* grouping as many orders together as possible to lower the unit cost. Obviously it can be improved by lengthening the delivery times offered to customers, enabling loads to be collected for transport to the same area. Alternatively, the company can specify a steadily higher minimum order level to ensure that vehicles are not travelling with small, uneconomic loads. Ultimately, however, there will be limitations to their use as the reality of load planning is that service priorities overcome pure cost considerations and compromises will continually be sought. Will it, for example, be more cost effective to use the largest possible load to service the largest possible number of customers; or use transport systems with smaller load sizes to deliver to a smaller number of customers? As the larger vehicle will have to travel longer distances, and will often be delayed at delivery points, the choice may not in reality be as cost effective as the use of smaller vehicles. In each case, the difficulty of obtaining an optimal journey plan will be considerable and a number of methods have evolved, from simple manual systems to more complex computer based approaches. For the majority operating their own fleet of vehicles computer optimization will be essential, but a brief review of manual methods is provided.

SDS, or Simplified Delivery Service, was the first manual system developed, and still is with variants, used by many small and medium sized companies. It involves the creation in the distribution department of pigeon holes for the geographic area serviced by the depot—one for each sub-area acting as a receptacle for orders for that sub-area. Loads are then built up from the most distant sub-area with the load planner working from the pigeon holes building up a load for the vehicle. The system is easy to install and very flexible but takes insufficient account of order priorities or the time that it takes to reach each sub-area, and as a result the solutions tend to be suboptimal.

A more commonly employed evolution of SDS is the TRANSIT (Timebased Routing and Scheduling of Industrial Transport) system. Using an Ordnance Survey map it breaks down the area into blocks of 10 square kilometres, each with the same delivery times from the central depot and broadly equivalent times within the block. The load planner is then able to allocate orders to the relevant squares and define the time necessary to service the deliveries. Loads can then be filled and drivers allocated. TRANSIT based approaches to load planning are far more effective in producing full loads and balancing the work between the various delivery drivers. It can also be effective in handling the problems caused by different order priorities—by insisting that all these orders are handled first, and the less urgent orders in the next, or following journey cycles.

Though TRANSIT based load management is an improvement over SDS systems, the interaction between the various grid areas tends not to be considered. The TRANSIT system can be said to be centrifugal in that the timings are determined from the centre and that routing decisions at the periphery of the delivery area are not optimal. The 'Savings' approach developed to improve the ability of the calculations to deal with the inter-connectability of the various delivery points in the network (Figure 12.1). From the basic savings equation it is possible to create a series of distance matrices and savings matrices from the various delivery points to the warehouse to determine the most cost effective routing.

$$S_{ij} = D_{oi} + D_{oj} + D_{ij}$$

Where:

S_{ij} = distance saving by linking together any two delivery points i and j
D_{oi} = distance between depot O and delivery point i
D_{oj} = distance between depot O and delivery point j
D_{ij} = distance between the two delivery points i and j

The 'Savings' method needs to be applied with the necessary constraints of maximum load and maximum journey time. For a normal delivery system in the UK this could be

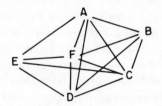

Figure 12.1 Inter-connectability between delivery points—the 'Savings' approach

put at 40 tons and $7\frac{1}{2}$ hours, though distribution systems employing smaller vans face differing constraints. The grid created can determine the gradient of savings from the greatest to the least. These savings can then be measured against the constraints operating for the specific type of vehicle employed.

Experience of the 'Savings' method reveals that savings are additive with further customers in the system, the closer the customers. The further customers are from the depot, the greater the savings achieved by linking customers. Arc type routes will provide greater savings than linear routing but total mileage may be higher than other types of routing. The 'Savings' method, however, works on the assumption that there is only one warehouse in the network, that drivers start and finish from the same point, and that each customer will have the same delivery requirements.

Separating local from distant deliveries

Because local deliveries are often cost ineffective for large vehicles some companies define areas to be serviced by third party distribution near the depot and keep company owned vehicles for longer distances. The main problem is how the company defines the local area for delivery, as changes in the level of customer demand and location continually alter the area in which third party transport is effective, especially if large customers are serviced by direct delivery from the production point.

Where a supplier has discrete areas of demand, for example major cities such as London, Birmingham, Manchester, separate supply 'hubs' or 'seed points' can be established and the load planning set from these hub points with the vehicle travelling directly from the warehouse to the supply area. Such solutions are generally suboptimal, as they ignore the possible economies of expanding the number of warehouse sites (see Chapter 7) and create artificial divisions between what may be very closely connected geographical areas, thereby excluding the possibility of improving on the load planning by having the vehicle cross over into other areas.

Computer methods for vehicle routing

The complex planning problems in organizing and controlling a wide distribution area can be resolved through the growing number of computer programs that identify the savings on route planning, and allow the distribution planner to enter the relevant constraints into the analysis. As the price of these packages is relatively low in relation to the potential savings, they provide the obvious solution to route planning for the majority of medium or large sized companies, (see below). In common with other problems in distribution planning the more complex the problem the greater the sophistication of the program and processing power required. Computerized routing generally substantially improves both the speed and accuracy of routing and provides the facility of interaction with other simulation systems to determine new warehouse locations. The main disadvantages are the high cost and level of the training that the systems demand and a slight lack of flexibility when, for example, road systems change, though even this problem has been overcome by updating the road information available within the system in certain programmes (see below).

Monitoring the effectiveness of the load planning system

High physical distribution costs make it important to continually monitor and evaluate the effectiveness of the method of load planning in operation. Circumstances change and it becomes essential to check the assumptions and calculations on which a load planning method is based. Here are some of the areas where change is likely to occur.

A key assumption in many load planning models is an estimate of journey and unloading time between delivery points and the depot. It is important to identify those areas within the delivery network where these assumptions are no longer valid, so that the schedule can be improved. The cost environment that initially favoured a particular type of load delivery system may not continue to be valid indefinitely. Introducing new types of vehicles with different load capacities and differing speeds into the calculations will permit the load planner to review the effectiveness of the vehicle types employed in relation to the distribution task.

COMPUTER SOFTWARE

Name: Dayload. Software House: Synergy Distribution. Supplier: NCR

Dayload is an interactive daily vehicle scheduling system. It will schedule vehicles, optimizing distances and ensuring maximum efficient loading. Late orders can be catered for without upsetting the schedule's resource savings.

Name: Roadnet. Software House: Synergy Distribution. Supplier: NCR

Roadnet is a computerized road map of the UK and Western Europe maintained with up to the minute information. It can be used to calculate and describe routes between any two locations or sets of locations, list the minimum times or distances between sets of locations and produce a matrix of minimum times and distances.

Name: Hyfleet. Software House: Hytec. Supplier: NCR

Hyfleet is an integrated fleet management system that covers maintenance/repair scheduling, vehicle inventory, vehicle running costs, tax and insurance renewal, vehicle replacement, VAT, and workshop management.

Name: Tranman. Software House: Perthcrest. Supplier: NCR

Tranman provides vehicle maintenance and operating costs, vehicle preventive maintenance, vehicle parts inventory control, tacograph analysis.

Name: V-Route. Software House: 3X. System: IBM

Comprehensive delivery optimization package. Allows for delivery window at each site, turn round times, trunking points, rest periods and maximum permissible driver hours, aggregates part pallets, prioritization of loads, use of contract vehicles. Provides printouts of distance and fuel utilization, and identifies best vehicles within fleets of varying size.

DISTRIBUTION ASSIGNMENTS

1 You are provided with the following grid containing the orders that need to be delivered in the next two days. There are available two lorries each of which can carry up to 20 tons. The average journey time within the region is 20 mph, and the drivers are limited to an eight hour day which includes their return to the warehouse. Devise a cost efficient delivery programme.

Distances between customer locations

	A	B	C	D	E	F	G	H	I
A		40	60	55	50	30	80	35	35
B			30	55	75	35	45	70	30
C				45	75	35	40	85	65
D					40	25	80	65	80
E						45	115	35	85
F							70	50	50
G								115	65
H									65

2 Using the savings method consider how transport should be organized for the attached grid of delivery points.

Grid areas

	1	2	3	4	5	6	7	8	9	10
1	5	8	15	6	7	22	29	4	—	25
2	16	12	22	—	45	55	12	11	17	8
3	7	32	9	2	1	6	27	15	11	13
4	13	15	12	22	14	11	18	6	7	65
5	12	11	5	6	*	2	7	11	9	14
6	13	6	31	12	4	5	4	3	2	—
7	11	7	13	8	3	22	21	19	—	—
8	8	2	11	1	2	—	11	8	5	23
9	12	—	11	16	11	5	23	14	9	4
10	21	11	12	14	15	—	—	3	1	1

*production point.

Each grid square is ten miles by ten miles.

Assume that each delivery includes 30 minutes unloading time regardless of load size.

Maximise efficiency of load planning in achieving deliveries within minimum time
—should extra vehicles be required, the plant will also have to include the cost and
time of these deliveries.

3 Using a road map of the area with your town as the centre, and making
assumptions about the journey time produce a TRANSIT delivery plan which will
optimize the delivery cycle for a company delivering product by road. Assume that
journey times are equivalent to road distance, that the average speed across the
ground is 30 mph, each town has five delivery points with an average unloading time of
30 minutes and that the drivers are limited to a total working day of eight hours.

4 The distribution planner in a company has the choice between two alternative
third party truckers for long distance deliveries to a particular customer which has the
following ordering pattern:

Annual sales	25 000 tons/year
Price	£400 ton
Transport loads	45 tons
Carrying costs	20 per cent per annum
Inventory stock level	95 per cent
Service level constant	2.00

The alternative services offer the following service:

	A	B	C
Transit time	5.4	6.8	7.2
Variation	2.0	3.0	3.5
Cost per load	£1000	£950	£920

Which alternative service should be chosen to meet the planner's requirements?

Order Processing

Throughout this book we have stressed that a major preoccupation of the distribution planner is the provision of an efficient and cost effective service to the customer. The customer is involved only indirectly in most aspects of the planning process and represents little more than this distant goal. For example, it is of little relevance to the customer where the supplier locates its factories or its warehouses. Nevertheless, there are areas of distribution that directly concern customers or channel members—that they receive from the supplier information about product and product availability, that they will receive their goods in the promised time and continued information about the orders' progress. Order processing is very much the visible part of the distribution iceberg. It is the part, along with the sales force discussed in the following chapter, that will epitomize the customer's experience of the supplier.

How the order processing system is organized is therefore crucial to achieving the service objectives of distribution by ensuring adequate speed, accuracy, reliability and information about the progress of orders. Table 13.1 shows how, as the order passes through the system, problems may arise for management at each stage. But from the customer's perspective it is the entire process that succeeds or fails.

EFFICIENCY AND ORDER PROCESSING SYSTEMS

The order processing system is also valuable to the supplier company for a number of reasons. It is a key source of *information* about day to day efficiency: how orders are being met, whether customers are getting their expected level of service, and where the main problems are being encountered. The role of the order processing system in providing much of the information necessary for long-term planning will be considered in Chapter 15.

Various *priorities* are implemented through the order processing system. In most companies where orders queue for despatch, order processing guidelines determine how they are handled: which order has priority and which can be delayed. Typically, small companies deal with orders as they come in either on a first in first out basis, or on the basis of their complexity with the more complex orders initiated first. As the

Table 13.1   Typical order processing cycle

Location	Customer to Sales Office	Order Processing	Warehouse	Transport	Customer
Days required	$1\frac{1}{2}$	$1\frac{1}{2}$	3	2	$\frac{1}{2}$
Cumulative days		3	6	8	$8\frac{1}{2}$
	Order Processing Phase			Shipment Phase	

company grows and distribution costs rise, there is a perceived need for better consolidation of orders, and larger companies establish order priorities based on customer categorization, establishing an order cycle target time for each particular type of customer. Much of the cost effectiveness of the distribution process hinges on the effective management of these priorities and on whether the order processing system is flexible enough to provide a mixed level of service—high for important customers and low for others.

The *documentation* function of the order processing system is important in ensuring that payment is made by providing legal evidence that goods have been provided and shipped. It will also serve as a source of information about the consignment for the customer and the company. In a previous chapter we discussed the problems of documentation in supplying overseas markets, but delays in documentation in all markets can lead to decreases in cash flow which is one of the main causes of business failure. Correct documentation will be most important when dealing with overseas markets, and earlier chapters have commented on the high rate of delayed payment due to shortcomings in the documentation of export orders.

Operating in the international environment will indeed require a whole range of new documentation to be generated during the order processing phase. Some of the more important are outlined in Table 13.2. In addition to these shipping documents, the company will have to consider carefully the documentary credit system that will

Table 13.2   Examples of documentation in export trade

Item	Contains
Bill of lading	Contents of shipment contract between shipper and supplier
Airway bill	Similar to bill of lading for air shipments
Certificate of origin	Notarized document by consular authorities identifying the point of origin of the goods
T form	Shows duty paid on non-EEC goods
Hazardous cargo declaration	Indicates specific stowage requirements
TIR Carnet	Applies to container transport overland for intermediate customs clearance

Source: West A., Marketing Overseas, Pitman, 1987.

Table 13.3 Integrating sales callage frequency with the order cycle

Customer type	Sales callage frequency	Order cycle	Service cycle
A	twice weekly	3 days	6 days
B	weekly	4/5 days	12 days
C	bi-weekly	6 days	20 days
D	monthly	9 days	40 days
E	quarterly	12 days	130 days

be used. Within the UK, the Board of Trade has developed a computer package called SPEX to help with the complexities of documentation in international trade, as part of their SITRO or Simplification of International Trade programme. Other computer packages have also been developed to aid in this area (see below).

Finally, order processing has a crucial role in *integration*. It will give hard information to measure the efficiency of the various departments against the requirements of both customer and the order cycle. One of the most visible is the relationship between sales callage patterns and delivery schedules. As minor customers receive sales calls infrequently, their expectations on delivery schedules will be limited. In contrast, major customers receiving frequent sales calls expect higher levels of service. The combination of the time between sales calls and the total order cycle time establishes a service cycle for the particular customer which will decide the number of days that the customer can conceivably be without stock. Reducing the order cycle time for particular customers or increasing the callage rate will lead to a decrease in the total service cycle. Table 13.3 emphasizes the ability of the order processing system to deliver a mixed service level to different categories of customers, enabling the distribution system to achieve the maximum flexibility and load consolidation.

Transport effectiveness, warehouse efficiency and inventory policies will also be measurable in a similar fashion against the demands of the order processing system.

CONTROLLING THE ORDER PROCESSING SYSTEM

Most order processing systems, whether manual or computer based, can be divided into component parts each providing information and generating documentation (see Table 13.4). An analysis of each gives an understanding of trade-offs that the company can explore to improve the speed, accuracy or reliability of the system by appropriate investment.

Order collection

Order collection refers to the transmission of a verbal or written order to the company. Order forms vary in level of complexity according to the company and product

Table 13.4 The order cycle and accompanying documentation

Phase	Associated documentation
Order collection	Order form
Order checking for inconsistencies	Minimum volume/delivery time
Credit checking	Credit clearance
Inventory check	Advice/production notes
Warehouse instructions	Packing slip/Third party advice/ commission statement
Order assembly	
Despatch	Invoice/bill of lading
Delivery confirmation documentation return	Posting delivery
Post-delivery	Receipt of payment

involved. At the simplest level the mail order company will receive an order through the post for a low cost kitchen utensil. At the other extreme a firm such as GEC may receive an order for generators for a power station. Although quite different levels of documentation are involved, it is still vital that it is as standard as possible. This helps to ensure that components of the order are clearly identified and coded to speed up the transfer of orders through the system, and minimizing possible sources of confusion within the supplier company with each unit and component having a unique method of identification. Multiple copy pre-printed forms such as those supplied by NCR in manual order processing systems have become a popular method of reducing problems of non-standardization. Products are clearly identified by code and multiple copies are available for customer and supplier recording requirements.

For companies in the industrial sector especially, it is the sales force that is mainly involved in order collection. Even so the company needs a high level of training and internal in-company information provision to minimize possible problems in order collection. The most important potential areas of conflict are the specific terms and conditions under which the goods are sold; the ability of the intermediary to negotiate on price; and the supply of detailed information on product availability and delivery times.

Investment in standardized order forms is not the only improvement that companies can make in order collection. Where postal systems are inadequate, the transfer of orders from the sales office or sales representative to despatch point often significantly delays the entire order cycle. UK surveys question the ability of the postal system to deliver within one working day over long distances. Investment in portable computer facilities or other electronic aids such as facsimile (fax) machines aid the transfer of orders from the field to head office. Where such systems have been introduced the benefits to the sales force extend to electronic mail and improved information transfer, updated pricing and other sales conditions. Such systems are increasingly used in a wide range of consumer and industrial sales forces, especially where the computer has become integral for the display of alternative finance schedules and payback periods, such as in the financial services and office equipment sectors.

Order checking

Action standards are needed to check orders for consistency. The most common inconsistencies concern pricing and discounts, closely followed by inaccuracies in product description. Standard order forms help greatly in reducing the latter. So do clear instructions to intermediaries or the sales force. The introduction of computer links between the sales office and the despatch point has also reduced the common errors in pricing and product description. Clear instructions to intermediaries and the sales force also limit confusion about minimum order levels but are insufficient where the order is complex, for example, in the installation of manufacturing equipment or computer networks. Here the preparation of a pro-forma invoice by the sales department will ensure that the order is checked and client agreement obtained before further action is taken.

There are other reasons why a company must check order consistency. A substantially raised order quantity may, for example, indicate that the end user is facing credit problems or is trading outside the immediate area which may conflict with other distribution arrangements. During the period of great expansion in the Middle East many companies attempted to maintain substantially higher prices by minimizing the ability of parallel traders—individuals buying in the home market and selling overseas outside the established distributor networks—to buy large quantities of product at low prices from the wholesale networks in the home market. Orders may be received from outside the traditional distribution channels or from an intermediary that is unwilling to co-operate with the company in maintaining particular price levels. As these types of order checking involve other departments within the company, marketing for example, senior management must establish clear guidelines about what orders will be met and what action should be taken if the order is not to be supplied. The legal consequences of not supplying an order on grounds other than that of payment must be understood by the personnel involved in the order processing system: for example, the Argos discount group took a number of companies to court for refusing to supply goods.

Credit checking

Part of the checking involved in order processing includes procedures and guidelines on credit—whether credit should be extended, and also what its limits are. A distinction is generally drawn between new customers and those that have had a longer-term relationship with the firm. For the new customer, laid down procedures should not allow credit above a certain sales value (or in many cases, not at all) without first checking credit worthiness and trading record, and receiving in certain cases trade references. For the established customer, records are needed on the level of any

Table 13.5 Example of a customer/credit analysis

Customer	Current order	30 days	60 days	90 days	Limit	Stop
A	300	500	100	—	1000	No
B	500	200	—	200	600	Yes

outstanding payments, and how overdue they are before further stock is released (Table 13.5), the 'credit ceiling'.

Credit ceilings are an important component of the credit checking procedure. Where a firm uses outside agencies to factor invoices—that is provide part payment or credit against the invoice value—credit checking can become more complex and time consuming, though in both cases the supplier's finance department will play a major part in carrying out the necessary clearance work.

Inventory check

Following the credit check, steps must be taken to ascertain whether inventory levels permit the order to be fully met and what action should be taken if it cannot be filled. This will almost certainly involve liaison between several departments and the completion of additional documentation. The sales administration or sales department need information about the proposed delivery dates and the likely non-availability of stock so that the customer can be informed; the production department about the stock movement to update the production schedule, or to initiate back ordering if necessary. Again, the effective transfer of information to the customer and the order taker especially is crucial to minimize potential problems. If a customer is kept well acquainted with the inventory situation most of these problems will not exist, and supplying the sales force with a weekly stock availability list (see Table 13.6) helps them to complete orders with few out-of-stock items. Of course, informing customers about the non-availability of stock has its disadvantages—it may mean that orders will not be placed. As orders are not placed, no inventory will be required, a classic example of a self fulfilling prophecy. Indeed it is rumoured that one major consumer goods retailer operated such a stock replenishment system for the better part of a

Table 13.6 Information listing on stock availability—week 11

Product	Stock availability	Next planned production
A	Ex-stock	—
B	Out of stock	week 15
C	week 12	
D	Ex-stock	week 13

year, explaining the long and mysterious absences of best selling lines, which could not be reordered as there had been no sales of them!

Motivation is also an important feedback to keeping intermediaries and sales representatives informed of stock availability (see Chapter 4). Achieving a sale which is then cancelled through lack of stock is considered one of the most demotivating issues in sales management.

Warehouse instructions

Information in the form of a packing slip gives the supplier's warehouse the go-ahead to initiate a picking routine for the order. Any special packing requirements accompany the packing slip which has the delivery instructions, and the delivery date. The warehouse manager can then assign priorities to the load completion. The packing slip will also generate information to other parts of the company and distribution system: to third party transporters if they are utilized, to update the warehouse information system on the availability of stock, to outside warehouses if delivery is to take place from regional depots, and the marketing and sales department for monthly sales figures. Commonly at this point, many firms prepare commission statements for the sales force as the packing slip finalizes the total size and value of the outgoing order rather than the value of the order booked. This further underlines the importance of maintaining an accurate flow of information on product availability to intermediaries or the sales force as restricted product availability will mean reduction in revenue for both.

Transport planning/post-delivery

The packing slip has a further role in delivery planning and transport allocation. Using the information on the packing slip, the load planner must decide how best to consolidate the orders for delivery to particular areas in the territory. Improving the speed of the order processing system may mean that an increased number of orders are available for delivery earlier than required by the customer. This substantially improves the flexibility of the load planner's task as it will make possible maximum load consolidation. The disadvantage of such an approach is that there will often be large quantities of static stock awaiting delivery—an order once picked is no longer available for other customers—a further example of a trade-off which the distribution planner must evaluate. Once the load has left the warehouse with the delivery note, a copy will be sent to accounts for the creation of the invoice and to sales administration in case there is need for further follow-up.

With the completion of the delivery, the order processing system must check that the documents confirming delivery are matched up with the initial packing slips. Any future enquiry can then be speedily and effectively managed. Copies of these documents are retained by the finance department.

TRENDS IN ORDER PROCESSING SYSTEMS

Computerization dominates trends in order processing systems. Many retailers, for example, are linking electronic point of sale systems (EPOS) with the order processing system. Some companies have provided sales forces with computers that permit a check with the central system for product availability, delivery times and the like. Orders can then pass straight through to the warehouse for despatch. The development of computerization has meant that more order processing systems are able to replace sequential order processing with systems that handle events in parallel, and reduce the total time involved in the order cycle. Integrated software packages allow a single strand of order processing information to be automatically transferred to the construction of invoices, the control of inventory, and the maintenance of accounts. This has done much to improve the productivity of order processing.

This level of sophistication achieved through computerization is, however, costly. Once installed, it must be maintained to a high standard as breakdowns in computer support will have a drastic effect on the entire order processing systems, in contrast to manual methods where duplicate copies of paperwork are retained to provide a record of all invoices generated within the system. Simpler systems are available for use on microcomputers and these are increasingly used by small to medium sized organizations to integrate order processing and the accounting system.

MONITORING THE ORDER PROCESSING SYSTEM

The most important monitoring information in the order processing system will be the speed of processing, the level of emergency delivery, and the total cost.

Though the average order cycle time yields valuable information about the system's efficiency, it is important to attempt to identify the slowest and fastest case in order to eliminate possible weakness, and to learn from the fastest cycle period which factors are important in achieving a speedy turn round of order processing. A key output criterion of the order processing system is the ability to deliver product within the stated time. Failure to achieve the standards set requires a reappraisal of the operating procedures.

Inefficiency in the order processing or stock control systems can make necessary emergency or special deliveries outside the normal planned delivery schedule. Though most companies experience this on occasion, and indeed will budget it as exceptional expenditure, a rising trend of emergency deliveries indicates a failure of the system to provide an adequate level of service under normal operating conditions.

As volumes change, so will the cost of the order processing system. It will therefore need monitoring to check that costs are not rising out of line with the percentage change in volume. This is particularly relevant for a rapidly growing company using a manual order processing system. As volumes increase the costs of ensuring that the system works effectively and smoothly may rise disproportionately if the number of people employed goes up substantially. This then is the point when the introduction of a computerized system should be considered.

COMPUTER SOFTWARE

Name: Goldcrest Business Systems. Software House: Goldcrest. System: NCR

Sales order processing, invoicing, stock control, sales ledger, sales analysis, purchase order buying, purchase ledger, nominal ledger, payroll, raw material processing, job costing.

Name: Stock Control and Purchase Ordering. Software House: 3X. System: IBM

Provides a multi-site, multi-supplier stock control system. Enables company to forecast based on usage, supply lead time, purchase orders due, minimum stock level.

Name: Perspective/700. Software House: LIOCS. System: Digital

Perspective/700 inventory management provides a multi-location, multi-company organization to record and control inventory transactions throughout the network.

Name: MAP Stock Control. Software House: MAP. System: PC Compatible

A personal computer package that provides a comprehensive stock control system for the medium sized company operating from a single site warehouse.

Name: Camsoft Stock Control. Software House: Camsoft. System: PC Compatible

A personal computer package that provides a comprehensive stock control system for the medium sized company operating from a single site warehouse.

Name: Multisoft Accounts. Software House: Multisoft. System: PC Compatible

Provides an integrated sales, accounts, purchase, stock and nominal ledger system for microcomputer systems at single locations.

DISTRIBUTION ASSIGNMENTS

1 Your company, which supplies bulk building materials to wholesalers, is approached by one of the leading builders in the country with a request that it receives supplies direct within three days of placing an order rather than the ten days that wholesalers receive their orders within. Write a report on the implications of such a change for the order processing system.

2 Choose a certain sector of the consumer durables market—carpets or bathroom equipment, for example—and investigate the delivery times that are offered by the various manufacturers. Would shortening the delivery time improve any company's competitive position?

3 A company is considering a range of expansion plans which include market development, product development and diversification. Write a report on the implications of these alternatives for the order processing system and the sales force.

4 A company has recently carried out a questionnaire of all its customers on their perceptions of how effective the company distribution is. The results of this survey are worrying. What action would you suggest and why?

Factor	Percentage of customers satisfied
Speed	55
Reliability	33
Completeness	47
Information provision	12

Sales Management—Its Role in Distribution

Previous chapters have mentioned the essential role of a sales force as part of distribution management. More than even the order processing system, the sales force is the visible part of the system for the majority of companies. How important a part of the distribution system it will be depends on the complexity of the selling task, the way in which the sales force is organized and the objectives the firm is pursuing in the market.

Every market sector makes specific demands on the way the firm organizes its selling effort. To start with, it will define the selling skills and personnel required. As an industry becomes more complex, the level of skill required rises. Sales tasks can vary from that of the van salesman who is essentially providing physical delivery of the product but who may also be taking some orders; through the classic picture of the consumer goods sales representative whose main task is to gain repeat orders from established customers for non-technical products; to the more demanding role of the sales representative facing the task of initiating purchase of high value technical equipment in industrial markets. The type of selling tasks and the skills required are outlined in Table 14.1.

The differences in the selling task influence the relative importance of the sales force in the marketing mix of both consumer and industrial markets. As the product becomes more complex and expensive the percentage of the firm's promotional budget that will be spent on the sales force will steadily increase. This is in part a reflection of the growing importance of direct delivery in the industrial market. Such considerations do not solely affect the industrial market, as firms operating in the consumer market with technical or complex products will face similar investment decisions—double glazing and insurance companies are two examples. Equitable Life, one of the leading life insurance companies in the UK, maintains a sales force of several hundred as it concentrates on direct sales to individuals and small companies and does not deal through intermediaries. Such varying sales tasks in various industries will require the sales representatives to gain different skills and knowledge.

At the simplest level of task specialization, the representative is performing a purely *administrative* role. Where the sales representative is acting as an order taker, the role will be essentially that of the *information provider*—a source of information, on pricing, promotional offers, and product availability. In more complicated sales environments, the sales representative is acting more as an *adviser*—attempting to provide the best solutions to problems that the customer is facing. Such jobs often have a high technical content and an understanding of how organizational decisions are arrived at, problems that other sales tasks tend not to face.

INTEGRATING THE SALES FORCE WITH COMPANY OBJECTIVES

The need for a sales force will be determined partly by the product policy that the company is pursuing, outlined in Chapter 2, and the type of distribution channel the company has chosen to fulfil its objectives.

These two factors will determine what type of sales skills are necessary to meet the demands of the customers, the type of individuals that should be recruited, how they should be trained, motivated and controlled. Dealing with wholesalers will, for example, demand a different range of skills from dealing direct with end users. The wholesaler based sales representative will have to be able to train and motivate wholesaler representatives, a task not required for direct contact with the customer. Expansion overseas will make extra demands upon the sales force with a wide range of required additional skills.

The type of sales task and the variation in the customer demands will secondly influence the way in which the sales staff are organized. Where the level of sales skill required is low and customers vary little in their product demands, it is logical to expect the same sales representative to service all customers within a specific area. This *geographical* basis for organization was the historical method of organizing the sales force and is still used in several industries—dividing the entire market into regions and allocating all customers within them to one sales representative. When the product range becomes too extensive for an individual sales representative to handle effectively though customers are still relatively homogeneous in their demands, a geographic division continues to be used with individual sales representatives within an area having responsibility for particular *product* ranges. Product divisions are most commonly found within companies with wide product ranges, notably wholesalers or industrial distributors.

Where there is an increasing demand for different and specialized solutions to particular problems, a sales force oriented towards specific customer groups with

Table 14.1   Sales tasks and requirements

Sales task	Complexity	Knowledge requirement	Negotiation skills
Van salesman	Low	Low	Low
Consumer retail	Low	Moderate	Moderate
Industrial equipment	High	High	High

common problems may become more and more essential. The sales representative is *customer* based, using whatever products and services the company provides to provide the appropriate solutions to the customers' problems. As might be expected, such organizational approaches will be most commonly found in companies selling complex equipment, such as computers or construction equipment. Thus ICL, the major British computer firm, has a policy of dividing its sales force on a customer basis. For example, there are education, defence, office and health service divisions each developing a detailed understanding of specific problems within each market sector. Education demands a very different type of computing system in general from that of the office, with many terminals all in constant use, requiring an entirely different system configuration.

For most companies the increasing concentration of buying power in a small number of large outlets has identified the requirement to augment the service provided to such customers. This has meant the development of a separate *national accounts* negotiating team. Such groups, which often include separate accountants, sales negotiators and marketing specialists, and often a specialist in distribution, have become crucial in the development of trade marketing or trade distribution agreements (see Chapters 4 and 15).

WORK LOAD ANALYSIS

High levels of service from the sales force, in common with high levels of distribution coverage, enable the firm to gain a competitive advantage in the market. However, the increase in competitive advantage must be judged against the steadily increasing cost. Organizing an effective sales force will require an analysis of the pay-offs between rising costs and higher levels of sales. The work load on the sales force will be a product of company policy, the number of customers in the market, and the callage or service demands of each customer type. From such calculations, the optimal amount of time that the sales representative should spend in front of each client, and the total amount of time required to support a particular distribution system can be evolved.

Company policy will again initially set the scene in determining the work load. As has been discussed in earlier chapters, product abandonment, market development, market penetration, product development and diversification policies will all have different effects on the customer/company interaction. Obviously product abandonment will be the most straightforward for the sales force, involving a reduction in contact with current customers. Market penetration policies, requiring a growth in consumption of current products by current customers, will require the sales force to spend more time on each sales visit attempting to expand the historic levels of orders. Market development by contrast will demand a much higher percentage of time being spent in developing new customer contacts. This type of selling is often called missionary activity, and the ratio between time spent and initial orders achieved will be reduced. Product development policies will also require an increased time spent in front of the customer in explaining new products. Diversification will make the most extreme demands on the work load of the sales force as they will be involved in selling new product concepts to new customers.

Each type of company policy will require a minimum amount of time to achieve an effective contact will the customer. Increasing this time spent in front of the customer will initially often improve the effectiveness of the sales force, but this will then be followed by a reduction, as additional time becomes less and less effective in achieving improved sales results. Where the optimum exists is a problem that each company will need to analyse carefully as it will affect the overall work loading of the entire sales force and the way in which the company budgets for the sales operation. Obviously, the optimum time spent will be different for large customers or important customers than for small, and this will further complicate the calculation. The computer based Callplan model allows the company to optimize the number of sales representatives based on the concept of optimum selling time. In addition to computer based methods there exist other more straightforward calculations that can be used to identify the likely optimum time.

In addition to an optimum individual callage time, customers will vary as to the number of times they will need to be contacted per sales period or company planning period. For important customers, the frequency will be determined by their stocking policy—large companies requiring frequent visits and rapid order cycles (see Chapter 13). For other and smaller customers, the callage frequency will be determined by the cost effectiveness of the call.

Customers can be effectively categorized according to both the frequency of the sales callage required and the amount of time that will need to be spent with each such customer. In practical terms in the consumer goods sector these categorizations are usually synonymous with distribution channels. For example, multiple chains would be categorized as A, requiring the most frequent visits and the longest sales times; regional chains category B, wholesalers category C, small stores category D and specialists category E. Similar approaches can be developed for the industrial market using criteria such as size of company, location, type of activity, technology used, buying methods, and price sensitivity.

For each market, there will be a number of customers in each category, and this information can be used to build up an analysis of the total time that will be spent by the sales force and also derive the likely load upon the order processing system and how it will interact with the sales force operation (see Table 14.2).

Table 14.2   Analysing customer service requirements

Customer	Callage time	Callage frequency	Customer numbers
A	0.50	52	55
B	0.25	26	125
C	0.25	13	225
D	0.25	10	345

CASE: HANDYMAN LTD

Background

Larry Smythe, the Midlands Area Manager of HandyMan Ltd, was examining the possibility of recommending the replacement of the company's existing policy of allocating sales territories on a geographical basis in his area. He was instead considering the potential in reorganizing the sales force either by product type or category of customer.

A family-owned maker of hand tools founded at the end of the nineteenth century, HandyMan Ltd had been taken over some two years earlier by Webber and Blackitt, one of Europe's largest industrial hand tool manufacturers. The group had previously allowed HandyMan to retain its autonomous sales force but spiralling costs were leading it to reappraise the situation with the help of area managers like Larry Smythe. The area managers as well as senior management were being asked to seriously examine the current organization of their sales forces with a view to maximizing efficiency and cutting costs wherever possible. In his brief to the group's sales force managers the Webber and Blackitt Sales Director also suggested that in considering the possibilities for improving sales performance through a reorganization of the sales force, they should also give thought to the proposal that what the group needed was a single sales force, finance department and managing director and common production control. They proceeded to ask the area managers of the operating companies to look at the possibilities of integration of the company's product range in their particular areas and what problems or opportunities would arise.

Webber and Blackitt and the hand tool industry

For a decade beginning in 1960 Webber and Blackitt had experienced a period of phenomenal and acquisitive growth. During that time it acquired control of various companies producing files, spanners and wrenches, precision measuring tools, and pliers. Its manufacturing output is currently about 155 million items across 3500 product lines, with certain specific areas of strength:
1. *Hand tools:* these included saws and saw blades, punches and magnets, nippers and files, spanners and wrenches.
2. *Measurement tools:* micrometers and chucks.
3. *Hydraulics:* jacks and hydraulic conveyor belts.

Strategy

The company had not been over-concerned with plant modernization and until quite recently production of hacksaw blades was so backward that they had to be hand moved from machine to machine eight times and hand shuffled on five other occasions. For the previous five years turnover (apart from acquisitions) in the UK had remained at about £50 million. Of this £36 million comes from hand and torque tools, £5 million from measurement tools with the rest coming from welding rods, cutting wire, hydraulic tube coupling and magnets.

It had also stuck to its old customer base, the engineering industry, selling products without a brand name across its range. Of the total UK hand tool market, including agricultural needs, imports had grown from 27 per cent in 1973 to 47 per cent in 1980. Webber had similarly seen its share of the files market eroded by Portuguese imports to about 25 per cent.

A halving of the Webber and Blackitt workforce formed part of a programme of cost-cutting, rationalization, and modernization initiated in 1980. Sales per employee, estimated at £25 000, however, remained at half of that of some of its foreign competitors. The product range was under investigation and it was inevitable that major changes would take place especially in the rationalization of the number of lines produced.

HandyMan

HandyMan had seen its slice of the British spanner sector eroded from 30 per cent to 16 per cent by 1980. The company also made wrenches, pliers and precision tools and acted as distributors for a substantial part of the parent company's product range.

In the Midlands, Larry Smythe's sales force sold products to four types of customers: engineering contractors, engineering distributors, small specialist shops and DIY superstores.

Engineering distributors

Engineering tool distributors, the company's traditional major market, now accounted for 35 per cent of sales giving HandyMan access to what had in the past been large industrial markets. Purchasing agents for these customers usually ordered equipment directly from the salesmen assigned to that customer. Since HandyMan had become part of Webber and Blackitt and handled the distribution of some of its products the task confronting the sales representative dealing with engineering tool distributors had grown to marathon proportions. Some 500 product lines were now involved. In the area of specialized machine tools, especially in the hydraulic sector, a substantial level of technical knowledge was required. HandyMan management were increasingly concerned about where this steady increase in product range was likely to lead to.

Engineering contractors

Engineering contractors, another important market in the past, accounted for another 20 per cent of HandyMan sales. The size of engineering contractors' operations had decreased substantially over the past decade. They were now mainly small organizations run by self-employed individuals who provided work for perhaps one or two others.

Because of their small size, the contractors were often very difficult to contact. Despite this, selling to them also required a good level of technical expertise.

The importance of the engineering tool distributors and engineering contractors as customers had begun to alter. Sales to them of highly specialized equipment remained stable. But their share of sales in other product areas had begun to decline. In the case of specialized tools they were mainly concerned with the quality of the HandyMan products, particularly reliability and durability. In the past, the price overall of the products bought by them had not been a major issue. As customers, they would continue to require the services of sales staff able to handle technical information.

Specialist shops

Diverse, independent, local stores throughout the area provided another most important market, accounting for about 30 per cent of the total volume. The shops varied substantially in their interests: some were builders' suppliers, others were general hardware shops giving a small amount of space to hand tools, still others were DIY operations and there were one or two specialist shops. These outlets typically also stocked competitors' products and were generally interested only in a comparativaly limited range of items, their requirements being quite different from those of the engineering specialists: spanners, pliers, saws. As customers they did not demand a high level of expertise from the sales representative but were concerned about other matters. There was an increased awareness about price and sales staff were finding that where there was a significant price difference between a HandyMan product and that of the competition the retailer would opt for the latter, particularly if the shelf space available was limited. Retailers were generally reluctant to give shelf space to any new brand especially if it was not supported by advertising. They complained that the recent introduction of brand names by Webber and Blackitt and the streamlined packaging, unsupported by advertising, had only served to confuse customers.

DIY superstores

About 15 per cent of HandyMan's sales in the area was with two DIY superstores. Their share of sales in a number of product areas was increasing at 5 per cent a year.

It had become increasingly clear to the West Midlands sales force that increasingly the engineering contractors were buying tools from these two DIY superstores. HandyMan's competitors had already established a strong presence in these outlets. However, the extensive HandyMan and Webber and Blackitt range provided good bargaining counters when dealing with the stores' buyers. The group could offer products which did not overlap substantially with those of competitors.

Major engineering outlets

Traditionally HandyMan had not sold direct to major engineering customers relying on the distributors to provide this service. Increasingly a number of major firms, particularly in the motor manufacturing sector, were buying direct and bypassing the classical distribution systems. This could become a major problem if more of the highly technical Webber and Blackitt range was handled by the HandyMan sales force.

Sales force personnel

The HandyMan sales force in the West Midlands area were currently geographically assigned. There were seven salesmen and one Area Sales Manager, Larry Smythe.

Over the years Smythe had consistently pressed management with the problems of the growing DIY sector and the changing purchasing pattern of the major engineering works. Previously he had been the most productive and far-sighted salesman. He had managed to get the two DIY superstores to open accounts with HandyMan and his good technical knowledge of the company's products had helped to maintain the level of specialized equipment sold to industrial customers and develop close links with contractors.

Basil Home, Smythe's most senior sales representative, also thought that there were greater opportunities for HandyMan products in retail outlets, superstores in particular, than the sales force realized. His area included the medium sized supermarkets and DIY stores bordering on housing estates. He had discovered that retailers were increasingly responsive to lower prices as a major influence on stockturn and was optimistic about the future. He had worked for HandyMan for over eight years and had moved territory twice within the West Midlands area.

Dennis Skinner's inner city territory was dominated by small retail shops which had been hard hit by the recession. To survive some had been forced into offering special trade price deals to contractors and Skinner found himself occasionally competing with the retailers for business from the contractors. The whole area itself was in decline, although there was talk of a special development programme. As a relative newcomer to HandyMan, young Skinner found his task a tough one.

The territory of Desmond Wilkins was a mainly rural one and his customers had changed little over the seven years he had worked for HandyMan, though Larry had tried several times to make him more active in other sectors. Self-employed contractors remained the bulk of his customers. Large amounts of his time were spent travelling as a result and his expenses were high. Many of the major engineering works had relocated themselves in Desmond's area but he had been unable to make any progress with them.

Before becoming a salesman, John Eliot had worked as an engineering distributor in his allocated sales area, having been a good customer of HandyMan in those times. A significant part of his sales were to friends and contacts he had established earlier in his career. He was openly contemptuous of the move towards selling to the retail sector which he regarded as selling shoddy goods.

James Grant had been very successful in developing the industrial engineering customer base in his territory. His technical expertise was often commented on by major customers including the army ordnance factory with which he had started to build up business.

Nigel Conradi had on many occasions just failed to win national sales competitions. He had aggressively build up his territory sales, particularly to the retail sector and the large DIY superstore that had become established in his area.

Alessia Brown had recently joined the sales force from the parent company. She was part of the management training scheme in operation at Blackitt and Webber which had recently been introduced by the new personnel director. Development of other sales expertise after a successful stint selling complex hydraulic equipment in the South of England to major clients was seen as a preliminary step to sales management.

Sales force organization

Larry Smythe considered three different organizational plans. First, a specific geographical territory would be assigned to each salesman, with the salesman in each territory being responsible for the entire range of HandyMan products and other products of the Blackitt range. Larry thought that this would cut down journey time and improve representatives' knowledge of the area. It would demand a considerable amount of retraining and increased product knowledge.

Plan 2 involved the specialization by customer type. Two salesmen would cover all the retail stores, two the contractors and two the industrial outlets, with a geographical division within the product specialization. Some Blackitt tools could be included also in this reorganization.

Plan 3 involved specialization by type of product divided into hand tools, measuring equipment and the hydraulic sector. This would have the advantage that the salesmen would be able to concentrate on the new range of Blackitt products that would be introduced.

Larry was also concerned that the changing nature of the products and customers might necessitate the development of a national or major accounts function. This had not initially appeared as part of his brief and he wondered what the implications within the rest of the Blackitt and Webber organization might be if he put this forward as another avenue of possible developments.

DISTRIBUTION ASSIGNMENTS

1   You are working for a company which concentrates solely on achieving sales volume of its range of soft drinks. Write a memorandum on the problems this might cause the company in the short-term.

2   You have recently been appointed as assistant sales manager for a company expanding from the North of England to the South and have been asked to write a report on the sales management issues that will need to be considered.

3   As a management consultant you are asked to advise on how a wholesaler should handle a steady increase in the range of industrial components that are sold by its sales force, with the breakdown of product and customer as follows:

	Per cent sales by customer type			
Range	A	B	C	D
1	10	30	40	20
2	35	15	25	25
3	60	5	15	20
4	15	45	5	35
5	5	25	25	45

4 You are asked to prepare a report on the proposal of a computer company that currently sells through 120 local distributors on its intention of moving towards supplying direct the main hospitals and colleges. What other implications will this have for the distribution system?

5 Analyse the stores on the high street. What does this tell you about the need for the establishment of a national accounts administration, and in which areas would locally based sales representatives continue to operate?

Implementing Change in Distribution

Discussion in this book has focused on the importance of the management of distribution not only in the reduction of cost, but also in the development of competitive advantage. How then, should a firm set about the task of controlling and re-evaluating its distribution system? Throughout our analysis we have shown that it is well nigh impossible to limit the impact of a particular planning decision to one area of company activity, and that many decisions will have knock-on effects in other areas.

However, for the sake of analysis we shall consider four main issues as being of overriding importance for distribution policy. Because distribution policy influences many areas of company activity, co-ordination is essential and the first key element is the need for effective *structure* within the firm to organize and implement the distribution plan. Building on this structure is the collation and analysis of *information* about the operation of the company's current organization of distribution, competitive trends and customer demands. This allows the firm to develop a new series of *goals and objectives* which will define where the company should invest to meet the changing market and customer requirements. From these objectives the distribution planner will be able to refine the components of the *distribution plan*—channels, production, warehousing, inventory, physical distribution and order processing systems, and from an understanding of the various trade-offs produce the most cost effective solution to the problems posed by those objectives.

ORGANIZATION DESIGN

Though the fine details of organization design are outside the scope of this book (indeed they are enough to fill, and do fill, many volumes) the tendency is for organizational issues to be totally ignored in any study of functional aspects of the firm. Rarely, therefore, will studies on marketing or product management consider the organizational issues that influence whether a particular policy will succeed, except in the case of studies on innovation. In such a multi-disciplinary area as distribution management it is hardly surprising that those firms that do not critically consider the organizational requirements for distribution management are unlikely to achieve effective implementation of the company's objectives. The major elements that influence the effective management of distribution are analysed in the rest of this section.

Matching responsibility and authority

Where an individual or department is responsible for implementing decisions it should have the authority to allocate the resources necessary to achieve the desired result. Within the context of distribution management, where the resources involved and the contribution towards the final costs of the product are substantial, it is logical for the control of distribution to be located at a senior level within the company. Therefore it might be expected that in industries with high levels of cost contribution from distribution, such as chemicals, paper, and metal manufacturers, a board level appointment with the responsibility of controlling the distribution activities of the firm would give the firm the best means of managing and improving the performance of this crucial activity, and thereby make a major contribution to improving the profitability of the firm.

It is, however, very uncommon to find a distribution director at main board level within such industrial sectors in Western Europe, though there is a growing tendency for a senior manager to be given this responsibility within similar companies operating in Japan. Some companies in high technology industries, with a high service requirement, and companies operating in consumer markets dominated by a few national chains, also appoint senior managers to co-ordinate service provision, but these too remain the minority. Even distribution managers are frequently without authority over areas which are central to the effective running of the distribution system. A survey in the US showed that distribution managers tended to control only

Table 15.1 Distribution management and authority

Function	Number of managers involved in decision making
Warehouse location	Most
Warehousing	Most
Transportation	Most
Order processing	Majority
Materials handling	Majority
Inventory control	Majority
Customer service	Majority
Forecasting	Minority
Choice of carrier	Minority
Finance method	Very few

Source: Adapted from Council for Physical Distribution Reports, 1982/88.

Table 15.2   Conflict areas concerning distribution policy

Department	Priorities
Production	Maximizing production runs
Transportation	Maximizing vehicle loads, minimizing delivery points
Marketing	Maximizing customer service (minimizing vehicle loads, maximizing delivery points, maximizing speed of delivery and stock levels)
Finance	Minimizing cost of delivery, cost of warehousing, stock levels, reducing customer base
Warehousing	Minimizing stocks, maximizing loads
Sales force	Quickest possible delivery, maximum filling of orders, minimum damaged stock

those that would meet the narrow definition of distribuion—that of lorries and warehouses mentioned in Chapter 1 (Table 15.1).

Reorganizing an established company presents grave difficulties. Yet many miss the opportunity afforded by major market changes to recognize the importance of distribution and to plan accordingly. Distribution policies cannot be effectively coordinated when the responsibility is split between four or five departments each with its own particular goals. The resulting conflict is almost inevitable. Some of the common areas of conflict that can occur are outlined in Table 15.2.

Conflict can only be effectively minimized where authority and responsibility are combined. But where responsibilities are separated, it can still be reduced by existing mechanisms in the company and in the distribution channel. In other words, the company will have to ensure that its internal 'motivational mix' operates effectively to reduce potential conflict. For example, the steady supply of information to all the operating divisions concerned with distribution will be vital in ensuring that common objectives are maintained and that personnel are rapidly aware of any problems.

Frequently, large organizations have either too many management tiers, or too few managers for the complexity of the task in which the organization is involved. Responsibility for too many employees reduces efficiency, though this is subject to the type of operation in which the firm is involved. Generally, the more complex and rapidly changing the environment and the more technical the employees' task, the shorter the span of management control. In the typical shop floor where large numbers of repetitive and non-skilled tasks are performed the span of management could be large, whereas in areas of the business where tasks are less repetitive and require greater levels of judgement and decision making the numbers reporting to a particular manager will need to be smaller. This concept of *span of control* has important implications for the organization of the distribution system.

First, as many firms attempt to replace personnel employed in distribution related activities with capital equipment, the skills required by the remaining employees will be significantly higher and in consequence the management span will need to be shorter, implying that there may be, for many firms, a need for greater management

**Table 15.3 Multi-layered organization struc-
ture in sales management**

Sales director
Sales controller
Regional sales manager
District sales manager
Area sales manager
Sales representative

involvement in the distribution process. Secondly, because distribution related activities are carried out within a number of departments, vertical management spans must be minimized. Take, for example, the interaction of the sales force with the distribution system. In many industrial sectors a close liaison will be necessary. In a firm organized like the one in Table 15.3 with many layers of control of the sales force, it will be difficult to obtain the necessary information from the sales representatives and often impossible to effectively integrate the distribution objectives into the firm.

Thirdly, the complexities of the distribution environment make it essential to define carefully the exact role of distribution personnel to maximize the efficiency of each individual. Detailed job descriptions are increasingly necessary to identify where the manager operates in the organization, to whom the manager reports, and the authority that the manager has to carry out the specific tasks (see Table 15.4). Such a job description has a number of advantages for the organization, establishing reporting structures and the number of staff each individual will be responsible for in addition to identifying specific tasks and the related authority.

With a rapidly changing external and competitive environment, companies must be able to alter and reappraise their distribution structure over a short period of time. Where responsibility for distribution is shared between departments, the system is less flexible and less able to respond effectively to environmental needs, further underlining the logic of concentrating distribution responsibility and authority within a single coherent division within the company.

A changing environment makes heavy demands on the acquisition of new skills. This is particularly important in the development of a distribution policy where the introduction and application of technology has become, and is becoming, more and more important at all levels. Companies must be prepared to train and retrain all staff as part of the continuing drive to maintain an efficient and responsive distribution system.

Although the *special requirements of the customer base* are frequently reflected in sales force organization (Chapter 14), few companies acknowledge that distribution activities would benefit from a similar approach. The growth of specialized distribution intermediaries creates the potential for some firms to provide specific levels of service for particular clients. Some firms have experimented with the appointment of specific distribution managers to handle particular types of delivery, national accounts being

**Table 15.4 Example of a job description of distribution manager employed
by a medium sized consumer goods company**

1. *Job title.* Distribution manager
2. *Job function.* To plan, control and operate the distribution system to achieve the most
   cost effective distribution that meets the company's strategic objectives
3. *Reporting structure.* Reporting to the production director. Day to day contact with
   other members of the company:
   Finance. Assisting in the planning and control of costs for transport and warehousing
   Sales. Liaison to ensure that customer service levels are achieved and to deal with delivery
   problems to specific customers
   Marketing. To help with the development of marketing strategies and new product launches
4. *Responsibility.* The distribution manager is responsible for the smooth and efficient running
   of the distribution function within the company. This will include:
   (a) all personnel operating within the warehouse and despatch areas
   (b) the maintenance and control of equipment and systems within the
       distribution department
   (c) the maintenance of a distribution information system which will enable the company
       to monitor the performance of the department against the targets set in the annual plan
   (d) to develop new links with outside contractors if necessary to improve
       distribution efficiency
   (e) to evaluate new equipment and report on their potential usefulness in achieving
       the objectives of the department
   (f) take part in preparing the annual plan
5. *Authority.* The distribution manager will be empowered to:
   (a) recruit (within company guidelines) personnel within the distribution department
   (b) spend up to £500 without reference to senior management within
       the distribution department
6. *Performance criteria.* The distribution manager will be expected to achieve the performance
   targets laid down in the annual plan and to report changes in the annual plan to line manager

---

separated from wholesalers, for example. The growing importance of certain customers is making the eventual creation of 'account managers' responsible for all aspects of client service, including distribution, a more and more vital organizational change, as has been identified in Chapter 14.

INFORMATION AND THE CONTROL OF DISTRIBUTION

Previous chapters stressed the need for continual monitoring and evaluation of the various components of the distribution system. Like other planners in the company environment, those responsible for distribution must be clear about the information essential to achieving their plan's goals—what types of information are needed to measure day to day performance; what data is required for longer-term planning; how much of each types of data is needed; and from where it should be obtained.

The effectiveness of the information system can be measured against four output criteria: collection cost, accuracy, simplicity and usefulness. The tendency with the advent of the computer is to collect a wide range of useless information. One company continued to print out each month and store a voluminous summary of all

Table 15.5 Information categorization

Category	Information type	Time scale
A	Frequent information	Daily but certainly every week
B	Infrequent information	Monthly or quarterly
C	Planning information	Six monthly or annual
D	Intermittent information	Review purposes

the items sold in that month. This practice was only halted when the cupboard containing the totally unused reports collapsed under their weight! The information supplied in this case failed to meet a key criterion—it was totally superfluous to the planning requirements of the organization. In the majority of cases, distribution planners can approach the problem by initially categorizing their information requirements on the basis of *how frequently it will be required* (Table 15.5).

Day to day information is necessary for short-term decisions on the management of the distribution system. No plan will be universally successful, and adjustments will have to be continually made. Most of the monitoring requirements have been considered in individual chapters, and will not be repeated at length here. In summary, we can say that short-term information requirements include stock levels, transport routing, load and production scheduling. They reflect the day to day requirements of the distribution planner needing to identify customer and load priorities and control over stock levels.

Changes in demand must be monitored too: the frequency, size, seasonal and geographic variations, the numbers of product lines in each order, and the trend in overall demand. This information is also vital to the marketing need to monitor the progress of channel members, especially where there are formal trade marketing agreements in existence. Changes in demand mean changes in reorder levels and in the number and type of vehicles used. Alterations must be made if production and storage costs change significantly, and if there are revisions in either the cost of different transport systems, either by weight or volume, or their availability. The information on the operation of the warehouse system, labour productivity and cost also requires monitoring to ensure that the efficiencies envisaged in economies of scale and consolidation are being maintained. A similar emphasis on efficiency and target achievement requires that the order processing system be monitored and information gathered on the percentage of orders completed within the target time, together with similar information on the productivity and performance of the sales force. The distribution planner must also regularly review the effectiveness of the forecasting system to provide accurate measurements of demand (see Chapter 9).

Planning information

Planning information concerns the data required for the development of a new distribution plan. As a result, it largely involves information which enables the distribution planner to decide between various alternatives. For example, to decide between different warehouse systems the planner needs all the available information on alternative systems: costs of space, equipment availability, impact of changing locations and so on. In physical distribution the planner will have to compare the costs of third party provision, the costs and performance of different transport systems, and the effect of changing packaging and containerization, together with the costs and benefits of improving the order processing system. Particularly important for planning is the analysis of potential trade-offs between the various components of the distribution system. Throughout earlier chapters the fact has been underlined that the cost contributions that make up the final overall distribution costing are obviously not fixed and interrelate, with an increased investment in one area leading to a reduction in another. To attain the fullest potential from this approach, the information system must be able to identify the key pay-offs that exist.

There will, for example, be possible trade-offs between single components: whether the additional costs of investing in new technology will be offset by the consequent reduced labour costs in, for example, the area of order processing, or warehouse organization; whether changes in working practices or the introduction of new technology will alter the cost structure of the operation. Then there will be a number of multiple trade-offs: speed of delivery will affect the firm's inventory level; warehouse numbers affect the level of all other costs. Finally there will be a series of inter-functional pay-offs. Distribution organization affects other areas of the company: production, marketing and finance. For example, delivering in bulk to a small number of customers will substantially reduce the requirements of invoicing and credit control that will be carried out in the finance department. For many companies distribution functions should be closely allied with credit control needs to ensure that goods are not despatched to customers that have not received credit clearance or to those existing customers that are over the accepted credit payment period.

A strategic or long-term plan can normally only be developed if the company understands the important influences operating in the market, both outside and inside the company. The distribution planner's contribution to the total company plan involves those broad factors analysed in Chapter 2. They are inevitably involved in the development of long range forecasts of major changes in the external environment (See Chapter 9). As distribution costs are a substantial part of the overall company operation, the distribution planner can also make a major contribution to the necessary analysis of future resource requirements—warehousing, investments in stock, order processing and the like.

Effective distribution planning requires more than an understanding of broad environmental factors. It also involves a strategic element—how to outperform the competition. Competitive improvement will depend partly on product, partly on price, partly on promotion (and for service based companies a range of other factors). But the distribution system can supply a competitive edge. A new company distribution plan has to consider how different customers perceive an effective distribution service, so that the necessary investment decisions can be taken to

Table 15.6   Competitive issues in distribution provision

Frequency of delivery	Minimum delivery levels
Emergency delivery facility	Time from placing of order
Reliability of delivery	Stock availability
Completeness of orders	Advice of non-availability
Sales contact frequency	Sales contact reliability
Sales contact skill	Customer query handling
Monitoring of stock levels by supplier	Ease of order placing
Accuracy of invoicing procedure	Competitive information
	Promotional information
	Availability of training

Source: Adapted from Christopher, the *Strategy of Distribution Management, Heinemann 1987.*

achieve the required level of competitive advantage. A number of distribution related factors are considered important across a range of industrial and consumer sectors. The range of factors mentioned are, as might be expected, very extensive (Table 15.6). Earlier chapters concentrated on a few key criteria being of greatest relevance across the majority of industrial and consumer sectors. For most customers time related distribution factors, such as speed, reliability, completeness, are used to judge the supplier's distribution service. However, not all sectors will have the same expectations of a distribution service, and any alteration in the nature of supplier's business should involve a reappraisal of the channel members' distribution requirements. The most important fact for the distribution planner to grasp is that not all customers will have the same service requirements, and that in order to establish effective and competitive distribution the planner must understand the specific demands of each main customer group.

To accurately achieve this service categorization, the planner will need to split the mass of customers into a series of categories or segments. Reality for the distribution planner is the individual member of the distribution channel which will service a particular marketing segment. Each market sector or distribution channel will therefore place a different emphasis on particular service criteria. It is essential for the supplier to rank the criteria accurately in order of importance within the particular market sector in which it operates. Against these criteria the effectiveness of each competitor in the market can be measured by some form of percentage achievement. An example is given in table 15.7.

The service criteria required for a particular market segment is an important issue in setting realistic objectives. A manufacturer with limited distribution cannot, for example, operate in a market environment where high levels of service are expected without planning a considerable increase in distribution resource allocation. For example a medium sized furniture manufacturer was approached by two of the major multiple retailers at an exhibition with substantial orders for a new range of garden furniture. The demands that these two companies placed upon the distribution

Table 15.7   Ranking competitive effectiveness

		Competitors' effectiveness			
Competitive factor	Customer weighting	A	B	C	D
Frequency of delivery	10	50	60	70	50
Minimum delivery levels	6	20	30	30	40
Emergency delivery facility	8				
Speed	2				
Reliability of delivery	6				
Stock availability	10				
Completeness of orders	5				
Advice of non-availability	4				
Sales contact frequency	2				
Sales contact reliability	2				
Sales contact skill	2				
Customer query handling	4				
Monitoring of stock levels by customer	2				
Ease of order placing	8				
Accuracy of invoicing procedure	10				
Availability of training	2				
Promotional expenditure	1				
Promotional timing	1				

systems were far greater than the supplier could manage with the limited resources at its disposal, leading to the eventual loss of both customers.

In addition to the information that the company needs for regular planning purposes there may be a variety of additional data for solving specific problems. Examples of such requirements include the analysis of new distribution channel members for overseas expansion, and production and supply alternatives.

SETTING NEW OBJECTIVES

It is possible to identify a range of broad objectives that will be generally applicable to most firms if we accept that the types of objective for each firm will vary. Each company will tend to set a measure of market share either relating to numerical distribution—the percentage of the total number of customers to which the company wishes to distribute; weighted distribution—the number of end users related to their importance as consumers of the particular product or service; a measure of return on capital employed (ROCE) and gross profit margin; and a measure of new product development success.

Once objectives are set, the company has to choose between the alternative action paths, and the timespan over which the plan will operate. The timespan obviously affects a number of key investment issues. Investment in the distribution system is often long-term with companies establishing particular market operations due to future strategic requirements. Short-term planning horizons tend to focus on flexibility as a central component of the implementation proposals. The Kuwait Petroleum Company has taken the long-term decision to retail petroleum products in the UK. As a result it has had to make a substantial initial investment in transport and storage systems in addition to buying outlets to sell the Q8 brand. The potentially slow payback on the investment is accepted as part of the longer-term strategic requirements.

The alternative action paths are considered in Chapter 2: cost reduction, product abandonment, market consolidation, market penetration, market development, product development, or diversification. Each of these alternatives has certain advantages and risks and a firm must consider which best meets its objective. In choosing the best action path the company must also define a second best or *fall back plan* should the preferred route be unrealizable. Each of these strategies will have different implications for the distribution system, as we have seen.

IMPLEMENTING DISTRIBUTION

Any implementation proposal must build up through an analysis of customers' requirements because of the differences in the service requirements of different customers and distribution channels. The first stage is to establish which distribution channels and channel members are most in line with company goals. By identifying the customers, the distribution planner can define a number of resource requirements necessary to support the company's progress with certain customers or market segments. For each distribution channel, a measure of volume, numbers of outlets, sales service requirements, and motivational costs can be established. It is likely that

Table 15.8   Customer service definition

	Channel 1	2	3
Large: numbers			
volume	12	55	120
sales calls	1000	500	300
service cycle days	600	250	50
agreements (£)	12	18	22
Medium: numbers	90000	—	—
volume			
sales call			
agreements			
Small: numbers			
volume			
sales calls			
agreements			
Total: numbers			
volume			
sales calls			
agreement			

not all members of the same channel will have identical requirements, and for most suppliers a separation of customer service on *size* of operation yields different expectations—separating each channel into small, medium and large companies. The specific requirements of each group must be identified through the process of *customer service definition* (Table 15.8). This permits the establishment of a differentiated service, matching service provision to customer requirements, thereby minimizing cost while maximizing competitive advantage. There is no point, for example, in providing the small retailer expecting a seven day delivery cycle with delivery within three days. It is expensive and fails to improve the supplier's competitive position. Table 15.8 can be reorganized to categorize all customers regardless of their distribution channels into numbers of clients with each receiving the same level of service. From the example in Table 15.8, the company would be able to produce four categories, A, B, C, D, each with broadly similar delivery cycle requirements (Table 15.9).

This data can also analyse the total load on the order processing system, as can the sales callage pattern and the optimum numbers of sales representatives required to implement the strategy, from a consideration of work loads involved in each of the callage types (Chapter 14). From the total order size and its geographical spread, it is possible to identify what percentage of orders can be supplied direct from the production point to the customer—and use the figures to establish what volume levels should be included in the trade agreements (see Chapter 4). The importance of the level of direct delivery is that it will influence the stock storage and warehouse requirement, and the physical distribution system by ensuring that full loads can be achieved. The greater the direct delivery of complete loads, the lower the overall distribution cost.

Once the timespan of order cycles is identified, the distribution planner can define the most appropriate physical distribution system for delivery from production site or warehouse to customer, and from production point to warehouse. Setting inventory

Table 15.9   Customer classification

Category	Number	Speed requirements	Accuracy requirements
A			
B			
C			
D			

Table 15.10   Inventory levels by product group

A	95%
B	80%
C	50%
D	50%

levels (Table 15.10) determines warehouse requirements and defining warehousing locations will provide the final links of the distribution system. For each decision there is an associated cost: the cost of direct delivery, storage costs, warehouse equipment and manning levels, other transport costs, and order processing costs. Obviously the longer the delivery can be postponed the lower the level of minimum delivery, as the load planner will be able to consolidate delayed loads with more urgent deliveries and thereby achieve full, cost effective loads. So there is a need for minimum order quantities for each customer category. Any agreed trade-off between delivery speed and order quantity would involve those departments controlling customer contact—marketing, sales, and finance, and are often a significant cause of conflict between departments—especially as they affect pricing and discount structures (Table 15.11).

Decisions on the distribution system will finally depend on the evaluation of the various trade-offs and the effects of changing volume. Breaking down the cost components of the distribution system into as many sub-sets as possible allows a critical appraisal of the various decisions taken. An optimal assessment of the total distribution cost can be made by comparing effects of different types of policy against the initial decision (Table 15.12), while maintaining the same output criteria established as part of company policy.

Table 15.11 Minimum drop by customer group

Customer category	Minimum drop	Price per case	Delivery cycle
A			
B			
C			
D			

Table 15.12 Costing structure

Factor	Initial	Modification 1	2
Volume	150 000	150 000	150 000
Direct delivery cost (£)	25 000		
Production to warehouse	15 000		
Inventory	80 000		
Warehouse equipment	5 000		
Warehouse fixed costs	25 000		
Warehouse labour	30 000		
Production and supply alternatives	25 000		
Warehouse to customer (standard)	110 000		
Warehouse to customer (emergency)	15 000		
Total			
Savings against initial analysis			

This system provides a method of recalculating the total distribution cost if the pattern of trade changes and alterations are necessary. Because of the complexities of the distribution environment, attempts to produce fully working commercially available computer simulations of all the possible interactions prove difficult. In their most advanced state, they are used by the big consumer goods companies and bulk chemical companies. The number of customers and the stock holdings that they need to maintain make such optimization critically important so they are investing heavily for systems to optimize within large geographical areas such as Europe post 1992. The main shortcomings of such large scale computer integration of the distribution system planning is that the assumptions built into the model are crucial for success, that corporate level decision making tends to be divorced from the reality of both the market place and the day to day problems of the operating units. Centralization of decision making will also reduce commitment within the organization to making a particular policy work.

For medium sized companies, a variety of software packages are increasingly attractive methods of modelling some of the interactions that exist within the distribution system. Examples of these software packages have been provided in the relevant chapters. Many of the users complain that some of the computer packages are not sufficiently flexible for their specific operating requirements, though many of these shortcomings are being overcome as new generations of systems become available.

Whether manual or computer analysis is used, the completion of the analysis enables the distribution planner to set a series of target achievements for the distribution system. Though they will vary, common levels of performance include measures of numerical and weighted distribution within a certain distribution channel, the speed, reliability and completeness of the distribution system. The targets can be monitored against the actual performance, and appropriate corrective action taken to improve the efficiency of key areas within the distribution operation. For each problem

Table 15.13 Problem solving in distribution—key issues

Problem area	Key factors
Market coverage	Distribution channels
	Channel members
	Channel agreements
	Sales force
Delivery speed	Order processing system
	Physical distribution system
Delivery reliability	Order processing system
	Inventory control
	Warehousing
	Load planning
Delivery accuracy	Inventory control
	Order processing system

there will be specific areas of concentration that need to be researched in order to define the most appropriate solution (see Table 15.13).

FALL BACK PLANNING AND THE CONTRIBUTION OF DISTRIBUTION

The final part of the evolution of the distribution plan involves contingency actions should the strategic direction of the firm alter; changing, for example, from a market penetration strategy to a product development strategy, and what actions need to be taken to minimize the consequences of failure in particular parts of the distribution system. As changes in strategic direction are generally implemented relatively slowly, the distribution planner will have sufficient time to react and to evaluate the necessary changes in the system, and to produce a new optimal distribution plan. By contrast, substantial failure in a part of the distribution system through natural causes—fire, flood, earthquake—or civil—strikes, civil unrest—will be of greater concern to the distribution planner. What actions are needed if there are shortfalls in production, warehousing, physical distribution, or order processing?

Answers would have to be found to some or all of the following questions. Where will stock be delivered from if there is production failure? Can third party warehousing be used if there are problems in the warehouse network? What alternative carriers or physical distribution system exists should the current one be unavailable? How can the company rapidly resupply the market if all the stocks currently held are seriously damaged? What manual systems of order processing should replace the current computerized system in the event of major breakdown? Worst case scenario plans will often prevent the firm from going out of business if disaster strikes and should be a vital part of the distribution process for firms operating in competitive markets.

CASE: CLADEX

Introduction

Cladex was consumer paint company, based in the Midlands, which had started in the early 1970s supplying own label paints to two small DIY retail chains. The company continued to grow with the expansion of the DIY market by concentrating primarily on supplying regional and some national chains with a proportion of their private label

Table 15.14 Cladex five year sales progression—(all figures in £ million)

	1983	1984	1985	1986	1987
Sales	15	17	19	22	25
Profit	0.8	1.2	1.4	1.5	1.6
Capital employed	2.1	3.0	3.5	3.5	8.9

requirements. By 1985, though they were continuing to supply own label products, they had also developed a range of branded paint products. Sales growth continued through 1986 and 1987 though increases in profitability were much more difficult to achieve, (see Table 15.14). Return on capital employed had dropped since 1983 as the large capital investment programme instituted by Cladex to meet rapidly rising sales volumes had failed to provide the anticipated return, declining from 38 per cent to the 1987 figure of 17 per cent. The board of Cladex were meeting to review the future of the company and were considering the following details which provided the information on which they would take their decisions.

The market

The market, which was valued at around £300 million at retail value (at an average of £2.25 litre, a consumption of 120 million litres per annum), had become progressively more competitive as paint production was concentrated by a series of industry takeovers into a smaller number of manufacturers.

The result of this steady increase in concentration was that Cladex faced a steady decline in profit margins as it could not effectively compete with the economies of scale both in production and promotion of the two market leaders. With sales totalling 15 million litres, Cladex had a 12 per cent market share, and was clearly the third largest manufacturer in the market. However, the market shares of the two other companies accounted for well over 60 per cent of total sales.

Customers

Cladex supplied their range of consumer paints to the high street, predominantly to the main retailers. It supplied part of the own label paint lines to:

> A.G. Stanley (operating as Ripolin, Decor 8, FADS)
> B & Q (a subsidiary of Woolworths)
> Woolworths
> Texas Homecare
> Homebase

and distributed its branded range, Homecharm, via a number of wholesalers, 200 in 1987, and to the smaller specialist DIY outlets of which there were an estimated 4000 nationwide. Own label product in 1987 contributed 68 per cent of total turnover, but only 42 per cent of total profit, and this followed a trend which had become established over the past five years (Table 15.15).

The attraction of the own label business was that the company produced on long-term contracts and did not need to hold stock, supplying their customers at regular and determined intervals. This was in contrast to the branded sector, which suffered not only from a high level of seasonality, but also considerable fluctuations in demand. Whereas external paints tended to be most in demand during the summer, indoor

Table 15.15   Percentage turnover and profit contribution by sector

	1984	1985	1986	1987
Own label: sales	55	57	63	68
profit	45	46	47	42
Branded: sales	45	43	37	32
profit	55	54	53	68

Table 15.16   Sales percentage by month by activity—1986

	1	2	3	4	5	6	7	8	9	10	11	12
Own label	7	7	8	9	9	9	9	9	10	6	9	8
Branded	4	3	4	5	9	12	16	15	8	7	7	10

Table 15.17   Sales percentage by month by activity—1985

	1	2	3	4	5	6	7	8	9	10	11	12
Own label	7	7	8	9	9	9	9	9	10	6	9	8
Branded	7	5	4	5	5	6	6	9	11	14	15	13

paints were most bought in the winter. This pattern was often changed by alterations in the weather patterns—a poor summer could drive demand of indoor paints up within a short period of time. Weather was not the only major influence on demand: changing disposable incomes and mortgage levels also appeared to have some impact on total sales. When the house market slowed down, people tended to spend more on DIY activity to improve the attractiveness of their houses, with an inevitable effect on the level of paint sales.

Such fluctuating demand patterns often make the branded market difficult to plan, especially for a company with fairly limited resources. Thus the sales record for 1986 (Table 15.16) showed a considerable difference from that of the previous year (Table 15.17), with most of the differences being explicable by differences in weather rather than economic change. In order to remain competitive against the two major companies in the market Cladex had to ensure that stocks were maintained against such variations in demand as the pressures on selling space within most retail outlets were becoming intense, and shortage of stock had in several cases caused them to be de-listed by three regional DIY chains.

Product range

The current branded product range consisted of ten colours produced in two tin sizes, one litre and two litres. Sales varied considerably within the range with the best selling

Table 15.18   Five year branded sales history by type (000 litres)

	1983	1984	1985	1986	1987
Brilliant white	400	425	500	600	750
Magnolia	325	400	420	400	425
Oyster	200	220	250	275	325
Sand gold	260	280	280	270	260
Black	225	380	380	400	550
Lime green	160	120	200	160	125
Clear blue	450	400	450	550	650
Aluminium	500	200	350	440	640
Bitumen	200	300	450	700	600
Textured white	300	300	300	500	450
Total branded	3020	3025	3610	4795	4775

line over the past five years varying between brilliant white, aluminium, and bitumen. The main lines are detailed in Table 15.18. Cladex had gained a reputation amongst the trade and the more knowledgeable customers for producing a higher quality exterior paint than the competition, and it was in this sector of the market that they tended to achieve their highest sales. The own label production was much more varied in colour and tin size, and the company over the past two years had produced around fifty different colours in up to five different tin sizes.

Production and warehousing

The company had invested heavily in modern, flexible manufacturing facilities, in the early 1980s, to meet what had been forecast as a steadily increasing demand for paint. The production plant could switch within thirty minutes from the production of one type or colour of paint to another, with a set-up cost of £550, a figure substantially below the competition. With its microprocessor control systems the plant was able to operate on a 24 hour day basis, with low staffing requirements. By 1987, the plant was continuing to operate substantially under capacity producing only fifteen of the possible 28 million litres which was the theoretical maximum capacity of the plant. This failure to achieve production targets meant that the company was failing to achieve the return on capital that the senior management had initially envisaged.

The company had built as part of its expansion plans a new warehouse alongside the production facility. The integration of the warehouse with the production facility and the introduction of advanced automation, allowed filled paint to be moved from the manufacturing point to the warehouse storage point with the minimum of physical involvement by factory or warehouse staff.

Current sales force

The company employed five sales representatives. Two of these negotiated with senior buyers at the major multiples for the supply of own label products; the other three were responsible for ensuring that the 180 main wholesalers in the country stocked the branded paint that the company produced. At present, the company negotiated annually with the multiples, and had loose agreements with the wholesalers which primarily consisted of attractive discounts on quantity. The company had decided as an issue of policy that it could not hope to compete effectively with the major consumer companies in media advertising—ICI alone spent £7 million on advertising in 1987.

Current physical distribution system

From their warehouse in the Midlands, the company used lorry transport to supply both their retail and wholesale clients. The average cost of delivery was £350 per round trip for their one 40 ton and £250 for the three 20 ton lorries that could carry 32 000 and 15 000 litres of paint, respectively. One of the advantages of the private label business was that Cladex were able to maximize vehicle utilization into the 55 central depots of the DIY multiples whereas deliveries of branded products tended to be only 35 per cent full.

Other possible avenues of activity

The company had special expertise in the production of technical paint products. The production department had one of the best reputations in the country which had helped in the acquisition and maintenance of the own label products. It was looking for avenues of activity that would exploit this technical strength, improve profitability and improve the current sales volumes. The main options were considered to lie amongst the following sectors.

Standard industrial metal work paints

There were an estimated 6000 consumers of standard metal working paint products in the UK, ranging from the smallest metal bashing firm operating from under a railway arch, to some very large concerns such as GKN. The total market was estimated to be worth around £17 million, at the average price of £3.5 per litre, or a total of 5 million litres.

Small firms tended to buy product from industrial wholesalers of which there were estimated to be around 120 in the country that stocked this type of paint, but the larger firms all brought direct from the manufacturers, who were mainly small regional companies. Price sensitivity was significantly lower than in the consumer market and margins in consequence higher. Estimates of the Cladex production department suggested that 55 per cent margins could be achieved when the company sold direct to the end users though using wholesalers would mean that margins would drop towards 40 per cent. The range of colours that were generally in demand was limited— research showed the following consumption pattern from a small sample of potential customers (Table 15.19).

Table 15.19 Percentage consumption patterns by customer for standard industrial metal paints

Black	55
Brilliant white	15
Aluminium	15
Beige	5

Research had also shown that the majority of users tended to hold low stocks of the relevant paint and would generally wish to receive new stocks within two days of starting a new production run of metal production.

Vehicle paints

Paints especially formulated for vehicles were on the surface an attractive outlet for specialist paints. There were an estimated 7000 outlets that carried out some vehicle paint work, though this varied from minor repairs to the seven or eight vehicle manufacturers that used paint in large quantities for original vehicle manufacture. The size of the market was estimated to be around £45 million, the bulk of which was accounted for by the vehicle manufacturers (an estimated £35 in paint per vehicle for the 1.2 million manufactured in the UK). The manufacturers determined which paint manufacturers were listed to supply both them and the repair market. The gross margins on the product that was supplied were high—estimated at 65 per cent—with a per litre price of £5. The small repairers tended to order the product via the spare parts departments of the vehicle manufacturers which held stock of all the colours currently used by the company. There was also a small retail market where consumers bought product for 'touching' up small defects in the paint work of individual vehicles.

Cladex would face a number of problems in this market sector. First, there was a demand for a wide range of colours: in 1987 a total of 45 would be required to service 85 per cent of the vehicles currently on the road in the UK. The large vehicle manufacturers also demanded not only exceptionally high technical specifications, resistance to chipping, scuffing and the like being especially important, but absolute guarantees on quality. Because of these requirements they tended to prefer to deal with large manufacturers which also could provide the technical expertise that was required. In addition, the introduction of computer assisted manufacturing systems such as just in time inventory control systems, meant that the suppliers had to meet 24 hour delivery schedules.

Powder coating

A growth sector of the metal manufacture was the increasing use of powder coating to protect metal work, especially furniture. The market was estimated to be worth £3 million in 1987, and there were currently 65 outlets that were active in the production of powder coated products. The current price for powder coated prouct was £7.50 a litre, which would provide Cladex with a 60 per cent gross margin. All the large companies bought direct from the two manufacturers that currently supplied paint to this market. Generally, each company would carry out powder coating in batch production and concentrate output in three or four days in a two week period. The powder coating companies tended to be able to forecast the production requirements several weeks in advance. Most of the paint requirements were in four colours which made up 85 per cent of total demand.

Structural paint

There was a large existing market for the supply of structural paint, the specialist product used to coat buildings and steel frameworks. Most of the work was carried out by small independent contractors which bought from builders merchants (of which there were an estimated 2500 in the country which sold significant volumes of structural paint). Some structural paint was sold through DIY wholesalers which were already Cladex customers, but this was much the smaller part of the market.

The market was estimated to be worth around £10 million, as much of the demand for structural paint was met by paints that were available from the consumer sector. Price competition was in consequence extremely severe. The average price was below that obtainable in the consumer sector, and there was substantial import substitution. Cladex estimated that they would be able to enter the market but that the potential margins per litre for the basic products were unlikely to be better than 10–15 per cent.

They were convinced that over time they would be able to develop a premium sector in the market based on their current product experience in the consumer sector in external paints. One of the directors was firmly convinced that they could gain up to 30 per cent of the market and improve margins to 30–40 per cent by marketing a product that would provide longer-term protection to steel structures than the current products at a premium price of 20 per cent.

Additional Reading

CHAPTER 2

Dicken P., *Global Shift*, Harper and Row, 1986.
Drucker P., *Managing in Turbulent Times*, Pan, 1986.
Peters M., *Managing with Chaos*, Free Press, 1987.
Porter M. E., *Competitive Strategy: Techniques for Analysing Industries and Competitors*, Free Press, 1980.
Smith G. D., Arnold D. R., and Bizzell, B. G., *Strategy and Business Policy*, Houghton Mifflin, 1985.
Tiffler A., *The Third Wave*, William Morrow, 1980.
West A., *Understanding Marketing*, Harper and Row, 1987.

CHAPTER 3

Christopher M., (ed.) *Effective Distribution Management*, Pan Books, 1983.
Guirdham M., *Marketing: the Management of Distribution Channels*, Pergamon Press, 1972.
Rosenbloom, B., *Marketing Channels: A management view*, 3rd edition, Dryden Press, 1987.

CHAPTER 4

Bowersox (ed.) *Management in Marketing Channels*, McGraw Hill, 1980.
Stern L. W., El-Ansary A. I., *Marketing Channels*, Prentice Hall, 1977.

CHAPTER 5

Brooke M. Z., Remmers H. L., (ed.) *The International Firm*, Pitman, 1977.
Dunning J. H., *International Production and the Multinational Enterprise*, George Allen & Unwin, 1981.
Hibbert E. P., *Principles and Practice of Export Marketing*, Heinemann, 1985.
Paliwoda S., *International Marketing*, Heinemann, 1987.

CHAPTER 6

Ballou R. H., *Basic Business Logistics*, 2nd edition, Prentice Hall, 1985.
HBR, *Manufacturing Management: Logistics, Materials, Inventory*, Harvard Business Review, 1985.
Hutchins D., *Just In Time*, Gower, 1988.
Monks J. J., *Operations Management*, McGraw Hill, 1987.
Moore P. G., *Basic Operational Research*, 3rd edition, 1986, Pitman Publishing.

CHAPTER 7

Bowersox, D. J., and Closs D. L., *Logistical Management*, 3rd edition, Macmillan, 1986.
Burton J. A., *Effective Warehousing*, 3rd edition, Pitman Publishing, 1981.
Buxton G., *Effective Marketing Logistics*, Macmillan, 1975.
West A., (ed.) *Handbook of Retailing*, Gower, 1988.

CHAPTER 8

Gattorna J., (ed.) *Handbook of Physical Distribution Management*, 3rd edition, Gower, 1983.

CHAPTER 9

Lancaster G. A., and Lomas R. A., *Forecasting for Sales and Materials Management*, Macmillan, 1985.
Owen F., and Jones R., *Modern Analytical Techniques*, 2nd edition, Pitman Publishing, 1984.
Brown, R. G., *Statistical Forecasting for Inventory Control*, McGraw Hill, 1965.

CHAPTER 10

Christopher M. *The Strategy of Distribution Management*, Heinemann, 1986.
Hill R. W., and Hillier T. J., *Organisational Buying Behaviour*, Macmillan, 1977.
Katz B., *How to Manage the Customer Service Function*, Gower, 1986.

CHAPTER 11

Germane G. E., *Transport policy in the 1980's*, Addison Wesley, 1984.
Lowe D., *Road Freight Transport*, Gower Pegasus Transport Library; Gower, 1985.
McTavish R., and Maitland A., *Industrial Marketing*, Macmillan, 1980.

CHAPTER 12

Robeson J. F., and House R. G., *The Distribution Handbook*, Macmillan, 1985.
Woodward F., *Managing the Transport Services Function*, Gower, 1978.

CHAPTER 13

Forsyth P., *Sales Management Handbook*, Gower, 1987.
Rogers L., *Handbook of Sales and Marketing Management*, Kogan Page, 1987.

CHAPTER 14

Scott G., *Principles of Management Information Systems*, McGraw Hill, 1985.

CHAPTER 15

Christopher M., *Total distribution: A framework for analysis, costing and control*, Gower, 1971.